THE 150TH OPEN

THE 150TH OPEN

CELEBRATING GOLF'S DEFINING CHAMPIONSHIP

with Iain Carter

R&A

HarperCollins*Publishers*

CONTENTS

Shane Lowry triumphantly breaks through the 18th-hole galleries to complete his 2019 victory at Royal Portrush.

Foreword

We all agree that the game of golf has a rich and storied past, but few championships can claim a place in history so special as The Open. And now it is turning 150 years young!

I have said many times that The Open might be the most enjoyable Major Championship I played over my career. It was so uniquely special and different than any championship we played in the United States. There is and was the rota of seaside links layouts that offer subtle nuances. The weather was always a factor and became its own inherent challenge in The Open. Then there are the fans. They all have a knowledge, respect and deep-rooted love for the game. Playing in front of them was an honour.

When I first hoisted the famed Claret Jug at Muirfield in 1966, the emotions that overwhelmed me were real and perhaps said everything about how special this Championship is to me. To be named the Champion Golfer of the Year provides a memory I will cherish for the rest of my life.

I am incredibly proud to have been part of this great Championship's long history and honoured to have my name engraved alongside so many other Champions on the Claret Jug.

The 150th Open is truly a milestone worth celebrating and gives all of us who love this great game an opportunity to reflect on the drama, emotion and elation that are part of the magic and mystique of golf's original Championship.

Here's to 150 years of The Open and to the next 150!

JACK NICKLAUS

Introduction

Four decades ago I set out on what was the biggest adventure of my life so far: leaving the English Midlands, along with two friends, to travel nearly 400 miles north to Scotland. Keen but not elite golfers, like thousands before us, it was time to fulfil our ambition to go to The Open, excitedly anticipating the great golfers we would witness contesting the biggest and oldest championship in the game.

Prior to this journey, we had followed the event from afar, and read of its humble origins, of Old and Young Tom Morris, Harry Vardon, Henry Cotton, Peter Thomson, Gary Player and Arnold Palmer. We had seen on television Jack Nicklaus toss his putter skywards in celebration, witnessed Tom Watson win an 18-hole play-off on his Open debut, delighted in the swashbuckling matador Severiano Ballesteros bursting onto the scene, and longed for a British successor to Tony Jacklin. And now it was time to see, hear, feel, smell and taste The Open for ourselves.

So, in July 1982, we drove to the outskirts of Glasgow, where we stayed with a relative of mine in her flat on the 11th floor of a council tower block. We rose early each morning to drive the 40 or so miles to the Championship at Royal Troon. We parked in a campsite at the southern end of the course, close to Prestwick, where the first dozen Opens were played. Ours was the 111th edition and we loved it.

Royal Troon's par-5 sixth hole, the scene of great drama at the 1982 Open.

Watching previous Opens on television, the courses carried a mystical feel. Whether it was the history associated with St Andrews, the frightful difficulty of Carnoustie or the raw beauty of Turnberry, these layouts seemed larger than life. After all, they filled the entire screen with their character and challenges. The players were also brought to life; the charisma of Palmer and Ballesteros, the pure competitiveness and grace of Nicklaus and the heartache of Ben Crenshaw (a serial near-misser and personal favourite). Appropriately chosen words from the most erudite of commentators always seemed to create a narrative that fuelled the Championship's legendary status.

Walking through the gates for the first time, there must have been potential for a sense of anti-climax, but there was none. The size and grandeur of the links were immediately striking, the challenge of the fiercely revetted bunker faces, the undulations of the dunes, the firmness of the fairways, the length of the rough, the freshness of the breeze all assaulted our senses.

Our first task was to seek the famous eighth hole, the tiny 'Postage Stamp' – a mere 126 yards in length but with card-wrecking trouble all around it. We had seen on television the great Gene Sarazen hole in one there in 1973, the last time Royal Troon had hosted The Open. 'And what do you think about that one?' was all veteran commentator Henry Longhurst needed to say. We knew what we thought – it was one of those glorious Open moments. Later in life, I described to BBC Radio listeners how Ernie Els did the very same thing. That little hole has always been an iconic setting for classic moments.

There were thousands of people gathered around the eighth when we arrived. We craned our necks and

saw a couple of groups come through. One tee shot landed close by with shouts of 'fore' and we ducked to avoid being clattered. This was the first of a lifetime of reminders that when you go to The Open you do not just share the theatre with the world's best players, you are actually on stage with them.

Next it was time to track down the names we had come to see; near the top of the list was Watson, who had won the US Open just the month before, chipping in at the 71st hole at Pebble Beach. Of course, the list also included Nicklaus, the man Watson beat in California and with whom he had so thrillingly shared in the famous 'Duel in the Sun' at Turnberry five years earlier. Nicklaus was the greatest living golfer and arguably the biggest sports star on the planet. It was the perfect Open to see many of golf's greats; Palmer, Player, Lee Trevino and Johnny Miller were all there, as were the irrepressible Ballesteros and defending Champion Bill Rogers.

We watched Britain's biggest name, Tony Jacklin – so thrillingly the Champion in 1969 – but there was little magic as he laboured to a disappointing first-round 77. Indeed of all those players we were determined to see on the first day, only Watson broke 70. His 69 left him two shots off the lead, held by a 22-year-old Bobby Clampett. Even though he had been beaten by only Watson and Nicklaus at the preceding Major, that US Open at Pebble Beach, the blond-haired American was not a player we had mentioned on our long journey northwards.

We joined in the applause as we sat in the grandstand at the 18th to see him complete the lowest round of the opening day. We did the same on the Friday, as he dispatched a beautiful 6-iron to six feet and knocked in the birdie putt in Champion style.

He was round in a course-record 66 to lead by five. The Open seemed done and dusted as we departed.

The following morning we read newspapers adorned with Clampett's photogenic smile. 'I'm not really concerned with the lead, I'm just concerned with continuing to play the same kind of golf,' reporters quoted the halfway leader. 'It is a mental challenge to see if I can continue to play the same shots. I am aiming to shoot the lowest score I can, and if someone can beat that, then that is great for them, but I'm playing really well.'

It felt as though this Open would not be one of those where an established great lifts the Claret Jug. We were going to see an American upstart, with a mechanical swing that showed no sign of breaking down, win the greatest golf championship in the world.

The Saturday morning was spent following Nicklaus, who had characteristically battled back from an opening 77 with a two-under-par 70 to make the cut. It was a tough day, the wind was blowing and the great man was battling as he put together a level-par 72.

We took up position behind the green on the par-5 sixth to watch the last groups come through. When the final pair arrived, Clampett seemed to have one hand on the trophy even though it was only Saturday afternoon. His position was even stronger, despite the hostile weather. The young American had picked up two more early birdies. Leaderboards showed him at

12 under par, seven shots clear of the field. Seven shots! We were being denied the close contest we so desperately wanted to see. By way of compensation we seemed to be in the presence of a commanding performance. A star was being born before our very eyes. We decided there and then, we would follow Clampett's every footstep for the rest of the Championship.

Peering through binoculars down that long sixth hole, we saw him disappear into a fairway bunker. A setback, but it was a par 5. Get back into position, take your medicine and move on with a safe par, and no damage is done. That has been the mantra of pretty much every Open Champion at some stage during their journey to triumph. There are no shortcuts to victory. Limit the damage, move on.

Except it did not work out that way for our leader. It took him three attempts to escape the hazard. He ran up a triple-bogey-8, and before our eyes his previously imperious, impregnable game fell apart. He never recovered. We followed the drama. Uncertainty replaced confidence as the fairways, the greens and the holes themselves seemed to shrink to his eye. What had been such an easy game was now unimaginably tricky. After rounds of 67 and 66, Clampett carded a 78. Yes, he still led – by a single shot – but this Open, which had seemed so closed, was now a yawning chasm from where one of any number of players would emerge triumphant.

The final day dawned and we drew up our plans. Clampett was to be abandoned and we watched a few of the early starters come through the 'Postage Stamp'. Then it was back to the 18th and the vast green-seated grandstand down the left side of the hole. The first fairway was to our back, the shoreline beyond that and the Firth of Clyde glistened in fleeting sunshine across to the glorious Isle of Arran. There are few views more grand but the one in front of us was even better with vast, packed stands surrounding the hole and the famous stone clubhouse sitting at the back of

the green. It was a classic Open scene, one replicated on the United Kingdom's best links year after year for decade after decade. And who knew what dramas would play out over the coming hours?

Plenty occurred all over the course. But the fact is we saw very little of the excitement. Instead we felt it, every step of the way. The giant yellow scoreboard sat atop the huge grandstand opposite. We did not have radios, mobile phones had not been thought of back in 1982 and there was not a television or big screen in sight. All we had was that big yellow scoreboard. And a procession of the greats coming down the closing hole. We stood and cheered as Crenshaw completed a 70 to finish 15th. Nicklaus raised the proverbial roof with his 69 to finish 10th, that opening 77 a distant memory. A young English lad by the name of Nick Faldo fired a 69 to come fourth. We could sense he'd be one to watch in the future! Faldo tied with Des Smyth and Masahiro Kuramoto, of Japan. Sandy Lyle was a shot further back in eighth place. That afternoon I watched Smyth, Lyle, Sam Torrance, Ken Brown and Bernard Gallacher come down that 18th hole. I cheered them all, oblivious to a future in which I would eventually work alongside them at golf events.

But that day, Sunday 18 July 1982, was all about celebrating the drama of The Open, and seeing very little of it. Our big yellow scoreboard showed Clampett continuing his retreat. 'He's done,' we nodded sagely, as his name tumbled from the top of the list for the first time since it had been hoisted there the previous Thursday. Up popped Nick Price, the moustachioed Zimbabwean, who earlier in the week said: 'I wouldn't want to be in Clampett's place with that lead; I couldn't handle it. I just want to finish in the top 10.'

Price was playing his fifth Open. He had never finished in the top 20 and we knew next to nothing

about him. Watson was on the fringes too. The scoreboard showed him eagle the par-5 11th. Nowadays The Open's Wi-Fi and app would provide those in the grandstands with instant footage of his perfect drive and brilliant 3-iron to three feet. But despite our ignorance we were still enthralled, whispers rattling around the grandstand as to how the three-time Champion had leapt into contention. Then came a collective sigh; a Watson bogey at 15 and Price was back in the clear. Price was going to win The Open!

This is a Championship that invariably identifies the greatest players but also has scope for upset. After all, Tom Morris was a huge favourite to win the first Open yet it was the dogged Musselburgh underdog Willie Park who took the honours.

Price led by three shots heading to the 13th, where a poor tee shot cost him a bogey. Up ahead Englishman Peter Oosterhuis was completing a 70 to set the target at three under par. We never thought that would be good enough and at no point entertained hope of a home winner. This was Price's to lose. The scoreboard showed him at six-under as Watson was finishing his round. Three rather prosaic pars followed his bogey at the 15th. The US Open winner set a new target at four-under. 'When I came off 18, I thought I'd lost,' he later admitted.

Suddenly they were again changing the number next to Price's name at the top of the leaderboard. The red '6' became a '4'. Collective gasps of shock rippled through the grandstands. Someone with a radio earpiece sitting two rows back told us the leader had been all over the place on the 15th. It cost him a double-bogey. Suddenly Watson, in the clubhouse, was in a share of the lead. Furthermore, Price still had

An honorary Scot, Tom Watson celebrates his 1982 triumph, a fourth Open win in golf's founding country.

to play the treacherous par-3 17th, and we had seen many a bogey posted from that hole during that afternoon. Sure enough the Zimbabwean was faced with a five-footer to save par, as the man with the earpiece's whispers were relayed around the stands. Sure enough he missed it.

And so Nick Price came to the 18th needing a birdie to force a play-off with the great Tom Watson. We all knew, experts that we now were, who would win that – should it come to pass.

At long last we could see the action as well as feel it. We held our breath as Price, with his brisk, rhythmic swing muscled an approach onto the back of the green. He had just over 20 feet for the birdie. Again absolute silence. The kind of silence you can actually hear. One man, with a stick in his hand, a ball on the ground and a hole to be found. It is so simple, yet so important. This is what The Open is all about. This is why we scrimped and saved to be able to afford the fuel to drive 400 miles in a cramped little car. We were there to watch history, to see which name would be engraved on one of sport's most precious trophies. Price tapped the ball forward. 'Looks good,' someone muttered. 'Nah, it's short,' swiftly followed a knowledgeable sounding Scottish burr. He was correct. The ball cosied up to the hole. It failed to disappear. The 111th Open finished with a frustrated groan and then respectful, sympathetic applause for the man who joined Oosterhuis in a share of second place.

And then came the presentation. Then came the throaty roars. Clad in his pale-blue sweater, Tom Watson was Champion for the fourth time, all of those wins coming in Scotland – Carnoustie, Turnberry, Muirfield and now Royal Troon. He held aloft the trophy but those moments are better remembered for him lifting and displaying a scarf proclaiming 'Scotland the Brave'.

The esteemed American golf writer Dan Jenkins later summed up Watson's triumph by saying in *Sports Illustrated*: 'His wasn't so much a charge to victory as it was a business-like journey designed to avoid all possible calamities while waiting for others, like your Nicky Prices, to suffer them.'

Yes, this was an Open lost more than won. Lost by Price on the closing holes of the final day, lost by Clampett over a weekend when he recorded scores of 78 and 77. Having led so handsomely, the 22-year-old shared 10th place with Nicklaus, who had started so dreadfully. There were so many stories from that Open, as there are at every one of these Championships. The overriding one in 1982 was that neither Price (his time would come) nor the young American halfway leader (his did not) were ready to become 'Champion Golfer of the Year'.

It is that quest which fascinates golf fans all over the world. It is a colossal journey to the very top of the game, one that has been embarked upon ever since golf's first undisputed Champion, a Scotsman named Allan Robertson, suffered his untimely death 10 days shy of his 45th birthday in 1859. From that moment the question has been, who will be the next Champion Golfer? This is why The Open was established the following year, when Willie Park upset the odds to become the first Champion and won the Challenge Belt.

From those humble beginnings in Prestwick, The Open has grown into one of the world's biggest and most historic sporting events. I detail here my experiences from the first occasion I was truly able to feel the magic of The Open. In truth, I could have picked any one of the 149 editions that have now been played. Each one has been special, very special. No one could have told me back then that I would become the BBC's golf correspondent and that my career would take me to so many Open Championships; that I would commentate on Nicklaus birdieing the last at St Andrews in his final appearance in 2005 and that

four years later I would be looking for words to describe Watson winning The Open for a sixth time at the age of 59. As it turned out, I did not need them because Watson bogeyed the last with the Championship at his mercy. That was another Open that was lost rather than won, but however they are settled a worthy winner emerges and the sport has its Champion Golfer of the year.

Now is a time to celebrate a golf event – and the people at its heart, players and fans alike – that has more than stood the test of time. It has grown exponentially through so many years. The first three Opens had no prize money, just the Challenge Belt, a trophy that was the forerunner to the Claret Jug. In 1863 the minor places split £10. A year later Old Tom Morris won £6 for his triumph, the first time a Champion received financial reward for winning what became recognised as golf's first Major. In 1982 we saw Tom Watson take home £32,000. Nowadays, the prize fund is paid in American dollars, with the winner claiming in the region of $2 million.

The financial side illustrates the growth, as do attendance figures. I was among 133,299 people who attended The Open in 1982. The last time it was staged at Troon when Henrik Stenson won an epic duel with Phil Mickelson in 2016 there were crowds of 173,134 for the week. Record attendances of 239,000 saw Tiger Woods win his first Open at St Andrews in 2000 and the first all-ticket attendance watched Shane Lowry's epic success of 2019 when the Championship returned to Royal Portrush for the first time in 68 years. It is all a far cry from the days when the pros teed off at the inconvenience of the Prestwick members to contest the earliest Opens.

But some things have stayed the same throughout. Winning The Open comes down to an internal battle of strength, heart and mind. It has to be won by someone who wants to become a true golfing champion. For most of us, there is only the opportunity to witness others fighting out such battles and it is always utterly

compelling to watch. I've known this ever since Royal Troon in 1982. I am convinced there is no other event that has offered such qualities so evocatively for so long.

Now we move towards St Andrews in 2022 and the 150th playing of The Open, staged at the historic 'Home of Golf'. There is much to celebrate and recall: triumph, despair, character and beauty. This is what this book aims to do.

Rarely was there a spare seat in the Troon grandstands of 1982.

ORIGINS: THE 'HOME OF GOLF'

ORIGINS: THE 'HOME OF GOLF'

Who is the best golfer never to have won a Major?

In clubhouses and bars all over the world, this is a ceaselessly debated topic and it is important because Majors define playing careers. It is also a pertinent question when we consider the origins of The Open, the oldest and most prestigious of these competitions. In the modern era, the Championship sits alongside the US Open, Augusta National's Masters and the PGA Championship in America as one of the four pillars of the men's game.

The First 'Great'

It is said that to be considered a truly great golfer, a player must win at least one of these elite competitions. Hence fevered debate over the merits of former world number ones such as Lee Westwood and Luke Donald who scaled the heights of world rankings without landing any of golf's most coveted prizes. Scotland's Colin Montgomerie was another to figure prominently in such conversations given his relentless domination of the European game in the 1990s, stellar Ryder Cup record but failure to land a Major title.

Go back to the nineteenth century, though, and consider another Major-less Scotsman, whose golfing prowess actually cuts this popular debate stone dead.

The only reason Allan Robertson did not win one of the biggest titles was because they did not exist when he was alive. But he carried enormous influence and the standard of his excellent play undoubtedly made him the most dominant golfer. The quality of his pioneering game prompted the creation of The Open, a tournament that was quickly regarded as golf's first and greatest Major Championship. Although he never lived to see it, he was the player who started it all.

Robertson was largely unbeatable because he was a brilliant player and he was astute enough to choose his opponents carefully. Born in 1815, he became the finest player of his day. Golf was his life as he followed the family trade of producing 'feathery' golf balls. He also controlled the course at St Andrews, the Fife town where he lived and worked and which has long been known as the 'Home of Golf'.

In the mid-1800s he occupied a house close to the course on the corner where today Golf Place meets Links Road. 'There is a myth about him never losing a match but that's not true,' says the renowned St Andrews-based historian Roger McStravick. 'But he was the best golfer and he was the Champion Golfer … He was canny in that he didn't accept every challenge, he picked his opponents and it was a title he guarded jealously.'

This was at a time when the best golfers competed in grand money matches financed by merchants and gamblers. They were huge betting occasions and choosing your partner was a skill in itself. 'There would be a bookie walking with the groups and people gambling after shots and sometimes they got too boisterous,' McStravick adds. 'I think it was their entertainment. They didn't have a TV or radio so

this was as exciting as could be. These were the origins of the professional game.'

One of the biggest of the 'grand matches' was played in 1843 when Robertson took on Musselburgh's Willie Dunne. It was an epic contest that spanned the Firth of Forth. The match was played over 20 rounds, a total of 360 holes. Robertson won it two rounds ahead with one left to play. Three years later they clashed for another epic duel and Allan emerged the victor once again. It was a match that generated huge interest in what was an increasingly golf- and gambling-obsessed corner of the east of Scotland.

In their book *Tom Morris of St Andrews: The Colossus of Golf*, authors David Malcolm and Peter E. Crabtree quote the *Fifeshire Journal*'s assessment of the winner of that 1846 match: 'We have no hesitation in asserting what everyone conversant in this difficult game admits, that Allan has proved himself the best player extant, and we are glad to add that we understand that a number of gentlemen have made arrangements to

present him with a handsome medal as champion, and well he deserves it, for he is the best golf player, but is quite a capital ball-maker, and with all a quiet, hard-boned, wiry little fellow, always as cool as a cucumber, and may be depended upon as doing his best at all times.'

Tournaments were organised in St Andrews and Robertson was sometimes barred from them because everyone knew he would win. He was a pioneer in using iron-faced clubs for lofted approach shots, which helped revolutionise the sport. Being the best golfer in Scotland, he was therefore the best player in the world.

Robertson was also part of a formidable alliance with Tom Morris, the son of a St Andrews weaver, who was developing into quite a player in his own right. The *Fifeshire Journal* reported that in October 1841 when he was a callow 20-year-old, Tom won the 'put-ins' or the 'in-puts', a competition where all the caddies (who were the better players) put into a kitty. Allan Robertson was excluded from the competition because of the inevitability that he would triumph. Tom emerged as the Champion, winning with a round of 92 strokes, which was the lowest score recorded at the time.

Robertson was a massive influence on Morris, who went on to become one of the most significant figures in the entire history of golf. 'I think Tom's time with Allan was priceless,' says Roger McStravick. 'It wasn't just learning the tricks of match play; all the little canny things that Allan did to pretend that he had hit one club when he'd played another and pretended that he had hit it as hard as he could when he plainly hadn't.'

They formed their impregnable partnership on the course and Tom joined Allan in the family golf ball manufacturing business. 'Court records show Tom only worked for Allan for around ten years, when people think it was for much longer,' McStravick adds.

It was skilled, painstaking work. The balls were made from three pieces of wet leather, stitched together and turned inside out, leaving a slit through which damp feathers were pushed. As they dried,

Allan Robertson's famous 'feathery'.

the feathers expanded and the leather shrank, making a tight, firm ball. They were then painted white so that they could be found and to give them a layer of protection.

Allan ran the family business from the age of 21 when his father, David, died in 1836. 'The old ball makers were very specialised,' says St Andrean author David Joy, who has written several books on golf's very earliest days. 'On a good day they could maybe make two balls. The ball cost about half a crown which was half a week's wages.' Such was Robertson's standing that to identify his handiwork he would simply stamp the balls with the name 'Allan'. There was little need to add his surname.

Their sphere of influence stretched beyond making golf balls and playing to the very highest standard. Between them, Robertson and Tom Morris laid the foundations for the modern game. Old Tom, as he became known, acquired not just the rudiments of making feathery balls but developed his golf, learned to tend and set up courses, and gained invaluable social skills. This combination of qualities ultimately made him golf's most significant ambassador, while his partnership with Robertson coincided with a boom period for the game, especially in St Andrews.

'Tom and Allan Robertson joined forces because the grand matches were rearing their heads,' Joy adds. 'There was the popularity of foursomes and gambling with the merchants, so they formed a team and they were never beaten.'

These were exciting times. St Andrews was coming alive with the extension of the railway to serve the town. Citizens had the right to use the 'links-land' for golf and the sport was growing in popularity.

Tom Morris's standing was also developing and he continued to work for Robertson until a fateful match in which Morris lost all his 'feathery' golf balls. His playing partner, Mr Campbell of Saddell, offered him a new-fangled rubber version, the 'gutta-percha'. It was made from gum that came from trees grown

'The Train to St Andrews'
by Garden G. Smith.

in Malaysia. Access to the material was a by-product of this period of industrialisation. It was a durable, all-weather golf ball that was virtually indestructible. It was also more affordable, costing only half the price of the old 'feathery'. David Joy insists: 'Nothing was more dramatic than the move from the feather ball to the gutta ball.'

In David Malcolm and Peter Crabtree's *Colossus* book, Morris was quoted by the writer H.S.C. Everard recounting what happened next: 'I took to it at once,' Morris said. 'As we were playing in, it so happened we met Allan Robertson coming out, and someone told him that I was playing a very good game with one of the new gutta balls, and I could see fine from the expression on his face, that he did not like it at all, and, when we met afterwards in his shop, we had some words about the matter, and there and then we parted company, I leaving his employment.'

Unlike his boss, Morris had no issues with moving with the times. 'Old Tom said it was a fight between tradition and technology and technology against tradition and he was caught in the middle,' says Joy. 'He was the right man at the right time the way the game was going.'

Robertson's fury also made sense. He eventually relented and did produce gutta balls but, at this point, his ancestral manufacturing skills were being rendered obsolete by his closest golfing ally. 'He came from a family who were ball makers for hundreds of years, going back to the 1600s,' Roger McStravick says. 'So when the gutty came in, that was a real threat to him. Famously he collected them and burned them rather than evolve with it. And this is why he and Tom fell out.' But the antipathy extended only to their working relationship.

'People make a big thing about them falling out but they still played a match as partners in the same year or a year later,' McStravick adds. 'If you see Allan's scrapbook it is full of clips about Tom Morris throughout. So it was not the end of their relationship at all.'

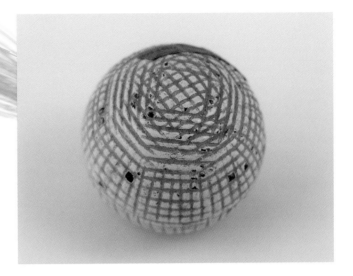

Old Tom Switches Coastline

In 1851 Tom Morris, his wife Nancy and their new-born son Tommy headed west to Prestwick on the Ayrshire coast, where the laying out and tending of a new course awaited. 'They knew Old Tom had lost his job so they invited him down to Prestwick to set up a course there which was a very compressed 12-hole course with the amount of ground they had,' says David Joy.

It was a big decision for Morris. Golf at the time was the preserve of the east of Scotland and he was heading to the western edge of the country, where the sport had yet to gain a foothold. 'For Tom Morris, I think it was a big risk because Prestwick didn't even have a course when he came to be the keeper of the green,' says Prestwick's archivist Andrew Lochhead.

Robertson continued in St Andrews producing golf balls but still playing to the very highest standard. In September 1858 he shot 79 around the St Andrews Links, which, at the time, was considered the best round ever to be played there.

Tom and Allan maintained their playing relationship through the decade but near its end Allan contracted jaundice. He was 10 days short of his 45th birthday when he died on 1 September 1859. The following day's *Scotsman* newspaper noted: 'His performances as a golfer were, it is admitted, without parallel; and being a man of the most amiable and obliging disposition, he was highly esteemed by every frequenter of the Links.'

Golf had lost its first genuine champion. How to find the next?

The obvious candidate was the highly talented Morris, who had been invited to Prestwick by the club's founding member Colonel James Ogilvy Fairlie, an Ayrshire-based landowner. Fairlie was a visionary and for a few years he played with the idea of creating a national competition. 'It was Fairlie's idea to set up a golf course,' Andrew Lochhead says. 'The reason that golf wasn't played on the west coast was because the weather was so wet and with the feathery ball it wasn't really feasible to play golf, especially with the higher rainfall in the winter.'

Fairlie helped instigate the 'Grand National Golf Club Tournament', the like of which had never before been seen. It was held in St Andrews in 1857 and

Robertson and Morris played key roles in running the event. In some respects it was pretty shambolic with teams failing to turn up and it was won by two Scotsmen representing the Blackheath club from London. It involved only 'gentlemen players', not the more talented caddies and pros, but nevertheless was deemed a success and with further refinements the event was staged again in the next two years.

Fairlie, along with his golfing partner the Earl of Eglinton, believed it was time to ditch the usual match play and set up a stroke-play tournament. This was the only way to determine a genuine champion.

'I think they were a kind of double act,' Lochhead says. 'They had both been members of St Andrews, they were the ones who were keen to start up golf at Prestwick. Eglinton was the more prominent, being the Earl of Eglinton, but Fairlie pretty much organised things. He would use Eglinton as his figurehead to promote events and get the top people from the east of Scotland to come and visit Prestwick.

'It took a while to get going but Fairlie then had the foresight to try and set up this event for the best professionals. It was a decent golf course and to try and get the professionals from the east to come and play in this event and start to build up the name of Prestwick.'

A belt made of red morocco leather with a silver golfing scene attached and costing £25 was commissioned to become the most handsome of prizes. As David Joy explains: 'James Ogilvy Fairlie said we need to acknowledge Allan Robertson. So let's throw out a challenge and see who will become the Champion Golfer of Scotland.

'And that was the instigation of the Open. It wasn't an open championship, it was by invitation.'

Indeed, the invitations had a rather limiting clause. Letters were sent by the Prestwick hosts to 11 clubs

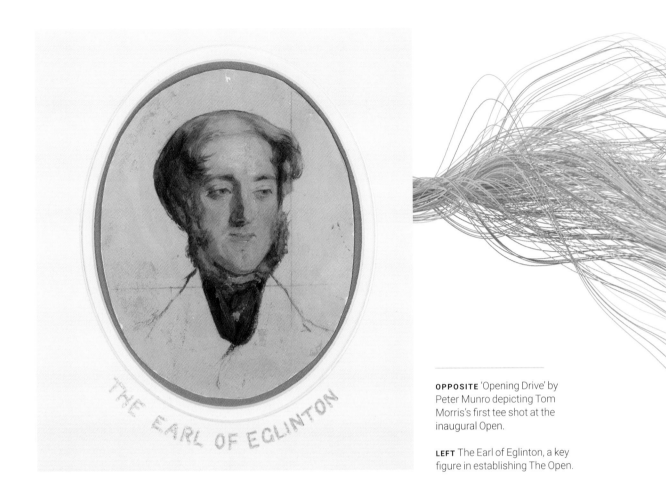

THE EARL OF EGLINTON

OPPOSITE 'Opening Drive' by Peter Munro depicting Tom Morris's first tee shot at the inaugural Open.

LEFT The Earl of Eglinton, a key figure in establishing The Open.

including St Andrews, Musselburgh, Bruntsfield, Leven, Carnoustie Panmure, Montrose, Perth, Blackheath and North Berwick. The letters invited them to send their best players, 'not exceeding three in number'. Furthermore, the letter stated: 'It is understood they must be known and respectable Cadies.' These professionals would also need to show a certificate of respectability from the treasurer of the golf club to which they were attached. As the archives at Prestwick show, Fairlie and Eglinton wanted to make sure that they avoided involving any 'objectionable characters'.

'These caddies, the artisan golfers, were known for being rough round the edges,' says Roger McStravick. 'They didn't come from the middle classes, they were from weaver families.'

This condition of 'respectable' ultimately impacted on the number of entrants. Only six players journeyed to Prestwick, to join two locals – Morris and Charlie Hunter – leaving a total of eight competitors for the inaugural competition. 'They weren't struggling to find players, they were struggling to find ones that they could rely on not to get intoxicated and let the club down,' McStravick insists.

There was also no prize money, just the Belt for which to compete. Potential competitors would have been able to find more lucrative money matches to play elsewhere.

Nevertheless, on 17 October 1860, the first formal attempt to find the Champion Golfer took place. The Open was born with competition over three rounds of a dozen holes on Tom Morris's 12-hole course at Prestwick, with a break for lunch at the local Red Lion pub. With Allan Roberston no longer alive, Tom was seen as the heir apparent. The bookmakers made him firm favourite to win the first Championship.

OPPOSITE Tom Morris, Open Champion 1861, 1862, 1864, 1867.

RIGHT Gold medal presented to Young Tom Morris in 1872, his fourth consecutive victory.

Park Prevails First but Morris Dynasty Established

When you see the grandeur of The Open nowadays, and the way the top names are so revered, it is difficult to imagine the Championship's low-key beginnings. Golfers in the first tournaments were a bit of an inconvenience. 'They had to squeeze out among the members,' McStravick says. 'Which is bizarre to think. It certainly would not have been "Oh, here we are at The Open, here's Tom Morris on the first tee, he's the favourite to win it" sort of thing. It was more like "Why are these oiks on our course? Get them out of the way as quickly as possible."'

But the tournament was properly run. It may have been low key, but it was not haphazard. 'Prestwick set up a committee,' says Andrew Lochhead. 'They set down the rules for the event, they bought a belt that cost a bit of money from the silversmiths in Edinburgh. They advertised the event in the newspapers and they wrote to other golf clubs to invite them to send players to come and compete. All these things together meant they were really quite serious about having a proper competition.

'Prestwick is very lucky, the archives from that still exist from that time. It's all laid down in writing from Fairlie in various letters for people to know about the event that was going to take place. Prestwick really wanted to be serious about having a proper golf event.'

Each pair was allocated a marker to keep score. Documents show Fairlie went out with the fourth pair. Each shot was marked on a dotted line next to the hole number and totalled accordingly.

While Morris was firm favourite, Willie Park was known to be a big threat. The bookies were, no doubt, altering the odds accordingly after Park claimed a three-stroke advantage by shooting 55 in the first round. Morris was in second place, and both he and Park shot 59s on the second circuit, meaning the man from Musselburgh remained three clear heading into the final loop. Tom outscored the leader 59 to 60 but it was not enough to prevent an upset. 'Tom was the favourite to win but got into trouble on the closing holes and didn't,' said Roger McStravick.

LEFT 'Tom Morris' by Sir George Reid.

ABOVE Robert Chambers of Bruntsfield, Edinburgh, won the second Grand National Golf Club Tournament at St Andrews in 1858.

Park came to the final green needing two putts from around 30 feet to win the Challenge Belt. The green was bumpy and hazardous, but Park's stroke was sure and the ball disappeared into the cup to complete a two-stroke victory in grand style. This made Willie Park the first ever Open Champion.

The home supporters and those with their roots in St Andrews had been firmly behind Tom Morris, but it was perhaps appropriate that Musselburgh supplied the first Champion. It occupies a highly significant place in the history of golf. Members of the Honourable Company, who drew up the original Rules of the Games, played their golf there along with players from other influential Edinburgh clubs such as Bruntsfield and Leith. 'Musselburgh was then arguably the home of golf,' argues Mungo Park, the great-grandson of Willie.

'The Edinburgh golfers, who in the 1830s were being crowded out of the two main centres – Bruntsfield and Leith Links – were channelled six miles down the coast to Musselburgh. There they could enjoy a quality of air that they wouldn't get in Edinburgh.'

Musselburgh also had a racetrack, was part of the fishing industry and was a mining town. 'Golf in the early years of the nineteenth century followed the money,' Mungo Park continues. 'There were merchants in Edinburgh, but it's also fair to say there were the "bad boys" of golf. A fairly raucous group of young men, aristocrats mostly, who rocked around the country gambling heavily, womanising and drinking.

'It's perhaps something that golf is not very proud of but they probably kept the game alive because they had the disposable wealth to support gambling on horses. So many of the early golf courses are in places where there was racing as well, and it's not accidental.

'There were also a lot of lawyers, some landowners from East Lothian, merchants from Leith and wealthy businessmen. Musselburgh was in the right place at the right time.'

Park came from lowly farming stock. One of six brothers, the census of the time showed him to be a farm labourer. 'I think he got into golf because they lived fairly close to the links, not right across from it as most histories say – Cottage Lane was about a half-mile walk away,' says Mungo Park. 'I think his life choices were to be a farm labourer like his dad, which would have been okay but not a good living. To strive to do something with his life he would have to go into service as a footman or a groom for the local gentry or play golf.'

Willie Park is often portrayed as a brash upstart, issuing challenges to greats such as Allan Robertson to play the big-money matches that prevailed at the time. 'I don't think he was a hustler,' Mungo adds. 'But I think out of need he had to put himself out there.

'He'd been through all the serious contenders in Musselburgh and he needed to extend himself to make a living out of it. If you could attract wealthy backers, it was like prize fighting, they were in your corner. They'd make matches for you and you would then earn a substantial cut from what they won from the bet that they placed on you. It was tough.'

Park's victory in the inaugural Open did not go down well. In a letter from London to the Prestwick treasurer, written two days after the tournament, a prominent Prestwick member, George Glennie, said: 'I regret exceedingly that our friend Tom was not successful.' Later he added: 'There is no doubt that Park is a fine player but in all the matches that I have seen him play, he is what I would call a lucky player. He goes bold at everything and is generally successful, especially with his long putter.'

'It's very sour,' Mungo Park says of the letter. 'I don't know what the source of that sourness is.

Maybe that slightly "look down your nose at Musselburgh" attitude was already creeping in because it was a mining town and not quite the place. The writer of the letter is quite outraged that Tom didn't win and that this rogue from Musselburgh should step in and take the first Belt. Almost an insult.'

There was also disappointment that the tournament only attracted eight players and for the second edition amateur golfers were also allowed to enter. In minutes of a Prestwick meeting held on 25 September 1861, it was said of the Challenge Belt competition: 'On all future occasions until it be otherwise resolved shall be open to all the world.' That meant amateurs could compete, but note the use of the word 'open'. That is the ethos which remains to this day. 1861 became the first time the event was truly open and all the leading professionals entered, including the Dunn twins, Willie and Jamie, who travelled from the Blackheath club in London.

Once again, though, Willie Park and Tom Morris were the dominant figures. Joint leaders after the first 12 holes, the defending Champion then earned a two-stroke advantage heading into the final round. But Park's renowned boldness brought trouble at the start of the final circuit. A daring second shot on the second hole put him in a severe hazard and it cost him three strokes. Morris went two strokes clear but the advantage was gone by the time they reached the seventh tee. From there, Park struggled and Morris birdied the short 11th, the penultimate hole, to go four clear. That effectively sealed it, although Tom's drive at the last was reported to have found a bed of moss close to a pool of water. He produced a fine airborne recovery and completed the final round in 53 shots for a comprehensive win.

Tom Morris beat Willie Park's winning total from the previous year by 11 shots. He was a popular winner of the Challenge Belt. McStravick has extensively researched Morris's life and concludes that he was 'gentle, funny, traditional and measured'.

LEFT Young Tom Morris wearing the Challenge Belt.

RIGHT 'Willie Park Senior', Open Champion 1860, 1863, 1866, 1875, by J.A.T. Bonnar.

Tom was also a man of the people who thought that his sport should be available to all. 'He was definitely for everyone playing the game, there was never a them and us. There was just golf – his attitude was a golfer is a golfer, anyone could play,' McStravick adds. His fellow historian David Joy concurs: 'When I started researching Old Tom, I could not find a bad word about him.

'He wasn't a showman, not at all, he was quite reserved and an example to us all. He was a great communicator and he'd speak to anybody from the captain of The R&A and royalty to the servants and the caddies.'

Joy, who has entertained thousands of people with his performances when he takes on the character of Old Tom Morris, also reveals: 'He had a face like an old leather pouch from being out in all weathers.'

Although the amateurs failed to mount any kind of challenge in that 1861 Open, it seemed appropriate that the best performer among their ranks was the man who had brought Morris to Prestwick and created the idea of the competition, Colonel James Ogilvy Fairlie.

So he was the Championship's first leading amateur and as the decades went by he was succeeded by many of the greatest players in the world in gaining that accolade.

Morris and Park's domination was somewhat counterproductive for the tournament. In 1862 only four professionals and four amateurs entered. There seemed little point in turning up, with those two Champions in the field and no prize money on offer. Tom matched his score of 163 strokes from the previous year to successfully defend the title and he beat Park by 13 shots, a record-winning margin that has never been beaten.

The following year Morris had the chance to win the Belt outright because anyone who claimed it three times in a row would be entitled to keep it. For the first time there was prize money: £5 for the runner-up, £3 for third place and £2 for fourth. The winner could make do with being presented with the Belt, which is what Willie Park did after a two-stroke victory over Morris.

Much has been made of the rivalry between the two players, particularly given the raucous support Park received from the Musselburgh miners during money matches. 'I think they got on,' insists Willie's great-grandson Mungo Park. 'Old Tom always said he liked to play against Willie. They were professionals with mutual respect and if there was a match being made it didn't matter where you came from. To think of it in terms of a solid and committed rivalry is artificial because these were guys who were just trying to make a living and it wasn't easy.'

Prize money for first place came in the following year, 1864, when Tom returned to the winner's circle and pocketed £6 as well as winning the Belt for the third time. The St Andrews-born Andrew Strath, who became Tom's successor the following year as the keeper of the green at Prestwick, finished second. Strath broke the Morris/Park stranglehold with that runner-up finish. And in 1865 he went one better. It was the sixth Open and Strath, an occasional playing partner of Morris, became only the third golfer to win it. He did it in rare style; his score of 162 strokes was the lowest to date.

Within a couple of years, though, standards rose considerably and in dramatic fashion. A new golfing force was on his way.

Young Tom Morris, as the record books refer to him, grew up with his illustrious father and the rest of the family in Prestwick. Tommy attended a fee-paying school, Ayr Academy. 'His education was a lot more middle class than a normal weaver's son's would have had,' says Roger McStravick. 'He was definitely brighter than average and forward thinking.'

Quickly, Tommy established a formidable reputation as a confident young golfer. He took on and beat one of his young contemporaries from Perth while his father was winning the main tournament that day, and it was the junior Morris who stole the headlines with his accomplished performance. By the time he was 15 he beat all of the top players in a tournament at Carnoustie. Tommy then beat Willie Park in match play for a £20 stake.

By the end of that year, 1864, his father had been persuaded by the Royal and Ancient to return to St Andrews and take charge of the links. But Old Tom and Young Tom went back to Prestwick the following year when the junior Morris entered The Open for the first time. Tom was out of form and his son was a stroke better than him over the first 24 holes. Neither player was in contention and Tommy pulled out of the tournament, perhaps wanting to take advantage of being back in Prestwick and having the chance to catch up with friends he had made growing up there.

Tommy Morris played with power and panache and possessed a wide range of shots that set him apart from most other players of the era. 'I just think he was very, very good,' says McStravick. 'I think Tiger in his early years was very similar, so he was definitely the Tiger Woods of his day. He played Open Champions from the age of 13 and he was beating them, and then they eventually allowed him to play in The Open Championship.'

Maturing physically and mentally, Tommy grew into an increasingly formidable golfer. In 1868 he romped to victory to land his first Challenge Belt with an extraordinary score of 154 strokes. It smashed Andrew Strath's 1865 record by eight. To use Roger McStravick's parallel with Tiger Woods, it was probably as significant an achievement as the American's 12-stroke Masters win on his professional debut at Augusta in 1997.

Tommy was only 17 years old and is still the youngest Open winner. His 47-year-old father finished in second place. Two generations occupying the top two spots in an Open is another notable record and one that is hard to imagine ever being matched. In 1869 the youngster successfully defended his title, winning by 11 shots from Bob Kirk. His triumph included The Open's first hole in one, achieved on Prestwick's eighth hole.

Young Tom was an invincible force wherever he played, and he matched Allan Robertson's record of 79 shots over the 18 holes of St Andrews. In May 1870

he then lowered it to 77 strokes and went to that year's Open as the overwhelming favourite.

The Championship was now causing a buzz in the press and attracted larger numbers of boisterous spectators. Tommy Morris, regarded as a local hero by the Prestwick population, was the main attraction. He began the 1870 Open by shooting a round of 47 over the 12 holes, which given the still rudimentary nature of the equipment and course conditioning is regarded as one of the greatest rounds ever played. 'That's one under fours,' notes Andrew Lochhead. 'The course measured 3,800 yards so on average each hole was 360 yards. That says it all. It was a course that didn't have proper fairways, the ball didn't run so much. It was a pretty fantastic score.'

With further rounds of 51 and 51, his finishing score was 149, 12 strokes better than anyone else. In the course of that triumph, he made an extraordinary three on the 578-yard opening hole, remember, with hickory clubs and the 'gutty' ball.

'When you see Tommy get a three on that opening hole at Prestwick you can tell these were incredibly skilled golfers,' McStravick contends. 'It was all about hitting the sweet spot and for them to nail that sweet spot, wow! I'd love to see him and Tiger. Just give Tommy a week with modern clubs and he'd be fine.'

So, back then, Young Tom Morris was indisputably the best. He had won The Open for three straight years and the Challenge Belt was his to keep. The only sadness was that Colonel James Ogilvy Fairlie, the inspiration behind the quest to find the Champion Golfer, had passed away before that year's Championship.

In the absence of his prompting and without a trophy to play for, there was no Open in 1871. But the Royal and Ancient, Prestwick and the Musselburgh-based Honourable Company agreed on a new trophy in 1872, a Claret Jug commissioned at a cost of £30. Furthermore the tournament would rotate between the three clubs and there would be a total prize fund of £20 with £8 going to the Champion, along with the new trophy and a medal engraved with the winner's name and his score, something that every Open victor still receives.

Prestwick staged the tournament in October of that year and Tommy Morris was again the winner from a small field, but he was pushed hard by Andrew Strath's brother Davie, who finished three strokes behind. So Tom Morris Jr was the first name engraved on the Claret Jug even though the new trophy was not completed until 1873. No other player has won The Open on four successive occasions.

The 1873 Championship was the first to be played at St Andrews. The weather was dreadful and quagmire conditions rendered it a lottery won by Tom Kidd ahead of Jamie Anderson, with Tommy finishing third. The home town took the top three spots, despite the conditions. The following year it moved to Musselburgh, where Willie Park's brother Mungo, who had returned from two decades at sea, was the Champion. Then, in 1875 it went back to Prestwick and Willie claimed his fourth and final title amidst a horribly tragic build-up to the event.

Tommy Morris was a newly married man at this time and his wife Margaret was expecting their first child. On 4 September 1875, Tommy and his father were playing an eagerly anticipated match against Willie and Mungo Park at North Berwick. The contest captured the imagination of the growing golf population of the east of Scotland, but the day will never be remembered for the golf.

There are various accounts of what happened. In their book *Colossus*, David Malcolm and Peter Crabtree quote what they believe was the most accurate account as recorded in *The Scotsman* newspaper.

The match had been completed and the Morrises had won when Tommy was handed a telegram 'announcing that his wife was dangerously ill and requesting that he should go back to St Andrews with all possible haste'. With no train from North Berwick that would make the connection with the last Fife train from Edinburgh, the Morrises were about to set off by road when Mr Lewis, a summer resident of the town, offered to sail them across the Firth of Forth in his yacht moored in the harbour.

They had just set sail when a second telegram arrived, 'stating that Mrs Morris had given birth to a son, but that both mother and child were dead'. It is believed Tommy only heard the tragic news upon his return to St Andrews. The Open was only a couple of days away and, understandably, neither Morris competed.

By the end of the year there was further tragedy as Tommy was taken fatally ill on Christmas Day 1875. He had been to a private party the evening before and went to bed as normal. Evidence suggests he suffered a ruptured aneurysm in the back of his chest. He was just 24 years old. Locals contend he perished as the result of a broken heart given the events of September that year.

Tommy led a remarkable life that in golfing terms remains indelibly inked in the record books. He has been described in some quarters as something of a tempestuous firebrand but Roger McStravick contends otherwise. 'He's portrayed as this upstart but he could not be Tom Morris's son and be anything but grounded. That would have been in his genes,' he said. And David Joy believes golf lost an incredible champion at precisely the wrong time. 'The great sadness of Young Tom's death was what he missed because the whole game was soaring.'

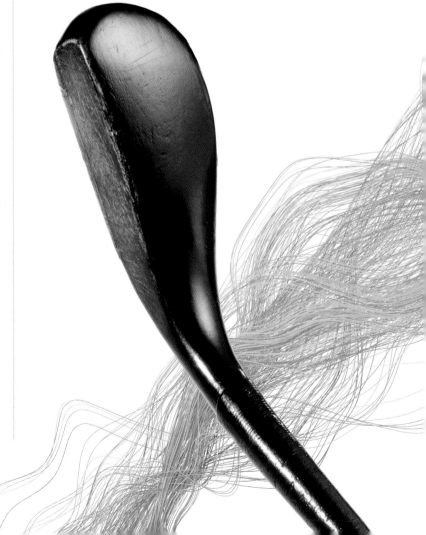

THE COURSES

THE COURSES

Browning, fast, firm summer fairways that snake through, over and around majestic sand dunes, surrounded by wispy longer grasses and punctuated by pot bunkers; they ultimately lead to the sanctuary of natural, verdant putting surfaces. This is what golf has looked like around the windswept coastline of the United Kingdom throughout the centuries the sport has been played. It is links land. It is where the game of golf originated and it provides a time-honoured environment for every Open Championship.

Fourteen courses situated at various locations in Scotland, England and Northern Ireland carry the distinction of staging The Open. They are the cathedrals of the game: grand, historic arenas that through the ages have allowed the best players to demonstrate their full repertoires of shot making and ball striking. These courses demand imagination, guile, power, precision and patience – the essential components that make the most worthy Champions.

Some are no longer used for The Open – Prestwick Golf Club and Musselburgh in Scotland, Royal Cinque Ports Golf Club and Prince's Golf Club in the south-east corner of England – but golf is still enjoyed at these locations and their places in history are assured. With the return of the Championship to Royal Portrush Golf Club in 2019, the other 10 courses remain at the disposal of The R&A. They ensure a uniquely historic feel every year the Championship is played. When The 150th Open is held at St Andrews in 2022 it will be the 30th occasion the Claret Jug has been competed for on the iconic Old Course. No other venue has staged the Championship more times.

Prestwick is the next closest with 24 Opens, but not since 1925 when the American-based Cornishman Jim Barnes was the victor. Each of the existing Open venues has undergone design changes through the decades, but all have preserved their original character. They still represent golf in its most natural form, providing the nearest test to how the game was originally played. The R&A advocate traditional maintenance practices and want greens and approaches to be firm and running. 'The threat of the wind and the ground game make it a much more three-dimensional sport than the target golf that is prevalent due to the climates and grasses in other parts of the world,' says architect Martin Ebert. He has worked on design and restoration projects at seven of the current Open venues.

'The beauty of links golf is that it's a ground game as well as through the air,' Ebert, a partner at Mackenzie & Ebert, adds. 'It's obviously a huge responsibility. What we've tried to do is study the history and evolution of the courses. It's amazing what we've learned from that.'

Many of the venues that stage The Open were first played by golfers using the old feathery and gutty balls but the game has obviously developed massively since those days. While Old Tom Morris could dispatch drives an impressive 220 yards or so in the nineteenth century, today's modern stars average 300 yards or more with their tee shots. So the courses have been

lengthened and altered to cope with an ever-changing sport. However, shot-making tests and strategic questions remain at the heart of a links challenge which is also at the mercy of often capricious coastal weather conditions.

The R&A invites clubs to host The Open and works closely with them on any alterations that might be required. Architects, such as Ebert, are contracted by the individual clubs to carry out the changes. But the work is often not straightforward and there are many more factors to be considered than simply providing a stiff and fair test for the world's best players. 'We always have to be aware that 99 per cent of the time the course has to be good for members and visitors,' Ebert says.

'Trying to find that happy medium of testing the world's best and still making it a pleasurable experience for everyone else is at the heart of any proposals, as is a good study of how the course has evolved over the years.

'What we've discovered is that a lot of good features can get either lost or diluted. Sometimes there are good reasons for that, but we think you should have a look and go back and see if there are features that should be restored.'

These courses carry the magical distinction of being known as Open venues. They have all provided magnificent tests of golf and generated many of the sport's most memorable moments.

PREVIOUS PAGE The par-4 first hole, Royal St George's.

OPPOSITE AND ABOVE Views of the par-4 sixth hole, the Old Course, St Andrews.

Prestwick

Few golfing layouts boast a deeper history than Prestwick on the west coast of Scotland. It is the course where The Open began in 1860. Founded nine years earlier, the club was formed after a meeting of locals at the nearby Red Lion pub.

'Prestwick is a seaside town,' says the club archivist Andrew Lochhead. 'It had a charter in the 1400s so it's a very old town with a population of 50,000. Traditionally it was where people came on holiday in the summer. It's very proud of its origins as the founding place of The Open Championship.'

Originally a criss-crossing 12-hole routing, it began with a first hole known as 'Back of Cardinal' measuring 578 yards. The notion of par did not exist in those days; the term was bogey. On the scorecard that monstrous opening hole was regarded as a six. The overall bogey was 48.

The first dozen Opens were played at Prestwick. The original keeper of the green and architect, Tom Morris, won four titles and his son Tommy claimed four in a row between 1868 and 1872. Young Tom set the lowest score with a round of 47 which started with

a remarkable three at that lengthy opening hole. This came in 1870, a year after securing the first Open hole in one at the 166-yard eighth. Originally measuring 3,799 yards, the penultimate hole at 132 yards was the shortest. The club acquired more land in time for the 1893 Open, which was played over 18 holes and won by Willie Auchterlonie.

Jim Barnes's victory of 1925 marked the last of the 24 Opens staged at Prestwick, but it was another American-based golfer who stirred the locals and simultaneously put paid to the course's Championship status. 'MacDonald Smith, who was originally from Scotland, was leading going into the final round and there were estimated crowds of around 15,000 that came to watch him,' says Andrew Lochhead.

'The course was overrun by all these spectators and the impression given was that Prestwick couldn't control the crowds and thereafter it was kept off the rota. It was probably fair enough because it was quite a quirky course and by this time courses were becoming longer.'

A magnificent clubhouse, which is a standing monument to the club's rich history, overlooks the present-day links, which is par-71 and measures 6,908 yards. 'Our name is in the history books as being a big part of The Open,' Lochhead adds. 'I don't think any of the members begrudge the fact that it won't come back here.'

St Andrews

'I've always loved this golf course,' said Tiger Woods when he arrived back at St Andrews for the 2015 Open, the last time the Championship was played at the 'Home of Golf'. The sport's most prominent and dominant figure has a special affinity for a unique layout which has staged more Opens than any other course. Twice Woods has won the Claret Jug in St Andrews, in 2000 and 2005, and it is no coincidence that he has flourished so well on the ancient Fife links.

The task of every Open is to identify the Champion Golfer of the Year and there are few better places at succeeding in such a quest. The list of Open winners on the Old Course is exemplary.

It is a who's who from every era of the game. Consider these names from the list of champions: Jamie Anderson, Bob Ferguson, J.H. Taylor (twice), James Braid (twice), Bobby Jones, Sam Snead, Peter Thomson, Bobby Locke, Kel Nagle, Jack Nicklaus (twice), Seve Ballesteros, Sir Nick Faldo and Woods (twice). These are all genuine greats of the game.

'If you're going to be a player people will remember, you have to win The Open at St Andrews,' Nicklaus famously commented. Woods, after his initial Open success in 2000, said: 'I am inclined to believe that winning The Open at the "Home of Golf" is the ultimate achievement in the sport.'

The 'Road Hole' and a view up the famous closing hole on the Old Course.

Former player and BBC Television commentator Ken Brown adds: 'St Andrews, strategically, is such an interesting course. It kept you absolutely at your wits' end the whole time. And then there's the place, the atmosphere and the history.'

It is an alchemy that seems to bring the best from the greatest players. 'I just love the creativity,' says Woods. 'You have to be able to hit all different types of shots. The first thing I ever heard about St Andrews is that all you do is hit it as hard as you can and aim left. That's basically not how you play the golf course.

'You need to have the right angles. Over the years of learning how to play the golf course under all different types of wind conditions, it changes greatly, and it's based on angles. You have to put the ball on certain sides of the fairways in order to get the ball close. That type of thinking and strategy is something I've always loved.'

The routing could hardly be more straightforward yet it is subtly changeable. The front nine is played down the right-hand side of a relatively narrow piece of land which stretches from the old grey town to the Eden estuary. It switches direction at the short eighth for what is known as 'the loop' and from the 10th players head down the opposite side of the course to continue an anti-clockwise journey.

Apart from the first, ninth, 17th and 18th holes, the greens are shared. They are vast areas. Players putting are largely oblivious to what is happening around the other hole on the same green because it is so far away. The second hole is shared with the 16th and so on. Add together the two holes using the same double green and the total always comes to 18.

'Golf has been played here since the 1400s; the first written record was probably in the 1500s,' says St Andrews-based historian Roger McStravick. 'I get asked all the time who designed the course and I say, "Well, mostly God." This is where the sheep slept, they bunked down – i.e. bunker – and they were all natural hills and hollows.'

But the hand of man has also played a significant role in enhancing and preserving this most natural of golf courses. Originally it was 22 holes, and played in a clockwise direction. In 1764 the Society of St Andrews Golfers (which later became the Royal and Ancient Golf Club) decided the challenges were too short and this led to a reduction to 18 longer holes.

Allan Robertson played a key role, bringing in the double greens in 1857, and Tom Morris oversaw a string of significant changes between 1866 and 1879. This was done thanks to funding from the Royal and Ancient and the town. 'The genius of Tom Morris is on the greens,' McStravick adds. 'If you walk up to the 18th it looks fairly flat, slightly up on the right. If you stand at the steps by The R&A Clubhouse you can see it's got such a slope. Whether deliberate or not there are so many optical illusions in his design. I think he had a really good eye; it was his natural talent, that's my gut feeling. He could tell what makes a green work.'

That 18th hole has a deep depression in front of the vast sloping green known as the 'Valley of Sin', which transforms a straightforward-looking home hole into a genuine challenge. Invariably it is made more daunting by townsfolk and tourists looking on. They inevitably gather in this historic area, no matter how humble the golfer to watch might be.

Before encountering the delights of the closing hole there are any number of iconic features to be negotiated. It starts with the Swilcan Burn snaking around the front of the opening green on a relatively short par 4 by today's standards.

The first and last holes are separated from the town by distinctive white-posted fences reminiscent of a horse-racing track. On the rest of the course, bunkers, little and large, litter the course. They are often obscured from view off the tee by the humps and bumps of the undulating landscape. On the second there is one called 'Cheape's', named after George Cheape, The R&A captain who complained against the use of the course for rabbit farming in the early nineteenth century.

The imposing 'Shell Bunker' guards the front of the seventh green while 'Hell Bunker' is the appropriately named monster that concentrates golfers' minds on the par-5 14th.

Most iconic is the 17th, the famous 'Road Hole', which is 495 yards of sheer terror for any golfer. The destiny of an Open played at St Andrews can never be confidently predicted until all the contenders have completed this imposing par 4. The drive crosses low-rise buildings at the back of the Old Course Hotel where once railway sheds were located. Out of bounds stretches down the right while rough provides trouble to the left of a narrow-angled fairway.

Guarding the green is the famous steep-faced 'Road Hole Bunker', a relatively small hazard that gathers balls that stray only slightly offline. To the back of the angled, upturned green – which is significantly wider than it is deep – lies the infamous road which is still part of the course with a stone wall behind it. This is an arena that serves great drama at every St Andrews Open and it is little wonder it is always surrounded by vast grandstands offering spectators the best view of the action.

And then comes surely the most stirring walk in golf, up to the closing hole. It involves crossing the Swilcan Bridge, an ancient stone structure thought to be 700 years old. You do not need to be a brilliant player to take this route; the vast majority who do are nothing more than average golfers enjoying public land which has been set aside for golf down the centuries. But it is true to say that pretty much every great player in the entire history of the sport has walked over that bridge while making that most evocative journey back into the magical, historic town known universally as the 'Home of Golf'.

The R&A Clubhouse. Its foundation stone was laid on 13 July 1853.

Musselburgh

Musselburgh is a short nine-hole course surrounded by a horse racetrack, but its importance to golf and The Open cannot be underestimated. The ultimate target of every golf hole is four and a quarter inches (108mm) in diameter. This is the width of the ancient tool used to cut the holes at Musselburgh and it was standardised for all golf in 1893 when the Royal and Ancient adopted the measurement. It remains unchanged today.

For nineteenth-century members of the influential Honourable Company, Musselburgh's East Lothian location provided an ideal escape from Edinburgh's stinking industrial fog. Golf has been in the area for centuries and it is alleged that Mary Queen of Scots played there or nearby in 1567. The course claimed to be the oldest in the world, records showing that a local lawyer, Sir John Foulis, played there on 2 March 1672. But Burgh documents reveal golf in St Andrews in 1552 and elsewhere in Fife, at Elie, in 1589.

Originally a seven-hole layout, with two extra holes added in 1838 and 1870, Musselburgh staged six Opens. The Championships held there were played over four loops adding up to 36 holes. Mungo Park, Willie's brother and a native of the town, edged Young Tom Morris by two strokes to lift the Claret Jug with a score of 159 in the first Open played around the tight links in 1874. The other players to win at Musselburgh were Jamie Anderson (1877), Bob Ferguson (1880), Willie Fernie (1883), David Brown (1886) and the son of the Championship's first victor, Willie Park Jr (1889). Thereafter Musselburgh lost its Open status when the Honourable Company shifted their base a few miles further east to Muirfield.

Today Musselburgh Links (Old Course) is maintained and run by East Lothian Council and is a 2,968-yard par 34 consisting of three par 3s, five short par 4s and a par 5. It is pretty much as it was when it staged The Open and visiting players can take on the course using hired hickory clubs. This creates an experience as close as possible to that enjoyed 150 years ago by the Park family and their fellow golfing pioneers.

Muirfield

Like the Old Course at St Andrews, Muirfield has an extraordinary record for producing champions of the highest calibre. The great amateur Harold Hilton set the trend in 1892 by winning the inaugural Open to be staged there, the first contested over 72 holes. Harry Vardon, Walter Hagen, Sir Henry Cotton, Gary Player, Jack Nicklaus, Lee Trevino, Tom Watson, Sir Nick Faldo (twice), Ernie Els and Phil Mickelson are other golfing legends who carry the distinction of claiming the Claret Jug on the East Lothian links. 'You look at all those guys – we all hit it pretty darn solid in our era,' noted Faldo, the winner there in 1987 and 1992.

'Muirfield, as a course, is as good as it gets,' says television commentator Ken Brown. The former Ryder Cup player posted his best Open finish of tied sixth in 1980 playing there in the final round alongside Champion Watson. 'If you ask all the players it would probably come out on top.' Brown notes the fair nature of the course with flatter than usual links fairways but insists it remains a formidable challenge. 'If it blows a bit you can rattle up an 80 in no time at all.'

The course's popularity stretches to the greatest names in the game. 'From the beginning, I liked Muirfield very much,' said 1966 winner Nicklaus. He made the comment after completing a career Grand Slam of Major titles with that victory. It remains his favourite course in Britain and the winner of a record 18 Majors chose the name 'Muirfield Village' for his own course near Columbus, Ohio. 'While it has the intrinsic qualities of a British seaside links, fairways that tumble every which way, magnificent low-cropped turf, deep bunkers, and hard, unwatered greens, it is a frank and open course,' he added.

Muirfield was first played over 16 holes initially laid out by Old Tom Morris in 1891. It was extended to the full 18 for the following year's Open won by Hilton. Over the first few decades much work was required to alleviate waterlogging while several sandy areas needed cultivation. Then came the most significant changes, made in 1923, when the Honourable Company acquired 50 more acres to the north of the course.

One of the great architects of the time, Harry Colt, was consulted and his recommendations led to the distinctive flow of holes that continues today. The front nine follows a clockwise direction around the outside of the course before returning to the clubhouse. Play then moves to an inside loop, with the closing nine holes played in an anti-clockwise direction. Tom Simpson re-modelled the short 13th in 1935 before the next major changes made ahead of the 2013 Open, won so thrillingly by Phil Mickelson in gloriously fast and firm conditions.

Those alterations were overseen by designer Martin Hawtree during the winters of 2010 and 2011. Subtle alterations were made to 15 holes, including the introduction of new bunkers to increase challenges off the tee, relocating bunkers to tighten entrances to greens and widening putting surfaces to provide more pin positions. The course was extended to 7,192 yards with a par of 71, but the essential character of what is regarded the fairest Open venue has been preserved.

'It's a fabulous test,' Faldo said when he arrived to play the 2013 Championship. The Englishman noted the demands Muirfield makes on the world's best players: 'You have to work the ball well, you have to drive the ball well. The greens have quite a bit of undulation on them so you have to stay on the right side of them.'

Muirfield is notable for killing Grand Slam bids. Nicklaus came to the Scottish links in 1972 having won the Masters and the US Open, and finished second to Trevino. Thirty years later, Tiger Woods was on an equally dominant roll at the Majors and hot favourite at Muirfield after he opened with rounds of 70 and 68. But if the golf course was fair, the weather most certainly was not. A fearful storm battered the links during the third afternoon and Woods scored a ruinous 81. Despite closing with a brilliant 65 he finished well down the field.

That Open in 2002 was won by Ernie Els after a play-off against Thomas Levet, Stuart Appleby and Steve Elkington. Two-time Champion Padraig Harrington was in the group who missed the shoot-out by a single stroke. 'This is unusual for a links golf course,' the Irishman said. 'It rewards somebody who is very consistent and can hit the middle of the fairway and hit the middle of the greens.'

Faldo, The Open's most successful player at Muirfield, added: 'If you go and play well out there, you'll score well.' It sounds easy, but it is a blueprint that only the finest players are capable of following. Look at the list of Muirfield champions, Nick included, and you find conclusive proof.

Royal St George's

William Laidlaw Purves was a much-travelled Scottish doctor who settled in London in the late nineteenth century and was a scratch handicap golfer at Royal Wimbledon Golf Club. The passion of his older brother, Alexander Pattison Purves, was archaeology and this somewhat random hobby ultimately proved highly significant to the history of golf. It led to the establishment of Royal St George's, a course that has staged 15 Opens.

Alexander was visiting his sibling in London when he suggested a trip to Sandwich Bay in Kent. He wanted to see the place where Claudius landed in AD 43. When they arrived there, the brothers climbed the tower of nearby St Clement's Church to survey the surrounding countryside. 'By George! What a place for a golf course,' exclaimed the intrepid doctor when he saw the vast expanse of spectacular sand dunes that dominated his view.

This story is detailed in *A Course for Heroes*, a history of Royal St George's, the golf club set up by William Laidlaw Purves after that initial trip to the Kent coast. He was correct: the land was perfect and it inspired the creation of a historic links which became the first to stage The Open outside Scotland. This would not be so much a local course but one to represent England. In terms of nomenclature, St George's was the equivalent of St Andrews in Scotland.

The course hosted its inaugural Open in 1894, a Championship that yielded the first of J.H. Taylor's five victories. The most recent, the delayed 2021 edition won by Collin Morikawa, was the 149th Championship. Other winners on this immensely challenging links include: Harry Vardon (twice), Walter Hagen (twice), Sir Henry Cotton, Bobby Locke, Sandy Lyle, Greg Norman and outsider Ben Curtis, who was ranked 396 in the world when he won in 2003.

'The funny thing is Ben turned up about four days before anyone else,' recalls former R&A Chief Executive Peter Dawson. 'I got to know him quite well; he was the only player there. I walked holes with him and his wife a few times so in the end I thought, "Wow, maybe that's the way to do it."'

The course has been a mighty test ever since the land was acquired from its previous owner, the Earl of Guildford. Play began in 1887. The original layout measured 6,012 yards and was designed by Dr Laidlaw Purves, who teamed up with fellow Scots Henry Lamb, a leading amateur and wine merchant, and William Anderson, who worked in the shipping industry. They were the driving force in setting up the Sandwich Golfing Association, which was the forerunner to the St George's club.

After his victory in the 1894 Open, J.H. Taylor described the course as 'a rather desolate and windswept spot'. In his book *Golf: My Life's Work*, Taylor added that with the old gutty ball, 'Some of the carries off the tee were rather frightening … The possibility of disaster was only too apparent from almost every shot one was called upon to play.'

Vardon won there in 1899 and 1911 and described St George's, which gained royal patronage in 1902, as 'the best course in the world'. The six-time winner detailed his reasons: 'There is scarcely a hole at which a player who only half hits his ball from the tee does not find himself in grave difficulties, demanding an unusually brilliant recovery and sterling play until he has holed out.' Writing in *The Complete Golfer* in 1905, Vardon added: 'The greens on that course are always well protected and they abound in character and variety.'

But not every player has shared Vardon's unbridled enthusiasm for the Kent course. Throughout its history, balls have occasionally bounced off firm fairways after what seemed perfect drives. This, though, goes to the heart of the nature of links golf. It is not always fair and the resulting adversity is not just a test of technique but also mental resolve.

'Royal St George's is a sleeping giant,' insists television commentator Ken Brown. 'It's not quite so popular with some of the overseas players because you get some quirky odd bounces. It's not necessarily the fairest but it is a very exciting, challenging course to play.'

And Open competitors have grown to like it. Phil Mickelson was no fan when he played Royal

St George's in 2003. Upon returning for the 2011 Championship, the left-handed American was able to much better appreciate the nuances of the challenges. 'The first hole is a great example of what I see throughout the rest of the golf course,' he said. 'There are three bunkers in front of the green that you have to clear, and the front of the green is pitched away pretty severely, so you have to be in the fairway to get the ball stopped.

'If you're coming out of the rough and it doesn't have any spin, there's no way you'll stop the ball on the green.'

The strategic complexities of the course, which measured 7,189 yards for the 2021 Open, provide another attractive element for Mickelson. 'The angles at which you have to approach greens, landing them 40, 50 yards short of the green, the way the bunkers are staggered, working around left of one bunker, right of the other, that is starting to come through on almost every hole,' he said. 'I'm starting to appreciate the golf course.'

Like Muirfield the holes flow in circular directions and the routing resembles an approximate figure of eight. The long par-4 fourth boasts the UK's tallest and deepest bunker, cut into a monstrous dune which needs to be by-passed with a resolute tee shot.

Changes have been made throughout its history, with the number of 'blind' shots required steadily reduced. After the First World War, the notorious 'Maiden' hole, the par-3 sixth, was altered so that tee shots no longer had to be played directly over a vast dune. The ninth and 17th greens were also moved from hollows to plateaus. It is thought Dr Alister MacKenzie, the architect who laid out Augusta National, was involved in the changes.

The long par-5 14th has proven a graveyard for Open hopes. In 1928 Gene Sarazen ignored his caddie's advice and ran up a seven on the 'Canal' hole, ultimately finishing second, two behind Walter Hagen. Bernhard Langer was hoping to pile pressure onto Greg Norman by choosing a driver in the final round in 1993, but the German smacked it out of bounds to kill off any hope of hunting down the Australian Champion. Norman's conquest in 1993 was as much down to his brilliance as Langer's capitulation on the 14th. The Champion fired a breathtaking front-running six-under-par final round 64 that included seven birdies. He set a new record aggregate of 267 for a win by two strokes over defending Champion Nick Faldo and became the first Champion to shoot four rounds in the 60s.

In 2011, a charging Dustin Johnson halved Darren Clarke's four-stroke lead with birdies at the 10th and 12th. 'I finally felt like I got some pressure on him,' Johnson recalled. Fatefully he chose a 2-iron for his second shot from 250 yards and it drifted right and out of bounds. 'I hit a terrible shot,' he admitted. It led to a ruinous double-bogey-7 and it was Clarke who went on to complete a hugely popular victory.

LEFT 'By George! What a place for a golf course.'

OPPOSITE Royal St George's formidable closing hole.

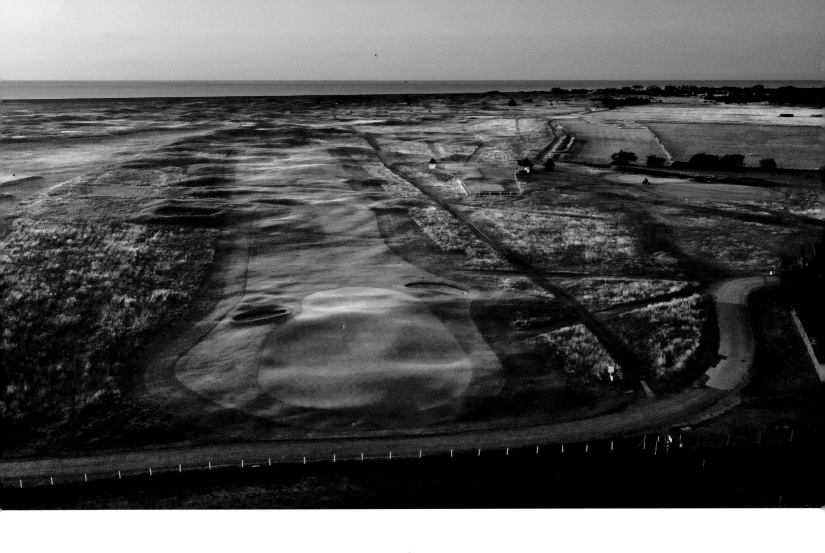

The course has continued to evolve and further changes were made ahead of the 149th Championship, particularly on the 18th hole. 'It's a mark of how the game has moved on, the tee couldn't go back at all,' explains architect Martin Ebert. 'There used to be three bunkers in the old days which used to be beyond driving distance, but with the advancement of the game they were clearly restricting how far the golfers could hit it in still or downwind conditions.'

The number of bunkers had been reduced from three to two, but Ebert felt further modifications were required. 'For this Open, the left-hand bunker was pushed much further left and further on and we wanted to see if this resulted in the golfers doing some slightly different things off the tee,' he said. 'Maybe they can thread the eye of the needle or maybe they can hit it a bit further beyond the very dominant dune in the middle of the fairway to clear that, but stop short of the left-hand bunker.'

Every modification has been aimed at preserving and enhancing the enduring challenge of a thought-provoking golf course. Its rich history has more than justified the instinctive reaction of the visionary doctor William Laidlaw Purves back in 1885 when he first caught sight of this extraordinary piece of golfing land.

Royal Liverpool

Tiger Woods ended a 39-year wait for an Open Champion to be decided at Royal Liverpool with a commanding performance over one of the most historic golf courses in England. That 2006 victory was followed eight years later by a thrilling triumph for Rory McIlroy, confirming Hoylake's enduring ability to inspire the most exciting players in the world.

The Liverpool Golf Club was founded in the Wirral town of Hoylake in 1869 and gained royal status within two years. The course was laid out on land also used for horse racing. Of English seaside courses only Westward Ho! in Devon is older. Hoylake quickly became an influential venue for the development of the game, staging in 1885 what became recognised by The R&A as the first Amateur Championship when Allan Macfie beat Horace Hutchinson 7&6 in the final.

Among its members the club boasted John Ball Jr, probably Britain's greatest amateur, who won the 1890 Open at Prestwick. Within seven years of that triumph, Royal Liverpool staged The Open for the first time and it was appropriately won by another Hoylake amateur, Harold Hilton. It was his second title following his 1892 victory at Muirfield.

The course became renowned for crowning landmark Champions. The Open's first overseas winner was Frenchman Arnaud Massy, who beat J.H. Taylor by two strokes at Royal Liverpool in 1907. Massy later chose Hoylake as the middle name for his daughter Margot. Taylor won there in 1913, then came a second

Royal Liverpool at Hoylake, with views across the Irish Sea.

title for Walter Hagen in 1924. He had already become the first American to lift the Claret Jug. Bobby Jones's triumph in 1930 helped him complete what was regarded as the Grand Slam – The Open and Amateur Championships as well as the US Open and US Amateur.

There followed wins for Alf Padgham (1936), Fred Daly (1947), Peter Thomson (1956) and then Argentina's Roberto DeVicenzo. 'That was a very sentimental victory in 1967,' remembers Donald Steel, a highly influential figure in Open golf course design and former correspondent for the *Sunday Telegraph*. 'I got to know him very well. He was a very, very nice man and everybody wanted him to do well and he was a considerable player.'

From the beginning of the 1960s The Open as an event started to significantly grow in size and stature. The top players were among the biggest sports stars in the world: Jack Nicklaus, Arnold Palmer, Lee Trevino and, from Britain, the 1969 Champion Tony Jacklin. Hoylake could no longer cope; it needed more land and a re-routed and re-modelled course, and so disappeared from the list of venue courses for nearly four decades.

Steel was at the forefront of the campaign to bring The Open back to one of its most notable venues. 'As The Open hadn't been held there since 1967, the club needed cajoling in the late 1990s,' he says. 'I was invited to an extraordinary general meeting

of members on a Sunday afternoon with a plan of what would be necessary in terms of radical change to the course. The R&A then needed to be convinced the changed layout would work.'

The old 17th hole was problematic with its green tight to the boundary fence, affording no spectator movement. A new putting surface was built and the par 4 re-shaped. For The Open it is used as the opening hole and the second is played as the 18th by the members. That hole also has a new green designed by Steel, who made myriad design alterations around the course.

Crucially, land was acquired from a school close to the sixth, which made room for a broadcast compound, and a deal was done to convert the public course on the opposite side of Meols Drive into a practice range fit for Open competitors for that week.

Routing the course to start on the 17th meant that the usual and distinctive opening hole, in front of Hoylake's grand clubhouse, which intimidatingly doglegs around the members' practice ground, became the third on the Championship card. It also meant an imposing horseshoe of grandstands could be built around the par-5 16th green, which would serve as the home hole.

That putting surface felt the tears of Woods as he completed his emotional triumph of 2006, a successful title defence and his first Major win after the death of his inspirational father, Earl.

Rory McIlroy escapes from the sand en route to the 2014 Open title.

Tiger Woods surveys a putt at a scorched Hoylake, where he won the 2006 Championship.

It was a stunning performance in classic links conditions, with parched, fast-running fairways challenging the shot-making skills of the world's best players. Greenkeeper Craig Gilholm had decided to stop watering the course at the end of 2005. 'It was a bit of a gamble in retrospect,' he later wrote in the *Daily Telegraph*. 'I wanted to produce traditional links golf on a brown golf course.' He succeeded in spectacular style, as did Woods, who used his driver only once – on the 16th in the first round – in the entire 72 holes. With a breathtaking display of iron play the American finished 18 under par.

Conditions were somewhat different for McIlroy's dominant performance in 2014, the most recent Hoylake Open. Indeed, forecast storms prompted organisers to bring forward Saturday's play, with competitors starting off two tees for the first time in the Championship's history.

McIlroy, who opened with consecutive 66s to lead, completed a four-under-par 68 to remain ahead. He was in the media tent when the storm struck and rain hammered the canvas with deafening force. After taking that unprecedented decision for an early start, The R&A Chief Executive Peter Dawson confessed: 'I was very relieved that the weather forecast had proven correct.'

McIlroy went on to triumph by two strokes and won his next two tournaments, including the PGA Championship, to secure a fourth Major title, confirming his status as the world's best player at the time.

Further course changes are planned before The Open returns to Royal Liverpool. Architect Martin Ebert drew up designs for a distinctive short par-3 17th on The Open card. Players will hit back towards spectacular sea views across the Dee Estuary. 'The original idea came from Alistair Beggs, who was captain of Royal Liverpool when Rory won and is Chief Agronomist for The R&A,' Ebert reveals.

The plan is for a memorable, iconic hole measuring 139 yards and called 'Rushes' that will surely figure prominently in future Opens. 'It was decided to get this hole playing up to a horizon and produce a much shorter hole,' Ebert explains. 'Miss it and perhaps a five or six could result, given the depth of the bunkers and the steepness of the surrounds. It'll be fascinating to see what drama that might produce.'

Royal Liverpool is steeped in golfing history, producing great and popular Champions. It is also making sure it continues to create more of the same in the future.

Royal Cinque Ports

Royal Cinque Ports Golf Club's challenging and charming links at Deal in Kent was the seventh course to stage The Open. Championships were held there in 1909 and 1920, but further attempts to host were thwarted by abnormally high tides that brought sea water sweeping across the course. This meant in 1938 and 1949 the destiny of the Claret Jug was decided instead at nearby Sandwich. By coincidence, England's Sir Henry Cotton was the defending Champion on both occasions.

Deal has not staged The Open since Scotland's George Duncan won in 1920, with J.H. Taylor winning the fourth of his five titles there in 1909. 'It is most worthy of such an event being held on it,' the winner declared after his triumph.

Deal continues to be a stern golfing test. At 7,367 yards, this par-72 layout hosts final Open qualifying events and the Amateur Championship was held here as recently as 2013. The third and fifth holes are early par 5s that sit either side of the short 'Sandy Parlour', which was originally a totally blind par 3. It has long since been played from an elevated tee that makes the putting surface visible.

The first three greens are located where they were originally laid in 1892 by Henry Hunter, Cinque Ports' first greenkeeper. Initially a nine-hole course, it was stretched to the full 18 within six years. Deal proved a popular venue with Kings George V, Edward VIII and George VI in the early to mid-twentieth century, and gained its royal patronage in 1910, which was reconfirmed 39 years later.

A traditional out and back links, most of the front nine hugs a coastline protected by a sea wall. 'It depends on the wind direction but you really have to make a good score on the front nine,' says Karen Stupples, the 2004 Women's British Open Champion who honed her skills there as a junior member. 'It gives you plenty of opportunities going out, with some shorter holes and some good par 5s. When you get to the ninth it really starts to take a turn in terms of difficulty.'

The course was damaged during the First World War, prompting the appointment of James Braid to make significant alterations. Further restoration work, overseen by Sir Guy Campbell and Henry Cotton, followed the Second World War. But the closing stretch remains, comprising longer versions of the original seventh, eighth and ninth holes from 1892.

'The bunkering is very strategic,' Stupples adds. 'There are some really long holes coming back and typically they play into the wind. You really have to be on top of your game and to have built a good score around that front nine to get it in the house with a good number.

'Once you turn and come back in, there are lots of humps and hollows and undulations. In the summer there are crispy top bits to those mounds and you have very lush green valleys. They will reward you with a great lie but typically it is a blind shot to the green.'

The course has always been a superb example of raw links golf. As George Duncan reflected after his 1920 victory: 'I think Deal is one of the best and one of the fairest courses I have ever played on.'

Royal Troon

Royal Troon Golf Club has been staging Opens since 1923 and is notable for its relatively gentle start and a fearsome finish. In between there is a spell of spectacular links golf, including one of the most famous par 3s in the entire sport. Situated in the neighbouring Ayrshire town to the Championship's inaugural venue at Prestwick, the club's Old Course has played host to The Open on nine occasions.

It boasts the most iconic short hole of any course that holds the Championship. The tiny eighth can strike terror into the heart of the greatest of players. 'A pitching surface skimmed down to the size of a postage stamp,' was how Willie Park Jr summed up this famous little hole and the description stuck.

In a practice round for the 2016 Open, Rory McIlroy took six strokes to escape the deep bunker that sits below the front right edge of a tiny, narrow plateau green. 'Every time I tried to get it out, it would go back into the same spot,' said McIlroy, who believes anyone who scores four pars there during an Open week makes ground on the rest of the field.

'How can a hole that is 123 yards long be so good?' muses BBC Television commentator Andrew Cotter, who has been a member of the club since his days growing up in the town. 'You stand up there and the target looks absolutely tiny, hence the "Postage Stamp" name, although it was originally called "Ailsa". It's because of everything that lies around the green.'

Another Troon native, eight-time European Tour Order of Merit winner Colin Montgomerie, agrees but says a weight of presumption adds to the hole's character. 'You are a professional golfer, it's your job and you're expected to hit this green at 123 yards,' he said. 'You could throw it on, really. I wish I could … and that's why that hole is fabulous, because you are expected to hit the green.'

There are five bunkers guarding the minuscule target. Cotter adds: 'It's usually into the prevailing wind and if you hit the green it's the easiest hole in the world but if you miss, it is almost certainly a dropped shot and possibly a double-bogey because of the depth of the bunkers.'

It can be a terrifying prospect and one that excites architect Martin Ebert, who incorporates the principles of the 'Postage Stamp' in his recent design of the new par 3 at Royal Liverpool. 'I've been lucky to referee at some Opens and Troon was one of them,' Ebert says. 'Just standing on the tee of the "Postage Stamp" in 2016 when it was playing only 100 yards on the Saturday, you could sense the tension in the players.'

Troon Golf Club was first established in 1878. Six greens were laid down by Charlie Hunter while keeper of the green at Prestwick. Driven on by the enthusiasm of the club's first captain, James Dickie, the course expanded to 12 and then 18 holes with George Strath's design and construction work completed in 1884. Much of that original layout is still played today, but long-time professional Willie Fernie made significant alterations. They included laying out the initial 'Postage Stamp' design and the formidable 'Railway' 11th hole.

England's Arthur Havers won the first Open at Troon in 1923, sinking a bunker shot for birdie on the 72nd hole to pip the great Walter Hagen by a single stroke. The others to win the Claret Jug on the Ayrshire links are South Africa's Bobby Locke, Americans Arnold Palmer, Tom Weiskopf, Tom Watson, Mark Calcavecchia, Justin Leonard and Todd Hamilton, and the Swede Henrik Stenson, who won an epic duel with Phil Mickelson in 2016.

Watson's triumph in 1982 provided Andrew Cotter with his first memories of The Open coming to his

home area. 'I only knew it as a place where I hit golf balls and then the biggest show comes into town and it was incredible,' he says. 'The atmosphere of it, the smell of it, the feel of it. That's where my love affair with The Open really started.'

Cotter was a promising youngster and graduated to the Scottish Schoolboys team while learning the nuances of his home club, which received its royal patronage in 1978. 'It's not just straight out and straight back,' the commentator says. 'You think the wind has changed direction but actually the angle has altered slightly, even on those relatively benign opening holes.

'I think of it as three sixes. The first six holes where you can make a score, including two par 5s, the fourth and the sixth. Then you have the six that meander around the middle, including the "Postage Stamp", and then the six coming back which are brutal.

'You stand on the 13th tee and you think, "I've got to hold on now" and it's just incredibly difficult. You can see the clubhouse in the distance and the town of Troon, but it feels a long way away when you've got those holes to play.'

That stretch has staged plenty of drama over the years. Palmer attracted vast galleries with his emphatic

win in 1962, a performance that helped inspire significant growth in the Championship. Forty-two years later the rather less heralded American Todd Hamilton showed extraordinary composure to cause a huge upset by beating South Africa's Ernie Els in a four-hole play-off.

And then there was Stenson's amazing win over Mickelson in 2016, which was the first Open to be screened live in the UK by Sky Sports. 'You were seeing two players at the very best of their form under the most pressure,' recalls lead commentator Ewen Murray. 'Mickelson did nothing wrong, Stenson did everything right.' The Swedish Champion finished at 20 under par, with his American rival finishing three strokes behind. The resulting roars throughout that astonishing Sunday told the story. 'I just sat back and admired it,' Murray adds.

Such low scoring suggested the par-71 course, which measures 7,190 yards, was something of a pushover but this was not the case. J.B. Holmes, who finished third, was only six under par. The results from the most recent Open there simply underlined Royal Troon's enduring characteristics. It rewards great play while still providing a stern and proper examination of golfing technique and temperament.

LEFT The great Bobby Jones is eagerly watched at the 1926 Open at Royal Lytham & St Annes.

OPPOSITE Despite being The Open venue situated furthest from the shoreline, Royal Lytham is still a spectacular setting.

Royal Lytham & St Annes

'I have to say Lytham St Annes is a great golf course, fantastic,' said Severiano Ballesteros, a two-time Open winner around the famous Lancashire links. The course is the most inland location of any to stage the Championship. It is surrounded by residential housing with no coastal views, but still provides an archetypal test of British seaside golf.

Ballesteros won his first Open at Lytham in 1979 in extraordinarily flamboyant style, repeatedly escaping unscathed from the course's numerous sand traps and in the final round breaking free from an area used for car parking to birdie the par-4 16th. He returned in 1988 to win a third Claret Jug in an Open that finished on a Monday because of weather delays.

Notable for starting with a par 3, the course boasts a vast number of bunkers. For the 2012 Open there were 206 in play but that number has subsequently been reduced to a mere 174.

The layout was originally designed by the first 'custodian of the links', George Lowe. Situated in

St Annes, the present site staged its first competition in 1896 after Lytham & St Annes Golf Club had been formed a decade earlier. Neighbouring Lytham was included in the title because it was a more recognisable place than the relatively new town where the club is located. They needed to move from the initial 1886 course because of limitations on the lease for the original land.

Before hosting its first Open in 1926, the year the club received royal status, Lytham held a number of noteworthy events to establish Championship credentials. Huge crowds, an estimated 6,000 spectators, gathered to watch a foursomes match in 1905. It featured four Open Champions: James Braid and Sandy Herd against Harry Vardon and J.H. Taylor. It was subsequently felt that the course needed toughening and the famed architect Harry Colt made significant alterations. Among them was switching the eighth and ninth holes to leave a challenging par 4 followed by a classic par 3 to conclude the outward half.

The 17th was extended by 80 yards, with the green moved to the left to create a difficult dogleg. It was made famous by the great amateur Bobby Jones's brilliant 175-yard recovery shot from a sandy waste area with a 'mashie' – the equivalent of a 5-iron – on his way to victory in the 1926 Open. A plaque marks the spot from where he hit before decisively taking the lead and making his way to the classic closing hole. Colt's clever pattern of cross-bunkering makes for a nerve-jangling climax to any round played there.

Jones's iconic victory came in the first Open where spectators were charged admission fees. His thrilling triumph set the tone for a course that has produced an excellent list of Open winners. Bobby Locke won his third Claret Jug there in 1952, Peter Thomson was Champion for the fourth time six years later and the elegant New Zealand left-hander Bob Charles won in 1963. Then came Tony Jacklin's memorable success in 1969, which ended an 18-year wait for a British winner. Gary Player landed the last of his three Opens five years later before Ballesteros exploded onto the scene with his swashbuckling triumphs.

Tom Lehman was the first American professional to win The Open there in 1996 and David Duval emulated that success in 2001. Ernie Els became the third South African to win at Lytham 11 years later. Els's victory capitalised on Adam Scott's collapse over the closing quartet of holes, highlighting the difficulty of Lytham's inward half. 'It's a very tasty nine holes,' reflected Ballesteros after his two successes.

'This is a great driver's golf course,' said Jacklin. 'If you don't drive the ball straight here, you've got no chance.' A par 70 measuring 7,086 yards for the 2012 Championship, it begins with that stern 205-yard opener. Tiger Woods highlighted the difficulty of this unique start, telling reporters: 'You have to be on your game right away, you can't just hit a ball in the fairway any distance you want. You have to hit the ball a precise number.'

LEFT Surrounded on all sides, a historic golfing oasis.

OPPOSITE No fewer than 174 bunkers pepper the links at Royal Lytham & St Annes.

The seventh and 11th are the only par 5s on the Championship card after the 492-yard sixth was reassessed as a par 4 for the most recent Open at Lytham. The course builds to a muscular finish with the closing two par 4s stretching to a combined 866 yards.

As well as staging the Championship on 11 occasions it has also held five Women's British Opens. The great Annika Sörenstam (2003) and British champions Catriona Matthew (2009) and Georgia Hall (2018) enjoyed victories at Lytham as did American Sherri Steinhauer, who won in 1998 and 2006.

'The bunkering is just so difficult,' says Karen Stupples. 'Wherever you want to hit a shot there's always a bunker ready to gobble up your ball. It is also a ball striker's golf course: you have to hit the ball really well and be very strategic with where you are placing it in order to get a good score.'

Carnoustie

For more than four centuries golf has been played over the links of Carnoustie, a course that seems to suit the bravest of players. It is the most northerly and arguably the fiercest test on the list of Open venues. 'It's got length, it's got great bunkering,' commented two-time Champion Ernie Els. 'You've really got to have your wits with you to play this golf course. It's probably the best bunkered course that you'll ever find anywhere in the world.'

It is also ancient golfing territory. Parish records refer to the game of 'gowff' as early as 1560. Situated on public land on the north-east coast of Scotland and now run by the Links Management committee, the course originally consisted of 10 holes laid out by golf's first professional, Allan Robertson. It was extended to 18 holes in 1867 by Old Tom Morris. However, it took significant changes, made by James Braid around 1926, to make Carnoustie a layout worthy of holding The Open. The prestigious Championship finally arrived on the course five years later.

Tommy Armour, who lost the sight of his left eye in a First World War mustard gas explosion as well as suffering serious injury to his left arm, was the first winner of The Open at Carnoustie. A native of Edinburgh, he had settled in the United States before starting to win Major titles, which also included the 1927 US Open and the PGA Championship of 1930. They called the former machine gunner the 'Silver Scot', and scores of 73, 75, 77 and 71 gave him a one-stroke win over Argentina's José Jurado.

In 1937 heavy rain threatened the Championship the next time it visited, with fairways waterlogged when Sir Henry Cotton won the second of his three titles. Ben Hogan then triumphed by four strokes in what was his only visit to The Open, in 1953. The determined American, who had been seriously injured in a head-on collision with a Greyhound bus only four years earlier, played an aggressive brand of golf that Carnoustie rewards if it is executed with supreme skill.

This was epitomised by Hogan's bold approach to the long par-5 sixth. In each round he courageously fired tee shots down the left side of the fairway, close to out of bounds, to earn the best angle to attack the green. His skill and steely nerve were rewarded with the win that gave him the career Grand Slam and his

third Major of the year. The sixth hole, once called 'Long', is better known as 'Hogan's Alley'.

Gary Player won his second Open in 1968 and seven years later Tom Watson marked his Open debut by winning an 18-hole play-off against Australia's Jack Newton. The Championship did not return for another 24 years until the new Carnoustie Hotel provided much-needed local accommodation.

It opened the year before Paul Lawrie's dramatic triumph of 1999. The Scot won a four-hole play-off against American Justin Leonard and Jean van de Velde after the Frenchman took seven at the 72nd hole, when a six would have given him the title. In hostile weather Lawrie, from nearby Aberdeen, came from 10 strokes behind to claim his only Major, with a brilliant final round 67.

For the third Carnoustie Open running, a play-off was required to settle the 2007 Championship when Padraig Harrington overcame Sergio Garcia.

The Irishman thought he had blown his chances because he drove into the Barry Burn off the final tee. 'The 18th hole is probably the toughest finishing hole in Major golf,' Harrington later said. 'It is based on circumstances, how you're doing and what sort of conditions you're playing in.'

After taking a penalty drop he dispatched his third shot back into the burn, which snakes in front of the home green. Harrington needed a brave up and down for double-bogey to scrape into a play-off, where he beat Garcia, who had led after each of the first three rounds.

At 7,402 yards par 71 off the Championship tees, Carnoustie has become an ever more popular venue. Crowds of 172,000 flooded the links in 2018 to see Francesco Molinari become the first Italian Champion. With weekend rounds of 65 and 69 on sun-baked fairways, he thrillingly fended off a chasing pack that included Tiger Woods and Rory McIlroy to finish two clear on eight under par.

'Carnoustie is the toughest and the fairest course,' says Ewen Murray, the lead commentator for Sky Sports, who played several top amateur events there in his formative years. 'You could play The Open tomorrow at Carnoustie. Put the markers on the back tees and off you go. It's a tough, tough golf course and yet it is tremendously fair.'

Thankfully this sport holds none of the military terrors endured by Armour before his Open success but this venue has certainly proven a place for players of courage who are capable of handling the heat of golfing battle. As Harrington says: 'The beauty of the golf course is that there are a lot of different ways of playing it, but eventually you're going to have to grow up and hit the shots.'

OPPOSITE The notorious Barry Burn in front of the final green, with the Carnoustie Hotel at the back.

BELOW A delighted Tommy Armour receives the Claret Jug after his 1931 victory.

Prince's

According to the legendary Gene Sarazen, Prince's Golf Club was 'Britain's finest course'. The seven-times Major champion had good cause to feel affection for the Kent links which occupies the same Sandwich Bay as Royal St George's. Sarazen won his only Open title on the one occasion the Championship was staged there, in 1932.

By then the course had established a fine reputation. At nearly 7,000 yards Prince's was built to cater for the extra length generated by the Haskell ball. The only Championship staged there was regarded a success and yielded a great Champion in Sarazen. He led from start to finish with a record low score of 283 in a five-shot win over MacDonald Smith.

Sarazen won with the help of Walter Hagen's old caddie 'Skip' Daniels, whom he first used while finishing runner-up to Hagen at Royal St George's four years earlier. At Prince's, Daniels had said he was no longer fit enough for the job, but at the last moment the Champion took him on because he did not like the bagman he had been using in disappointing practice rounds.

Prince's may well have staged more Opens had it not been ravaged during the Second World War, when it was requisitioned as a battle training ground. Seventeen of the original greens remained after the course was restored by Sir Guy Campbell and John Morrison in 1950. They created three loops of nine holes – the 'Shore', 'Dunes' and 'Himalayas' – which all return to the clubhouse.

'The "Shore" and the "Dunes" are the real meat of the course and form the Championship layout,' says Karen Stupples, a Kent native and 2004 Women's British Open Champion. 'It is very strategic and a lot flatter than Royal St George's or Royal Cinque Ports because the dunes separate the fairways. They are always full of really thick rough but the fairways are fairly flat in between. You don't get any strange, weird bounces into the rough.'

The course is used by The R&A for Local Final Qualifying. For the 2003 Open, former Masters winner Ian Woosnam chipped in to birdie the first hole of a play-off to secure his place in The Open at Royal St George's. Eight years later local professional Francis McGuirk qualified around his home course to realise his lifelong dream of playing a Sandwich Open.

Royal Portrush

Venturing outside Scotland and England for the first time, The Open arrived at Royal Portrush in Northern Ireland in 1951, but it took a further 68 years before the Championship triumphantly returned to the Dunluce Links for Shane Lowry's tumultuous victory in 2019.

Set among rolling sand dunes, the course provides spectacular coastal views that make it one of the most breathtaking venues in the world. Originally a nine-hole layout when it opened in 1888, it was swiftly extended to 18 and originally was known as The County Club. Gaining patronage from the then Duke of York, it was named Royal Portrush when the Prince of Wales (later King Edward VII) was made a patron in 1895. Club members enjoyed classic golfing ground and it hosted a series of top events including the inaugural Irish Open Amateur as well as Irish Professional and British Ladies Championships.

But not until 1929 did Harry Colt lay out plans for the Dunluce course, which quickly became a regular home for the Irish Open. 'I love the simplicity of his designs,' says Irish former Ryder Cup captain Paul McGinley.

'Harry Colt courses are not the most difficult to play. He always gives you a side to play on. If there's a bunker on the left, the right-hand side will be open and he generally lets you chase the ball into the greens, so the handicap golfer can still get in that way.'

The spectacular seventh at Royal Portrush.

Nevertheless, Royal Portrush was regarded a stern enough test to stage The Open and in 1951 it produced a memorable two-stroke win for the English showman Max Faulkner. A combination of reasons, the relentless growth of The Open and political troubles in Northern Ireland, meant Portrush then slipped off the list of Open venues.

It proved a long road back. 'A lot of advisory visits took place in the 1980s and 1990s with emphasis on the days when it was hoped The Open might return,' remembers architect Donald Steel. 'Even then, it seemed unlikely that the 17th and 18th holes could be retained.'

Bit by bit the campaign to return The Open to the Antrim coastline gathered momentum. Northern Ireland embarked on more peaceful times following

the Good Friday Agreement of 1998, and this more settled and secure background encouraged the thought that such a massive international event could be held there.

Furthermore, Irish golf was enjoying unprecedented success. There were Open wins for Padraig Harrington, Darren Clarke and Rory McIlroy. Graeme McDowell, a Portrush native, won the US Open in 2010 and this just two years after Harrington had added a third Major with his US PGA Championship triumph.

'There is something about this place which is very special,' McIlroy said of a Portrush course that was a big part of his formative golfing years. 'It holds great memories for me. When you grow up so close to great courses like this you take them for granted. Then you play all over the world and come back and realise just how good it is.'

A hugely successful Irish Open was played at Portrush in 2012 and The R&A officials were among massive galleries monitoring how well the tournament played. A decision on whether to venture into what was still uncharted territory for the modern era eventually fell to R&A Chief Executive Peter Dawson.

'I was very, very affected by the enthusiasm of the members and the staff at Portrush and of the Northern Ireland government and civil servants,' Dawson says. 'It was clearly a huge deal for them. I thought if there was that much goodwill and desire this is going to work. And it turned into a rip-roaring success.'

Course changes were needed. The land occupying the original 17th and 18th, which were rather prosaic closing holes compared with the majesty of the rest of the course, was required to house the spectator village. The club's neighbouring Valley Course provided the eventual solution. 'The ground that we had to play with was unbelievably blessed with natural features,' says architect Martin Ebert, who oversaw the alterations.

'It was just a question of massaging that to create holes that did justice to Harry Colt's redesign back in

the thirties. This was another great example of historic research and what it allowed us to glean about the evolution of the course. When we looked at Portrush, Harry Colt's original layout had a clubhouse up in the town, his first hole and last hole had both disappeared over the years and were replaced at that stage by the eighth and ninth holes. Holes he gave his blessing to but didn't actually design.'

Ebert constructed a formidable uphill par-5 seventh and superb risk and reward par-4 eighth to replace the lost closing holes. The new design finishes on the old 16th, a cunning dogleg par 4. 'We were able to assure members who are very proud of their Harry Colt heritage,' Ebert says. 'Without wanting to put words into Colt's mouth, you could argue that if he came back today and was given that same brief he would say, "Well, actually that's great." Hopefully he would have given his blessing.'

Colt would surely have revelled in four extraordinarily ebullient days in July 2019. They thrilled a sell-out crowd, as Lowry completed his win by six strokes with scores of 67, 67, 63 and 72 to finish 15 under par. The par-71 course measured 7,344 yards, which was 542 yards longer than the layout upon which Faulkner won his only Major title.

Unsurprisingly, the course received universal acclaim, summed up by McGinley, who commentated on his compatriot's success for Sky Sports. 'Royal Portrush delivered, no doubt,' he says. 'It was always going to justify The Open being taken there.'

Royal Birkdale

Although Royal Birkdale was a relatively late addition to the list of Open venues, it enjoys a reputation for being arguably the finest golf course in England. It has consistently demanded great play from great champions who have thrilled vast galleries with their performances.

Since the Second World War no venue has staged more high-profile golf events. It has held 10 Opens along with the Women's British and Senior Opens, the Ryder, Walker and Curtis Cups, as well as The Amateur Championship.

Formed in 1889, it was decided five years later to move the club to the Birkdale Hills, land that was perfect for links golf. It comprised multiple sand dunes and was situated in an area noted for magnificent golfing terrain, north of the city of Liverpool and just to the south of the town of Southport. The grand and distinctive white art-deco clubhouse, resembling from the outside an ocean-going liner, was opened in the summer of 1935.

The course was upgraded to Championship standard by architect Fred Hawtree and five-time Open Champion J.H. Taylor. They had a simple philosophy to route holes in valleys between the sand dunes and they did a superb job. 'Birkdale is the most amazing test, given a bit of wind,' says Ewen Murray.

Many of Royal Birkdale's holes are lined by sand dunes, offering spectators excellent views.

Opens at Birkdale attract large galleries who take advantage of excellent views from the huge sandy mounds that surround the action. 'I always feel each hole is its own little stadium created by nature,' says BBC Television and Radio commentator Andrew Cotter. 'All the fans are on sand dunes looking down on the holes, and because you have such big crowds and they all have such fantastic viewpoints, it is very hard to beat.'

Royal status was granted in 1951, the year Birkdale held the Walker Cup between the amateurs of Great Britain and Ireland against the United States, who completed a 6–3 victory. America has a strong affinity with the place but so does Australia. As the course took its first steps towards being regarded as one of the finest Open venues, Peter Thomson – a Melbourne native – was embarking on his journey to becoming one of the true greats of the Championship.

Having been thwarted in 1940 by the war, Royal Birkdale held its first Open in 1954. It was Thomson's fourth visit to the event, having been runner-up in the previous two years and sixth in his debut at Royal Portrush. The Australian eventually put his hands on the Claret Jug with a dramatic one-stroke win over Dai Rees, Bobby Locke and Syd Scott. A five at the last proved enough; Rees could not make a four to win and Locke needed a three (he nearly holed his third shot from 12 yards) after Scott had set a target of 284.

It was the first of five Open triumphs for Thomson and he went on to win the next two Championships. His last Claret Jug also came at Royal Birkdale in 1965 and he described the course as 'man sized but not a monster'.

In between those victories Arnold Palmer came to Birkdale and landed his first Open amidst awful weather in 1961. Rees again finished in the runners-up spot by the narrowest margin. Storms and high winds forced the cancellation of the final two rounds on the Friday and the Championship was completed the following day.

Palmer scored a superb-second round 73 in 50 miles per hour winds on the Thursday, a round he regarded as one of the finest of his career. There was also an incredible 6-iron second shot from punishing rough on the right of the 15th (now the 16th) in the final round. Somehow he muscled the ball 124 yards to the green. 'I never hit a ball so hard in my life,' he later stated. A plaque marks the spot from where he struck his unlikely approach.

The much-celebrated American went on to win despite a sensational finish from Rees, who scored three at the demanding last in an inward half of 31. Palmer's triumph lit the blue touch paper as the Championship embraced its most charismatic winner. He, along with Jack Nicklaus and Gary Player, formed the 'Big Three', and they relentlessly drove the expanding global popularity of the game.

A decade later another captivating American, Lee Trevino, won The 100th Open, the first of his two successive titles. Trevino, who had won that year's US Open, held off Lu Liang-Huan – better known as 'Mr Lu' – a player who captured the hearts of the galleries for the engaging way he raised his hat to acknowledge their applause.

In 1976 Johnny Miller ended the hopes of the extraordinary teenage talent Severiano Ballesteros. Tom Watson won the last of his five Opens in 1983, his only victory outside Scotland, before Australia celebrated another Birkdale victory thanks to Ian Baker-Finch. The 30-year-old famously covered the front nine in just 29 strokes as he collected five birdies in the first seven holes of his final round.

'Royal Birkdale is my favourite links in the world,' says Baker-Finch. 'The course is laid out with flowing fairways and tucked in greens among the dunes. It is so natural, so playable and a great viewing course for the crowds. It's in a classic golfing region and just oozes old world links championship golf.'

Mark O'Meara was the reigning Masters champion when he won a play-off against his unheralded American compatriot Brian Watts in 1998 before, a decade later, Padraig Harrington successfully defended his title despite carrying a wrist injury into the Championship.

Royal Birkdale is a course capable of inspiring extraordinary golf and this was never more evident than when Jordan Spieth won the most recent Open staged on the English links in 2017. During the final round, the young American was in trouble with a massively wayward tee shot to the right of the par-4 13th. He was the wrong side of the dunes and needed to take a penalty drop among the manufacturers' trucks, located to the side of the practice ground. Somehow Spieth escaped the hole with only one dropped shot before embarking on an extraordinary run of form to hold off fellow American Matt Kuchar.

Spieth nearly holed in one on the downhill par-3 14th. 'That tee shot was, for me, the shot of the year,' says Ewen Murray. 'It is a tough par 3, and then there were the putts that followed that.' They dropped one after another, from long range for eagle on the par-5 15th and for birdies on the par-4 16th and the long 17th, where Harrington had decisively eagled back in 2008.

The unfortunate Kuchar did nothing wrong over the closing stretch but ended up losing by three strokes to give Spieth his first Claret Jug. His triumph was achieved in an awe-inspiring manner which was a perfect fit for its majestic setting.

Turnberry

Known for being the most picturesque of The Open venues, Turnberry's Ailsa course now carries a reputation for being one of the very best in the world. Even before recent improvements it was a worthy test, and in four Opens to date Turnberry has been the stage for more than its fair share of drama along with golf of the highest quality.

'You just can't fake it around this golf course, you just have to hit good golf shots,' Tiger Woods commented when the Championship was last played on the Ayrshire links in 2009. 'You have to make sure you really know what you're doing out there … and you've got to understand why the last three Champions here are some of the best ball strikers.'

The winners to whom Woods was referring were Tom Watson in 1977, the first time The Open was played at Turnberry, Greg Norman in 1986 and Nick Price, the Zimbabwean Champion of 1994. All were at the very top of the game when they lifted the Claret Jug at this rugged, photogenic Scottish links.

Golf was first played here at the beginning of the twentieth century after Willie Fernie, the Champion Golfer of 1893, laid out 13 holes at the behest of the third Marquess of Ailsa. He was looking to capitalise upon the opening of the railway line between the towns of Ayr and Girvan.

The treacherous 10th green at Turnberry.

However, this prime area for the links game suffered significant disruption because it was used as an air base in both world wars. This ultimately prompted a comprehensive redesign by Philip Mackenzie Ross, ahead of the reopening of the Ailsa course in 1951.

His was the layout that staged the 'Duel in the Sun' of 1977 when Watson pipped Jack Nicklaus by a single shot after both had separated themselves from the field during one of the most famous and sun-drenched weeks in Open history. Norman claimed the first of his two Open titles there nine years later before Price pipped Jesper Parnevik to the trophy with a blistering finish in 1994. 'The roar for Price's long eagle putt at the 71st hole is still the loudest cheer I've ever heard on a golf course,' says BBC Radio's longest-serving summariser Andrew Murray.

The cheers were replaced by collective groans the next time The Open returned to Turnberry in 2009. Galleries were on the verge of witnessing one of the greatest sporting stories when Watson, at the age of 59, had a par putt to win a sixth Claret Jug. Alas for the romantics this stubborn seven-footer failed to drop and Stewart Cink went on to win a play-off against the veteran.

Nevertheless, it was another vivid chapter in Turnberry's folklore which, no doubt, added to the attraction when, in 2014, Donald Trump bought the resort, including its three golf courses and luxury hotel. This purchase prompted radical enhancements to the par-70 Championship course, including a remodelling of the scenic stretch around the ninth, 10th and 11th holes.

Architect Martin Ebert was commissioned to carry out the work after a recommendation from the then Chief Executive of The R&A. Among the changes was turning the par-4 ninth, with its famed back tee on an exposed rocky outcrop, into a long short hole. It is a spectacular hole measuring 248 yards and played across the rocky bay. 'It is brutally difficult off the very back tee, which would only be played occasionally and depending on the wind conditions,' says former European Tour player Andrew Murray, who is also a Turnberry brand ambassador.

Turnberry's relative remoteness means it is used sparingly on The Open rota. Whenever it returns to stage the Championship for a fifth time it will provide a rare treat for golfers and spectators alike.

ST ANDREWS
AND THE R&A

150

ST ANDREWS AND THE R&A

For centuries the Scottish town of St Andrews and its
Royal and Ancient Golf Club have fostered an environment
for golf to grow across the planet. They developed
The Open into one of the world's most significant annual
sporting events and quietly innovated to make the sport
bigger and better. Simultaneously they preserve and
enhance the unique traditions of this distinctive pursuit,
one that has more than stood the test of time.

The Metropolis of Golf

There is a mutual benefit from the existence of the organisation which has been at the forefront of golf for nearly 270 years and the town in which it is based. St Andrews provided fabulous golfing ground and the game prospered on links land made for the sport. But without the golf club, which came into being in 1754, it is highly unlikely that the town would have evolved into one of the most popular tourist destinations in the sporting world. 'The R&A were fundamental to the development of golf and the town of St Andrews,' says historian Roger McStravick. 'The town council didn't look after the course, the gentlemen golfers did. They paid for the upkeep and maintenance work.'

Today St Andrews has a resident population of around 17,000 people. It is home to a historic university, the seat of learning where Prince William met his future wife Kate Middleton. It was named one of the 'best places to live' by *The Sunday Times* in 2014. 'Royal connections have boosted the University's appeal,' the newspaper stated. 'And with affluent students come the kinds of bars, restaurants and shops normally found in the capital. Throw in the coastline and golf courses and St Andrews becomes a seriously attractive place to live.'

PREVIOUS PAGE The Royal and Ancient Clubhouse commands a view over the opening and closing holes of the Old Course.

OPPOSITE The Royal and Ancient Clubhouse, overlooking land that has been golfing ground since the 1400s.

- Approximately 700,000 visitors arrive each year, around 40 per cent from overseas, generating more than £100 million for the town's economy.

- The association with golf accounts for around one in five visits to this glorious corner of the Kingdom of Fife.

- The St Andrews Links Trust manages seven courses, including the Old Course, upon which alone 45,000 rounds a year are played.

- The overall links covers 300 hectares, the largest public golfing complex in Europe.

- There is a golf academy with swing studios and more than 60 practice bays, three clubhouses and four shops selling distinctive memorabilia marking the 'Home of Golf' and employing around 400 people in peak season.

It is an extraordinary legacy. 'Golf has been played here since the 1400s,' McStravick says. 'The first written record was probably in the 1500s, so golf has always been here. There was so much going for golf in St Andrews, the setting is just beautiful, so natural.'

The initial recorded mention of the game in the town comes from 1552 in a deed bearing the seal of Archbishop Hamilton. It refers to public ownership of the links; uses of which included grazing of livestock and the 'playing at golf, futball, schuting, at all gamis …'. A picture from around 1740 shows golfers on the links with the Swilcan Bridge clearly visible. The image shows the town set further back than is familiar. Today this oil painting hangs in the Royal and Ancient Clubhouse.

A letter from one of the university's professors, sent in the late seventeenth century, describes St Andrews as 'the metropolis of golfing' and this perhaps reflects the way players were beginning to gather and formalise the sport. Among them were several 'Noblemen and Gentlemen of Fife'. They canvassed support from the Gentlemen Golfers of Edinburgh, who were modelled on a similar society for archery in the capital city. A silver golf club was put up as a prize to be played for at St Andrews in

March 1754 and with it the seeds of the Royal and Ancient Golf Club were sown in the form of the Society of St Andrews Golfers.

Minutes from that year show that 22 players gathered for the Challenge for the Silver Club on 14 May. They were 'admirers' of golf and had 'the Interest and prosperity of St Andrews at heart'. These men were not the original members of a newly formed golfing society, they were effectively the trustees of the Silver Club. But further evidence from a minute book dated 1766 indicates that an organisation had been formed. 'We the Noblemen and Gentlemen subscribing Admirers of the Ancient and very healthfull Exercise of the Golf ...' began an entry, with the key word being 'subscribing'. It goes on to refer to 'Members of this Club' and confirms the existence of a 'Captain and his Council'.

The Silver Club was played for under complex match-play rules until 1759, when this was changed. 'Whoever puts in the ball at the fewest strokes over the field, being 22 holes, shall be declared and sustained victor.' This, seemingly, was the birth of the stroke-play form of the game which has been used throughout the history of The Open. At that time it was still a century away from inception.

Some of the rules were fascinating, including one that stated a ball unplayable could be lifted and thrown back 'at least six yards' while incurring a one-stroke penalty. Around 1764 came the move to reduce the course from 22 to 18 holes when four relatively short holes were turned into two longer ones. This was still a century before 18 holes became the standard length of rounds elsewhere.

TOP Dated c.1740, this is the oldest-known painting of golf in St Andrews and shows familiar elements of the skyline.

RIGHT The Silver Club is adorned with solid silver golf balls, engraved with the names of Captains of The Royal and Ancient Golf Club of St Andrews.

The Foundation Stone

Progressing the club was not always straightforward. At the start of the nineteenth century came a crucial period regarded as 'the Rabbit Wars', when the Pilmour Links – as the area for golf was known – came under threat from a furry enemy.

The town was declining and after the council sold the land to raise funds, a set of deals led to a father and son, Charles and Cathcart Dempster, renting it to farm rabbits. This inevitably led to damage to the golf course and a long and expensive legal battle. In their *Colossus* book, David Malcolm and Peter Crabtree refer to court records in which Tom Morris's grandfather, John, is quoted. 'These [rabbit] scrapes have become very numerous since Mr Dempster got the links,' John Morris testified. He added, they are 'a great prejudice to the playing of golf'.

It is believed that had the Society of St Andrews Golfers not ultimately fought their legal war with the Dempsters, golf could easily have died or remained merely a curious Scottish pastime. It would no longer have had the drive of the influential club behind it

and may well have withered. They were also helped by a virus which wiped out the rabbit population.

The golfers emerged stronger while St Andrews Town Council was left poorer because of the cost of the dispute. It ultimately became easier for the club to acquire land to build a clubhouse. The foundation stone was laid on 13 July 1853 and work was completed just over 11 months later. It grew into a structure that became arguably the most iconic building in golf.

King William IV had conferred royal status on the Society in 1834 and its name was changed to the Royal and Ancient Golf Club of St Andrews. It was an organisation of ever-growing influence, particularly when The Open took off and became the world's pre-eminent golf competition.

The sport began to grow across Britain. At the start of the 1880s there were just over 100 golf clubs, with only 20 in England. Within a decade there were 300 clubs and a third of those were based south of the border.

There was growing clamour for uniformity in how the game should be played and clubs looked to The R&A to provide a lead. Original Rules drawn up by

the St Andrews Club in 1851 were formally adopted by the Honourable Company in 1883. The establishment of the Amateur Championship also created a forum that brought together leading clubs. After a series of often contentious meetings it was agreed The R&A should form a Rules Committee. It comprised 15 members drawn from Scottish- and English-based members and was chaired by Benjamin Hall-Blyth.

A Great Influence

From these origins grew the Royal and Ancient's role as the organisation that set the Rules of Golf internationally. With the evolution of The Open and The Amateur Championship, the influence and standing of the club continued to grow. The town also prospered, with golf facilities at the heart of its success. The neighbouring New Course was set out by Old Tom Morris in 1895 and the Jubilee came along two years later as a course primarily for women and beginners.

'Without The R&A I don't know what we would have, but it certainly would not be the links we have today,' says Roger McStravick. 'I genuinely believe it would be a very different place without the gentlemen golfers of the Society of St Andrews Golfers because they paid for everything. It's inconceivable trying to measure how brilliant this place is thanks to The R&A. Everything you see around you is thanks to those early golfers.'

St Andrews, known as the 'Auld Grey Toon', has become one of the most famous places on earth. Its university is a world-class establishment and the town's buildings, historic walls and ruins provide unique character and the richest of legacies. And much of its international fame is also due to the area's deep relationship with golf and The Open Championship.

'There's nowhere in the world with such a sense of theatre as St Andrews, with all its heritage and its ghosts through the mists of time as the centre of golf,' insists historian David Joy. 'In the 1950s, when the game really took off, people would come to the town because of the golf, just to be in St Andrews.'

Between 1897 and 2003 the Royal and Ancient Golf Club was responsible for three areas of huge importance to the game. They ran The Open, the world's oldest Major, and were custodians of the Claret Jug, still among the most sought-after trophies in sport. They ran other tournaments of great prestige in the amateur game, including the Great Britain and Ireland team for the Walker Cup. The club also set the Rules for the worldwide sport, in conjunction with the United States Golf Association. And they embarked on growing the game, particularly in parts of the world that had not yet widely discovered the joys of golf.

For a single club based in a town of fewer than 20,000 people living in a relatively remote corner of the Scottish coastline, it built an astonishing sphere of influence. From establishing 18 holes as the standard length of a golf course, to beating the challenge of a humble rabbit farmer, to driving and developing one of the biggest sports in the world is an extraordinary journey.

In 2004 the club celebrated its 250th anniversary but the year also marked a significant structural change. The roles of running The Open, setting the Rules and developing the game were devolved to a newly formed set of companies, known as The R&A. 'I think it was necessary,' says the former Chief Executive Peter Dawson, who oversaw the restructuring. 'It was done for a number of reasons; mainly because it was right to have a degree of transparency about The R&A's activities that being a company gives, which a private members' club might not want to give.

'It was also becoming increasingly difficult to sign large contracts as a club as opposed to a corporation and all the protections that corporations get. People said at the time that this was all because of members' personal liabilities, but it wasn't really – that was a side issue.'

Royal and Ancient members still filled positions on R&A committees and played significant roles in the running of the game. But the objectives of the golf club were simplified. It remains, first and foremost, a members' organisation with a Clubhouse and high-quality facilities. It enjoys access to first-class golf on the courses of the links. The club plays competitions and matches and hosts spring and autumn meetings for its members. It continues to help the St Andrews Links Trust, with the aim of preserving the town's position as the 'Home of Golf'. There is also a key role of preserving records and artefacts relating to the history of the game.

The Royal and Ancient Clubhouse stands proudly overlooking the first tee and the vast fairways of the opening and closing holes on the Old Course. It is the most historic and evocative scene in golf. All the world's best players have trodden these fairways, from Morris to McIlroy, Watson to Woods, Jack Nicklaus, Harry Vardon, Severiano Ballesteros, Bobby Jones and Walter Hagen, to name a few other legends who have graced this glorious land.

Millions of rounds have also been played and enjoyed by players of all standards; visitors lucky enough to emerge from the daily ballot of Old Course tee times. Others enjoy the delights and challenges of the New, Jubilee, Eden, Castle, Strathtyrum and Balgove courses. They combine to create a golfing mecca. No one leaves without being intoxicated by the uniquely heady air of the 'Home of Golf'.

In that famous Royal and Ancient Clubhouse, members can sit among imposing bay windows, surrounded by artefacts and paintings that provide a permanent reminder of how this delightful, maddening, occasionally deeply satisfying pursuit originated. They survey an outdoor scene that has endured and prospered for centuries, charming golfers from every corner of the world.

On the first floor above is situated the office of the Secretary and Chief Executive of The R&A. It is hard to imagine a better work station and it is there that decisions continue to be made to significantly influence and shape golf in the twenty-first century.

The Magic of St Andrews

By Donald Steel

One topic that runs and runs is the strength of the Old Course's defence against the world's finest golfers. St Andrews is where everyone wants to play and where everybody wants to win. So, does anything else matter?

What set the cat amongst the seagulls was The Open victory in 1964 of Tony Lema, having never played in Britain before and with barely a single practice round. It may sound an over-simplification to suggest that all he did was borrow Arnold Palmer's caddie and obey orders, but it is the truth. Tip Anderson knew his way round blindfolded and, in next to no time, Lema was playing low pitch and runs as though born in Granny Clark's Wynd.

It was such a remarkable victory that the Championship Committee of The R&A were left to consider the alarming possibility that the Old Course might have become too easy and in need of attention. After much heart searching, under the chairmanship of Gerald Micklem, they decided they did not mind what the winning scores were, provided they were produced by the best players of the day.

Recognising its historic eminence and iconic status, it was a way of saying you accept the Old Course for what it is or not at all. There was a fear of turning it into something it was not. They also felt minor change would have little effect while major change was unthinkable. After all, huge greens are impossible to ring fence. Another interpretation was that lower scores were inevitable and there was nothing to be done to stop them. How right they were.

Against such a background, a checklist of the nine subsequent St Andrews Open champions is most revealing. In chronological order, they are Nicklaus, Nicklaus, Ballesteros, Faldo, Daly, Woods, Woods, Oosthuizen and Zach Johnson. Go back to 1946 and you can add Snead, Thomson, Locke and Nagle, the golfing equivalent of *Debrett's Peerage*.

Micklem emphasised, 'I am not so precise as to insist that the best man wins but, rather, one of the best men wins, thereby proving he understands the challenge of St Andrews and its strategic as opposed to penal qualities.' Going further, the list of near misses or, in several instances, not-so-near misses, is equally distinguished. Not-so-near misses are relevant since Lema won by 5 strokes, Faldo by 5, Tiger by 8 and 5, and Oosthuizen by 7. In 2010, only Oosthuizen bettered Lema's total of 279 46 years earlier.

Golf feasts on such famous moments, but they are only part of the story. In the interim, golfers cross continents to win a place in the ballot and walk in the footsteps of their heroes. In summer, the Old Course is open from dawn until the long northern twilight holds the night at bay. It takes some getting to know and is not always love at first sight. However, there is comfort that the opening drive confronts the widest fairway in all golf, although the holes soon narrow into avenues of unique double fairways and familiar double greens. It is the world's best thinking man's course, the ultimate and complete test.

One peculiarity is the allocation of just two par 5s and two par 3s, even if nowadays four par 4s are in range from the tee. At St Andrews, five courses run virtually side by side and, if the layout of the Old had been more expansive, there might have been room for only three. Nowhere else could five courses occupy

such a small acreage, but, whatever the occasion or the state of play, it is on the closing holes of the Old, with its wonderful skyline, that the visual magic of St Andrews, the oldest seat of academic learning in Scotland, is so apparent. In the awe-inspiring return to the town, golf also comes increasingly under public gaze, with many non-golfers taking time to stand and stare.

The amazing truth, too, is that golf on the links preceded The Open by some three hundred years, while the Royal and Ancient Golf Club was founded more than a hundred years before Prestwick housed the first Open in 1860, a mere nine years after Prestwick's own formation. Not until 1920 did

The R&A assume full administration of the oldest Championship, although the message is unmistakable. Whether Champions, members of local clubs or pilgrims from afar, all golfers are equal. Nobody has any special privileges save that of enjoying an experience quite unmatched anywhere.

'Champagne' Tony Lema is presented with the Claret Jug at St Andrews, 1964.

BROADCASTING: BEST SEAT IN THE HOUSE

BROADCASTING: BEST SEAT IN THE HOUSE

Bringing The Open to homes and cars around the world via TV, radio, smartphone and tablet is one of the most vital, challenging, complex and cutting-edge jobs in sports broadcasting. Ever since the days of crackling radio signals and black and white television, extending right up to today and our touch-screen age of HD, this has been the case. Like the Championship itself, those who convey the sights and sounds of golf's oldest Major have been on an epic and evolutionary journey and one of ever growing complexity.

The challenge is to convey thrilling, captivating, atmospheric moments so they are enjoyed by millions across the globe – to put the Championship at the fingertips of the entire world.

For everyone involved, the objective is the same: to tell the story of The Open.

Victory on the Airwaves

Bobby Jones's successful title defence at St Andrews in 1927 was the first to be covered on the airwaves of BBC Radio. Sandwiched between 10 minutes of the Daventry Quartet and a special programme called *Les Cloches de Corneville* there was quarter of an hour set aside at 7.55 p.m. on Friday 15 July for The Open Golf Championship, a studio broadcast from Dundee.

The following year, for Walter Hagen's triumph at Royal St George's, the *Radio Times* carried a picture showing galleries around a green. The caption said: 'FIGHTING FOR THE BLUE RIBAND OF THE GAME' and beneath read this explanation: 'This view shows a portion of the great crowd that followed Bobby Jones in the final round of The Open Championship at St Andrew's [sic] last year. This year's contest has been followed with no less interest by sport-lovers all over the country, and for their sake it has been arranged that Mr. Bernard Darwin, the famous golfer and golf writer, shall broadcast a review of the morning's play in the final round today [11 May 1928] at 1.30 and at 7.00 he will give a full account of the play and the result.'

Darwin, a grandson of the British naturalist Charles Darwin, was a semi-finalist in The Amateur Championship of 1921 and a distinguished golfing figure who went on to be captain of the Royal and Ancient. His pioneering broadcasts were termed 'Eye-Witness Accounts' and his role brought alive the Championship for golf fans unable to attend.

It is a philosophy that continues today. 'We should be giving you the best seat in the house,' says David Mould, the executive producer for European Tour Productions, who generate the pictures supplied to worldwide broadcasters who screen The Open, including Sky Sports in the UK and NBC in the United States. 'If you can't actually go and be there, I want you to sit on your couch and feel part of it.'

A Global Championship

That audience could be anywhere because The Open is big news across the globe, especially in America. NBC and the Golf Channel make significant investments to cover the Championship and follow the likes of ABC and ESPN, who were long-time providers of US coverage.

'It is huge over here,' says presenter Cara Banks. 'They absolutely love it. NBC have been very big supporters of The Open and there is no stone left unturned. They have the main broadcast, Golf Channel has Morning Drive on site and they even do a Midnight Drive through until 2 a.m. on the Wednesday night into the Thursday morning to kick off coverage of the opening tee shots. That leads into live coverage starting at 7 a.m.'

Pictures are fed from ETP under the guidance of David Mould. He heads a team of more than 450 people, operating around 120 on-course cameras to bring the sights and sounds from the fairways. 'It is a massive operation for us,' Mould says.

'I can't think of a better Major for the way it looks and that helps us because it just looks so special.'

ETP also employ 15 commentators to help tell the story. 'We try to make sure the commentators are not just all English; we need Australia, the US and Asia represented as well,' he adds.

Those commentators are heard on a generic world feed taken by multiple broadcasters from different territories. Others – including NBC and the Golf Channel as well as Sky Sports – use the pictures, but generate their own bespoke coverage. 'Our job is to add the layers and make it into a Sky production,' says Sky Sports' executive producer for golf Jason Wessely. He is responsible for a 220-strong team during Open weeks. 'We add our commentary, our voices and our personality. We are constantly trying to tell the viewer what the story is and its complexities.'

Sky Sports first screened The Open live in 2016 after 60 years of BBC Television coverage. The Championship has always been a most challenging event for broadcasters. 'I did 15 FA Cup finals and six grands prix but nothing beats doing The Open,' says John Shrewsbury, who with Alastair Scott was the long-time boss of the BBC's coverage.

'The atmosphere and the buzz that you got from it was amazing because it was such a complicated thing to do. It's like putting a huge jigsaw puzzle together. You're talking about 30 odd thousand golf shots in the four days and if you can catch 10 per cent of those you are doing well. The selection has to be pretty damn good to get the story of the event.'

The technology was nowhere near as sophisticated. 'We used to have an engineer come in four hours before rehearsals just to switch on and warm up the cameras,' Scott recalls. 'You think now it takes four microseconds before a camera is ready to use. I think we just had 15 cameras in 1972; in 2000 we had 46.'

Despite fewer resources, the demands were the same as today. Scott devised a cardboard scoring system so that producers were up to date with the state of play, including which holes the leaders were playing. Later he came up with the system that allowed the BBC to record shots while others were being shown live so that nothing crucial would be missed. 'You are trying to keep tabs on 18 football pitches, so to speak, and choosing which story to follow in pre-electronic scoring days was the hardest thing.'

Producers and directors had 72 monitors in front of them to keep track of the action. Breaks were taken sparingly, if at all. 'If you went out for an hour and came back it would take you a good half an hour to find out who was where again,' Scott recalls.

Commentators provide the accompaniment to help the viewer make sense of the images. The BBC's Peter Alliss became the undisputed 'voice of golf' after a producer overheard him regaling fellow players with tales of woe on a flight back from a tournament in Ireland. 'He quickly worked out I could talk a bit,' the veteran broadcaster reflected not long before his death at the age of 89 in December 2020. Alliss was a leading professional and Ryder Cup player who competed in the last of his 25 Opens in 1974. He made his first broadcasts at the 1961 Championship at Royal Birkdale.

Storytellers

'Listening to Peter was just heaven, he was wonderful,' says Sky's lead commentator Ewen Murray. 'You just remember his performances at The Open and the joy he gave to so many.'

Alliss initially joined the legendary golf writer and broadcaster Henry Longhurst. 'I didn't speak to him for the first three or four years,' Alliss admitted. 'It was very much a gentlemen and players atmosphere back then. But once we started talking we were almost inseparable, and he was godfather to my eldest son. I was Henry's sort of minder. He was quite self-effacing in a strange way because he looked the most snobbish and difficult man ever, but he wasn't in the least and actually hated pomposity.

'Henry was very economical in his commentary; he didn't say that much. Rather like Dan Maskell at the tennis it would be "Oh, I say!" He had a fruity voice and an economy of words and he was able to state the obvious without it sounding as if he was stating the obvious.'

Following Longhurst's death, Alliss became the lead voice of the BBC's coverage in 1978. He was part of a popular team that included the swing analysis of Alex Hay, the erudite vocabulary of former Walker Cup player Bruce Critchley, on-course reporting from Clive Clark and the astute, articulate commentary of Ken Brown. But Alliss was the star performer, with a wit and charm that gave golf broadcasting a unique flavour.

'Peter has done some fantastic stuff throughout his career,' says Brown. 'His ability, his vocabulary, his voice – he had the perfect commentary voice. He spoke with clarity and editorially he could sum things up. And he had a totally unique way of delivering the stuff. He'd never have any notes but he'd have a lot of things in his mind. He'd have a draw and the programme and that would be about his artillery.

'One year at The Open he had 400 letters. I had one. My letter was to ask Peter Alliss something. His were all addressed on the envelope as just Peter Alliss, The Open Championship and whichever course we were at.'

Throughout the BBC years the television coverage grew in sophistication. Alastair Scott's first memory of working at an Open was seeing Jack Nicklaus being pushed up a ladder at Muirfield to be interviewed by Harry Carpenter after winning in 1966.

'The commentary box was built over the greenkeeper's toilets to the left of the first tee. Fortunately they weren't in operation that week,' Scott recalls. 'Jack didn't have a head for heights but he had director Slim Wilkinson behind him edging him up to the studio.'

It used to be very rudimentary. Nowadays it is all about cutting-edge technology and the venues are suitably equipped with a colossal broadcast compound. The cabling is part of permanent infrastructure buried beneath the fairways and becomes accessible whenever the Championship comes to town.

'In the old days cameras would go down at the drop of a hat,' John Shrewsbury admits. 'There'd be about 90 miles of cable around the course, which is mind blowing these days. If you got water in the joints you just lost it until the engineers could get out and put it back together again.'

Until relatively recently it was impossible to cover every hole on the course. The BBC would have positions at 11 locations, the first six and last five.

'We didn't do the full 18 holes until around 1990, I think,' Shrewsbury says. 'After Greg Norman birdied the first six at Troon in 1989 we thought if he goes on and birdies any more we are in trouble because we didn't pick it up again until the 14th. There was a huge gap in the middle despite it being already a huge operation.'

Coverage has moved on significantly. The BBC introduced camera hoists for panoramic shots and lenses were buried in bunker faces to enhance the drama. The relentless innovation continues in Sky's coverage, which is fuelled by European Tour Productions' pictures. The demands on ETP's David Mould and his director Jim Storey are much as they were for the BBC pioneers who went before. 'I sit there for seven hours, I don't move,' Mould says. 'You are solely focused on what's in front of you. I don't go to the toilet because I feel if I step out then I lose my thread. You don't really want to take breaks.'

LEFT Colin Montgomerie with Golf Channel's Todd Lewis after teeing off first at Royal Troon in 2016.

OPPOSITE Camera towers follow the action, Royal Lytham and St Annes 2012.

Mould decides which players the viewers see and when. He relies on experience picked up from more than two decades in the business, covering tour events throughout the year. He takes three course walks in the week leading up to the Championship to work out how long it takes players to move from greens to tees. 'When Graeme McDowell makes his weird noise, I know that gives me ten seconds before he hits his shot,' Mould reveals. 'When Louis Oosthuizen puts on his glove and wraps it round, that's a 15-second trigger for him to play his shot.

'If two people are putting and they are both in with a chance of joining the lead you have to trust that you are going to pick the correct one to show, and those sort of tricks come naturally. There's a massive feel to what you are doing, an acquired instinct in a sense, doing it for a long time under pressure.'

Sky's executive producer Jason Wessely admits his coverage 'lives on the glory of the world feed production'. But to provide their comprehensive dawn till dusk offering remains a massive undertaking. The key is to convey the tension being felt by players; to show that this is no ordinary tournament but one of life-changing prestige. Ewen Murray and fellow commentators such as Paul McGinley, Richard Boxall, Wayne Riley, Andrew Coltart, Mark Roe and Rich Beem, among a host of others, play vital roles.

'The lead commentator is telling the story,' Wessely says. 'The colour commentator is adding insight to that story, the on-course commentator is telling you what nobody else can see. They can feel, see, smell the atmosphere out on the course and that the tension of the leader is palpable. It's the on-course reporter's job to bring that to life.'

Holding it all together is the presenter. Sky's Sarah Stirk insists the Championship provides her favourite week of the golfing year. 'It was such a massive deal for us, we probably didn't think we would ever get The Open,' she admits. But the long hours are embraced and she loves broadcasting from remote presentation positions on course among the galleries.

'Being on home soil is such a big thing because you are interacting with your audience a lot more. They're all golf fans and driving on your buggy through the spectators you are interacting and engaging … much more so than the other Majors.'

There is no escaping
the camera's beady eye.

Engaging the World

When Sky took over in 2016 it seemed a somewhat controversial move away from the much-loved BBC coverage; however, the corporation still attracts millions of viewers for its daily highlights shows. 'Sky's commitment to golf was growing all the time,' recalls Peter Dawson, the former R&A Chief Executive, who brokered the deal. 'I think Sky do a magnificent job of the on-course stuff. The BBC did more of total event coverage. Leaving the BBC was sad but inevitable, I think.'

Being a dedicated sports provider means Sky's coverage is able to begin with the very first shot of the Championship at around 6.30 a.m. on the Thursday of Open week. 'We were on the first tee for Darren Clarke when he hit the opening tee shot at Portrush,' Stirk recalls. 'We opened the show and Clarke walked on and interacted with us live on air and that's priceless. You can't get that in a studio.'

Television producers and The R&A consider carefully the pairings for key times in the broadcast day for both sides of the Atlantic. It was quickly realised marquee names would also be needed to sustain the very early coverage. This is why Ryder Cup legend Colin Montgomerie struck the opening tee shot in his home town of Troon in 2016 and Clarke was chosen when The Open came to his native Northern Ireland.

'You arrive at the television compound around 4.30 a.m. and you wait for that moment when the programme starts and off you go,' says Ewen Murray. 'You open the book early on Thursday morning and then the final chapter is written late Sunday afternoon and there are so many stories in between.'

It builds to the crowning of an Open Champion. Murray, who made his Open debut as a player in 1973 and first visited the Championship as a nine-year-old in 1964, has numerous voices from directors, producers and video-tape operators in his ear while maintaining authoritative, calm and insightful delivery. 'You learn to sift out what you need and what you don't need,' he says. 'If I didn't have that noise in my ears I don't think I could do it. It's just ambience and your voice goes over that.'

Murray's job is to provide the words to accompany the images captured by the cameras. 'The pictures give

you the words and sometimes they give you silence,' he reveals. But calling the winning moment is always very special. 'It's a tremendous surge of adrenalin, more so than any other event,' he says. 'You don't want to mess it up.'

While Murray can allow the pictures to tell their story, that is not the case in radio coverage where the spoken word in consort with the unique, natural sounds of an Open create a compelling offering for the listener. BBC Radio has been ever-present at The Open since the days of Darwin's 'Eye-Witness Accounts'.

Former head of BBC Radio Sport Gordon Turnbull spent more than a decade producing and editing his department's golf coverage and recalls one of his predecessors describing how the event used to be reported. 'I remember John Fenton saying reporter Tom Scott would go up onto a high dune somewhere and at the appointed time, perhaps one minute past 11, he would just start his report and end after a minute,' Turnbull says. 'That was how they did it.'

Gradually the coverage expanded to incorporate live commentary of the shots as they were hit. The veteran writer and broadcaster Renton Laidlaw was at the forefront of the coverage and remembers it being a pretty precarious business. 'The old commentary boxes would be quite high up,' he said. 'Getting up the ladder was very difficult, carrying a case with notes and things. There was no health and safety and the wind would be blowing. We wouldn't be allowed to do it nowadays.'

Ken Brown has vivid recollections of how these broadcasts inspired him to pick up a microphone after playing in the 'Duel in the Sun' Open of 1977. 'I drove home in the car and listened on the radio,' Brown recalls of how he kept up with Tom Watson's thrilling win over Jack Nicklaus. 'I enjoyed it so much. The drama was spectacular and listening on the radio brought the golf, surprisingly, to life.'

It is often said that live golf should not work on the radio, but it is a most malleable medium, which means that the listener can be taken to exactly the right moment at the correct time. 'Golf on the radio is just absolutely wonderful,' says Tony Adamson, my predecessor as BBC golf correspondent. He is correct. There is no greater broadcasting experience than describing the key moments, standing inside the ropes

and sharing the stage with the world's best players. The contrast between the silence that accompanies shots and the roars that go with their brilliant execution makes for magical listening.

'The atmosphere of an Open Championship, I still maintain, is better than the atmosphere of any other Major Championship,' Adamson contends. 'It's the atmosphere that gets to you in the end and we had the massive privilege of being inside the ropes.'

There is no other form of broadcasting quite like it. 'You're with the crowd and next to the players,' says Andrew Cotter, who performs commentary for both radio and television. 'When you are commentating on radio you are almost part of the Championship itself. They are long, long days but they were the best days.'

TOP LEFT The Sky Sports team quiz Darren Clarke at Royal Portrush.

TOP RIGHT Never hurry a Murray: veteran 5 Live summariser Andrew takes a moment with commentator John (no relation).

With it comes a responsibility to encourage listeners to stick with the broadcast. Normal programming on BBC Radio 5 Live is interrupted by the arrival of comprehensive coverage of the four days, so it is important to reflect every aspect of this massive event. 'It wasn't just about the leaderboard,' recalls John Inverdale, who presented coverage of 25 Opens from 1994. 'It was talking about what breed of bird might be sitting on top of the leaderboard, while you were also reflecting that Nick Price was leading or whoever it was.'

As one of the top sports broadcasters of his era, Inverdale reported from pretty much all the world's biggest events: the World Cup, Olympics, Wimbledon and international rugby. He recognises the capability of a close and exciting Open, such as the Henrik Stenson/Phil Mickelson epic of 2016, to stir the sporting soul. 'Very, very few sports sustain drama like that over four hours in the way that golf can,' Inverdale says. 'It can be absolutely captivating and that is when radio is in its pomp. On those days there are very, very few other days like it on the sporting calendar. It builds and it builds to a fantastic climax.'

It is those times for which broadcasters live, whatever the medium. They are providing contemporaneous accounts of pure sporting theatre, not knowing which way the plot will twist and turn. It is what makes The Open so compelling to an audience near or far from the action – some of them even beyond the earth's atmosphere.

'We've had interaction from space stations,' says Steve Tebb, IMG's head of audio, who edits and produces the bespoke At The Open radio service. Tebb's team provides a service broadcast within a 10-mile radius of the Championship and it is carried internationally via The Open website and syndicated radio stations. 'We've had nuns listening in orphanages in India,' Tebb adds. 'There have been some really far-flung places. You get a lot of Americans listening when they are driving because Sirius XM is embedded in car radios. That's the beauty of radio: they can be doing other things, but these listeners still want to be across the action because they are massive golf fans.'

Tebb's 16-strong team start broadcasting on the Tuesday of Open week and, along with live commentary from inside the ropes, their work is wrapped up into daily podcasts to create a comprehensive audio service available digitally anywhere in the world.

Opportunities are plentiful in the digital world and The R&A have been innovative in making the most of the current era. Spectators are able to watch action on their smartphones via The Open app while sitting in grandstands. 'We were the first green-field sporting event to have Wi-Fi across the Championship,' says Malcolm Booth, The R&A's director of sales and marketing. 'We did a test at Lytham in 2012 and then ran it out at Muirfield the following year. I think that's the kind of innovation that people don't necessarily associate with The R&A but it was a demonstration of being forward thinking and finding new ways to heighten the experience for people at the event.'

There have been up to 10 million visitors to TheOpen.com along with two million app downloads during a Championship week to help satisfy golf fans' thirst for more information and coverage of the event. Innovations such as 'The One Club', an online

membership, allow subscribers to experience and enjoy The Open on a year-round basis.

'It will continue to grow as more and more people have a multitude of digital connections,' says Booth. His digital team provide a complementary service to sit alongside the more traditional broadcasters in a way befitting the twenty-first century. 'The bigger the audience we have and the more regular the engagement, the higher the audiences we can drive to watch the four days of the Championship through our broadcast partners.'

Anyone involved in telling The Open story feels an enormous sense of privilege. It began with Bernard Darwin nearly a century ago and given that his grandfather gave us the theory of evolution, it is perhaps fitting that what his grandson started has evolved beyond imagination into a vast and vital role.

It has been another epic Open journey. Sky Sports' Jason Wessely will never forget walking into the broadcast compound for the first time in 2016. 'The sheer scale and size and enormity and the feel of it just absolutely blew me away,' he says. 'I've been on hundreds and hundreds of TV compounds but that one was incredible.' So proved the coverage of that Troon Championship, winning a prestigious BAFTA for the way it reflected Stenson's iconic triumph.

'The R&A are keen to get their uniqueness across. The yellow leaderboards and the ancient history of The Open, the links ground, the weather challenges, the real, authentic down and dirty gritty sense of golf,' Wessely says. 'The players are battling out there and they make for great brand qualities.

'Golf is not an easy sport to broadcast, let alone with all those additional challenges that you have on a links course by the sea in terrible weather. So the practical challenges and the philosophical challenges are pretty hard but that's kind of what makes it fun.'

Volunteer Stories

By Tim Culshaw, Open Volunteer

The Open needs not only the might of The R&A and its affiliated organisations, hundreds of companies, sponsors and television; it also relies on thousands of volunteers. They are responsible for crowd marshalling, working leaderboards, helping on practice grounds, assisting the media and merchandise tents. There are walking scorers, scoreboard carriers, rubbish collectors and programme sellers. The volunteers are generally golfers of all ages from all walks of life. They want to be there to simply be part of The Open. Marshals around the course generally come from local golf clubs, each allocated a hole. Around 50 members from tee to green work in two shifts each day, controlling crowds, stands and crossing points as well as ball spotting. Geoff, a friend of mine, was spotting on the 17th at Birkdale 2008, keeping an eye on balls landing in thick heather. A caddie approached and asked, 'Have you got it?' Geoff, looking down at the lie, replied, 'Yes I've got it, but you are not going to like it.' By this time, the caddie's well-known American player had arrived and, hearing this, he quipped curtly, 'What do you know?' Geoff stood back, without response, then watched as the player squirted his 3-iron horribly low and left into the rough on the other side. As he walked off hurriedly, head down, Geoff took great delight in grinning at the caddie and retorting, 'Told you!'

He was also at close hand on the 17th fairway when Padraig Harrington and his caddie had the discussion about whether to hit his now famous 5-wood, which led to the eagle that cemented his Open victory. Geoff, the only person within earshot, loves to relate their discussion. Listening to him 12 years later, the story has been embellished and the mists of time decree that it was actually marshal Geoff who gave Padraig the advice to hit the 5-wood and was therefore instrumental in deciding the destiny of the Claret Jug!

With each group the volunteer team comprises a referee or 'walking Rules official', a scorer, scoreboard carrier and bunker raker, generally a member of the British and International Greenkeeping Association. The scoreboard carriers are boys and girls between the ages of 16 and 18, who display players' scores for the benefit of the on-course spectators.

On the par-4 12th tee at Royal Birkdale, a young scoreboard carrier I was with decided to rest the board on the barrier behind the tee. In awful wet conditions, I could see it starting to slide and, with impeccable timing, just as Justin Rose got to the top of his backswing it fell to the ground with an almighty clatter! Justin pulled out of the shot, thankfully, and glared at the red-faced lad. After several seconds of an icy stare he re-focused and hit it to four feet! The lad was mightily relieved when Justin made the weekend exactly on the cut number.

A top volunteering role landed by another friend, Doug, at Muirfield in 2013 was to sit in the locker room and organise players' start times for the practice days. We were all quite envious. On the Monday and Tuesday evenings over a beer he was full of it: 'Sergio said this, Poults said that, I put Lee with Darren, Dustin wanted to play with Phil.' etc., etc. On the Wednesday morning I watched as Phil Mickelson, Ricky Fowler and a couple of others were followed by another four, including Tom Watson. There were now eight on the tee. Tom said, 'I've booked 8 o'clock.' Someone from the other group said, 'The guy gave us 8 a.m.' I listened to all this in stitches at the thought of Doug, happily sitting inside tinkering with his start sheet, unaware

of the mayhem in front of me. They all looked at each other as I texted Doug: 'Don't know what you are doing in there, mate, but it's chaos out here!' In the end Watson threw the balls up and his four went off first. Doug, amidst the ribbing and laughter later that night, blamed it on a glitch in the computer system.

The scorer with each group keeps everyone informed of how the players are faring. Every shot is inputted into a hand-held device, recording where it is played from, fairway, rough, bunker, green and so on, as well as the length of putts. These statistics are relayed to the electronic leaderboards around the course, the media centre and computer systems around the world. Once the 'send' button is pressed the score for the hole is final, and can't be changed with the device. However, each scorer has a radio and can talk to 'score control' if need be, where adjustments can be made by them. In the recorders' cabin the numbers the scorer has recorded through the system appear on a TV screen above the players' heads.

The players double check with their own cards in silence. As a scorer you sit there praying they agree with you! It is a great volunteering role I've been lucky enough to have on many occasions.

The players of course are still ultimately responsible for signing for each other. In 2003 Mark Roe and Jesper Parnevik famously, after a mix-up with each other's cards, signed for the wrong score and were disqualified. Mark Roe was in contention. Thankfully a few years later the rule was changed.

To be out there scoring is always exciting, but the first time it is also a daunting and quite nerve-wracking experience. On a lovely sunny morning at Muirfield I set off making my debut and focused on the three players, D.A. Points, Brett Rumford and Marcel Siem, concentrating on recording their every shot, from every location correctly. After a few holes I was getting into the routine, and with everything running smoothly began to relax and enjoy myself. By the time we came up the 18th hole I was now feeling very confident and

totally in control. Nothing had gone wrong. As any professional golfer who's done it knows, the walk up the 18th in The Open Championship is an experience, a moment to savour. Club golfers imagine what it must be like, and here I was, being able to walk inside the ropes down the middle of the fairway behind the players.

I took it all in: the famous clubhouse behind the green, the huge iconic yellow scoreboards, crowds in the grandstands flanking both sides of the fairway, the players doffing their caps and lifting putters to acknowledge the applause. As we walked to the green, my mind drifted back to Jacklin and Trevino and later Faldo in his yellow sweater all treading this same path. However, in that moment I had taken my 'eye off the ball'. On the green it was the American D.A. Points to play. My device said it was his third shot, but as I looked down at my paper sheet in horror, I had written three shots already, including fairway bunker: 'T, FB, F', so surely it was his fourth shot? Absolute panic took over. Had I missed inputting the fairway bunker into the system or was the 'FB' wrong on the sheet?

Had he played from the fairway bunker or was it another player? My mind went blank. He putted, then tapped in – was it a four or a five? My finger hovered over the 'send' button. There was no time to ask as the others still had to play. My heart was thumping – it was decision time. I pressed and off it went; a par 4 was registered into the system, to the leaderboards, the media centre and off around the world.

After Siem and Rumford had putted out and during the handshakes D.A.'s caddie confirmed the news I feared, that it was actually a 5. Suddenly my moment of glory crumbled into a nightmare as I had failed my scoring debut at the final hurdle. There was no time to alter by radio. I was ushered by The R&A official into the recorders' cabin, but this wonderful privileged experience was turning into a panic, all of my own doing. I explained my error. As I went through the detail, with The R&A recorder frowning and with all eyes on me, I felt like a naughty schoolboy. The adjustment was rectified, cards signed and, still shaking, I skulked away from the cabin.

Although it was a fraught moment, it was a valuable lesson! Now when I walk up the 18th my eyes don't leave the play – I concentrate on the job in hand, scoring for the players and leaving the dreams of Open glory to them. Sometimes you get some awful conditions. The rain at Birkdale in 2017 springs to mind – it was horrendous that Friday afternoon for the second round. The computer stopped working and the paper was wet even under a plastic cover. It was hard work for us, never mind for the world's best players having to play in it!

On the tough sixth hole Justin Thomas blocked his second shot into the sand dunes on the right. He played his third and fourth hardly moving the ball as his hand came off the club. The fifth shot only went about two yards into the deep grass in front of him. At that part of the sixth there are no spectators, so it was down to Justin, his caddie Jimmy, a marshal and myself. I was only four yards away and saw exactly where it went in, so I got down on my hands and knees but we couldn't find it. Justin dropped another under penalty, played his seventh onto the green and two-putted for nine. Justin turned to me and asked, 'How many was that?' He had lost count. I confirmed the nine and we moved to the next tee. From being in contention a day earlier he missed the cut, but only three weeks later he won the US PGA and became a Major champion. The ups and downs of professional golf!

In 2019, scorer Ronnie Nicholl couldn't have imagined how frenetic his day would be as he set off with match 18 on day one at Royal Portrush. On the seventh, David Duval had to play three balls from the tee and, having found one, realised nearer the green that he had played the wrong ball. Ronnie recalled: 'The referee and David went back to look where he had played and then eventually went back to the tee. I was up at the green recording the other two players and didn't know what was going on. Twenty-five minutes went by. The ref came back ashen faced and wasn't sure of the score and penalty accrued. It was a bit chaotic;

the media were all quizzing me. Score control said put 15 down for now, we'll sort it later!'

At St Andrews another friend, Ian, was scoring an early group out on Thursday morning. Sweden's David Lingmerth, playing his first Open, scored seven birdies in nine holes to go out in a record-equalling 29! To Ian's frustration score control kept radioing him. 'Score control to match four, are you sure that's another birdie?'

One of the great things about volunteering each year is that you bump into the same people, whether it be the referees, bunker rakers, marshals or the army security lads who walk with the top players. There is great camaraderie and everybody has their own stories of Open experiences to trade during the round. For the walking team of volunteers who were allocated match 13 at Royal Birkdale on the Saturday morning in 2017, it was to be a special occasion. As the round unfolded, and the birdies dropped, South African Branden Grace was to achieve something no one in the previous 145 Opens had done and return an Open Championship low record score of 62.

The thousands of volunteers at The Open Championship each year do so to get involved in The Open and be a part of the oldest and most prestigious Major golf championship there is. The volunteers who were out on the course that day at Birkdale will all have tales to tell relating to Branden Grace's round.

The marshals whom the group passed by, the students peering down from the large yellow scoreboards, the referee, the scorer who recorded each of those 62 strokes to keep the world informed, the scoreboard carrier and bunker raker – they were all there and witnessed it. They also contributed to the occasion and were part of Open history that day. For Open Championship volunteers, it really doesn't get any better than that!

Quiet, please! Marshals ensure perfect silence for players aiming to sink a crucial putt.

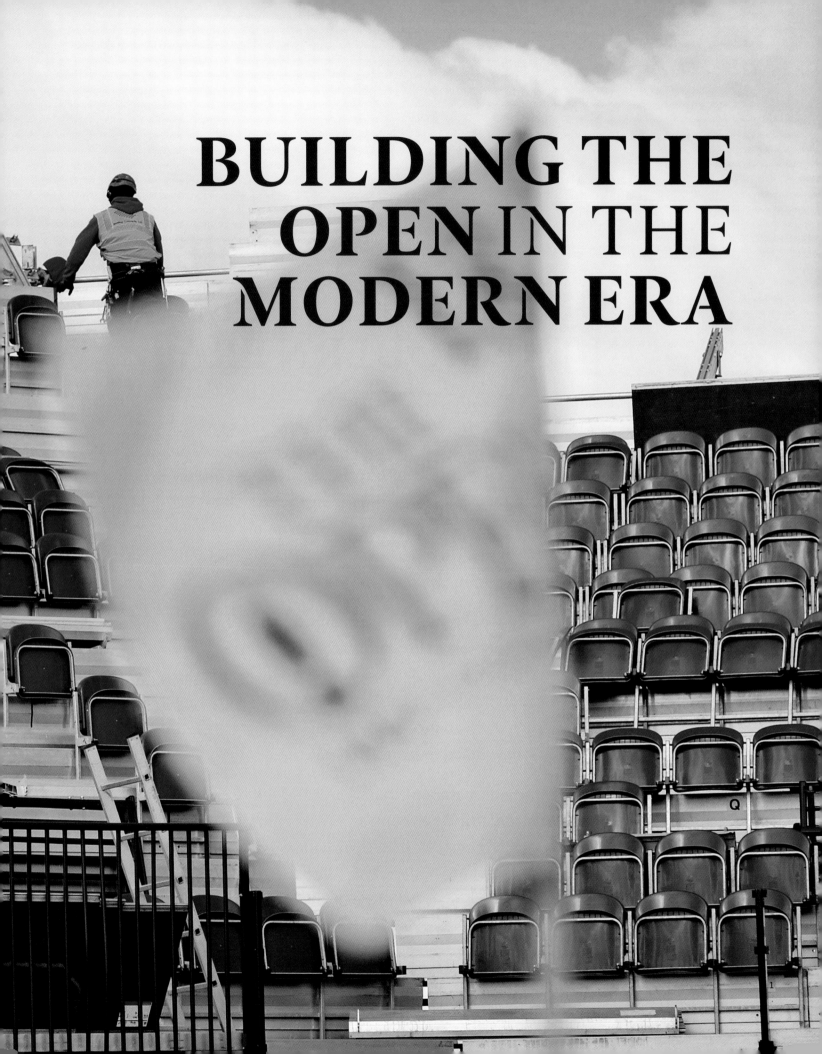

BUILDING THE OPEN IN THE MODERN ERA

BUILDING THE OPEN IN THE MODERN ERA

'We create a temporary town on a 450-acre greenfield site,' says Johnnie Cole-Hamilton, The R&A's Executive Director for Professional Championships. He is describing the task of staging The Open. 'We have to provide infrastructure to support 40–50,000 people on a daily basis. There are a lot of towns in Scotland and England smaller than that.'

Throughout its history this Championship, dreamed up by the nineteenth-century folk of Prestwick at a meeting in the town's Red Lion pub, has grown and grown ... and grown. How might those pioneers, who put on that eight-man Championship in 1860, react if they were to hear Cole-Hamilton reel off the figures and demands that must be fulfilled to stage The Open these days?

'We have to provide marquees, that means 20–30,000 square metres of tentage,' The Open boss says. 'We put in about 70 kilometres of power cables. We have to provide water and waste management, which is a huge undertaking. We have to build around 15,000 seats in temporary grandstands, and on it goes ... And then we have to take it all down again!'

From Raincoats and Trilbies to Technicolour Glory

Peter Alliss vividly remembered his first visit to an Open back in 1947. He travelled with his father, Percy, from their home in Dorset to Royal Liverpool. 'I was obviously excited,' the former Ryder Cup player and veteran TV commentator said. 'The journey up was on the train, going to Bournemouth from Ferndown. We went on the bus with golf clubs and suitcases and everyone looked at us if we were mad. "What the hell have you got in that bag?" they would ask. Then it was the train up to London and on to Chester and then we had a bus along to Hoylake.'

Alliss was immediately struck by the golf course, its beautiful greens and dangerous opening hole with the practice ground out of bounds. He also recalled the scale and feel of the Championship. 'There were a lot of people,' he said. 'All the men in raincoats and trilby hats. All the women seemed to have two-piece costumes on, tweed suits with a hat and handbags. Not everybody had golf shoes, they had sturdy walking shoes.

'It felt like you were at a big occasion. There were masses of people. Of course there was no TV at the time and there was a fellow called Eddie Carter who put up scoreboards. He made them all himself. He dug holes in the ground, four posts would go in and then he'd put the cross bits in and then he slotted in these big pieces of wood. At The Open there would be around 120 competitors and he would sort out all of the names and numbers on pegs. He'd put "Alliss P" up there and then he'd have a little wedge of wood which he'd knock in and then the scores, 78, 79, 81, 84 – whatever it was. And he'd work on it all on his own, maybe with one young lad helping him lift the timbers.

'I got to know him; he was a real Londoner. He had no teeth, he was only about 50 and he used to roll his own cigarettes. He'd take two minutes to roll it and then he'd light it and half of it would go up in flames because it was just paper without any tobacco in there!' Alliss recalled with laughter.

In comparison with today, when The Open is one of the world's biggest annual sporting events, it was a

pretty homespun environment. 'They used to wrap a bit of hessian around some trees and that's where the men went for a pee,' Alliss continued. 'I don't know what the women did.'

Another veteran broadcaster and writer, Renton Laidlaw, attended The Open from the 1950s. 'It was like a glorified monthly medal,' he chuckled. 'It was all so natural. It was a golf tournament and still a special event because it was a Major. We knew all the people who had won were big names, but it was just a relatively quiet event, very genteel.'

In 1959 when Gary Player won at Muirfield, Laidlaw was a budding reporter. 'We had a little press tent,' he says, recalling a week when his job was to collate scores for his paper, the *Edinburgh Evening News*. 'There were 14 or 15 of us and we drove into Muirfield and parked our cars right by the tent.

'The secretary of Muirfield would occasionally come into the tent and he would say, "Here's a pretty good score from so and so, a 69." Everything was so relaxed and easy.'

This was all about to change, however. An irresistible force was on its way, bringing with it a massive injection of interest, presence, energy and excitement.

The next Championship in 1960 marked its centenary, but even more significantly it was the first time the field included a character from Latrobe, Pennsylvania by the name of Arnold Palmer. When this most charismatic of sporting figures arrived at the 'Home of Golf', he was on his way to becoming one of the most famous sportsmen the world has ever seen. At the time Palmer was looking to emulate Ben Hogan's feat from seven years earlier of winning the first three

Majors of the year. He already had the Masters and US Open titles to his name.

A modern-day Grand Slam was a notion that was taking hold and Palmer put The Open at the heart of it. He had a ready smile, instantly connecting with fans and television cameras. He oozed personality and throughout his career galleries willed him to win because they could see how manfully he was striving for success. The American's first attempt at winning The Open was typically valiant. He battled horrendous weather and came up only one stroke shy of success, with Australia's gutsy Kel Nagle the man prevailing.

But Palmer's presence and unadulterated respect for The Open made an important impression amongst fellow Americans, some of whom had been more reticent to travel to the UK. 'That was what really brought players back,' says former R&A Secretary Sir Michael Bonallack. 'The top ones wanted to come.'

Palmer returned in 1961 and won a weather-affected Championship held at Royal Birkdale. It was the second successive Open to finish a day late on a Saturday. Weather forecasts were far from promising and The R&A had controversially stated that the competition would be declared void if it could not conclude before the Sunday of that week.

Palmer did not necessarily agree with the ruling and who knows how the Championship would have been influenced had he been thwarted by the stormy weather of that week? Perhaps that lasting love affair with The Open might not have materialised? The Championship may never have felt the full dividend of what ultimately proved unstinting support from the world's most charismatic sports star.

Arnold won again at Royal Troon the following year, by which time the ranks of 'Arnie's Army' of supporters had swollen to almost bursting proportions.

OPPOSITE Keeping up with the action at Royal Liverpool in 1924.

LEFT Arnold Palmer visits the merchandise tent in the week of his 1961 triumph at Royal Birkdale.

OPPOSITE Bobby Locke in 1952 receiving the Claret Jug in front of a scoreboard telling the story of his third Open triumph in four years.

RIGHT Arnold Palmer watched from all angles in 1961 at Royal Birkdale.

It became clear for the first time that proper ropes would be required to keep galleries in position, largely because of Palmer's popularity. A young Jack Nicklaus was also arriving on the scene and Gary Player completed an exciting triumvirate known as the 'Big Three'. 'The Open was transformed once Arnold, Jack and Gary started coming to it,' says Sir Michael.

Brigadier Eric Brickman was the man in charge at the Royal and Ancient during this period. He ushered in a new television era and had the foresight of allowing engineers to dig up sacred fairways to bury TV cables as early as 1955, the year when The Open's first prize rose to £1,000. By the mid-sixties the event was being beamed into homes on both sides of the Atlantic and crucially it was still being championed by the most influential sportsmen of the moment. It was certainly no longer the genteel occasion of old.

In 1967 Brigadier Brickman was succeeded as Secretary of The R&A by a formidable personality in Keith Mackenzie. He was just the man to pilot The Open and take advantage of a new and even more intoxicating age of colour television. It was also vital to capitalise on Palmer's influence in making The Open attractive to big names from overseas. 'Keith had this great drive and personality and he used to go out to America trying to talk to people and persuade the players to come,' says Sir Michael, who succeeded Mackenzie in 1983.

'The players didn't all have managers then so he and his secretary had to arrange their accommodation. The players were okay, but the wives would complain about the bathrooms and views. Keith was a showman and he was a good administrator. He knew what he wanted and he knew how to get results. He would have tremendous arguments with people but he knew what he was doing for The Open.'

There was another key figure in this period of rapid growth, Palmer's manager, who was an American lawyer called Mark McCormack. He, better than anyone, recognised Palmer's true earning potential, and it was vast. From their relationship, McCormack founded the influential International Management Group, an organisation that has worked closely with The R&A for decades growing the commercial side of the Championship.

'Mark was extremely straightforward,' says Sir Michael. 'He loved golf, he loved sport and if he said you'd got a deal, you'd got a deal. He was committed to The Open and that was such a big bonus for The R&A.'

Growing a Global Footprint

A total prize fund of £10,000 in 1965 rose to £100,000 by 1977. The financial growth was sustained by increasing revenue streams, several of them spotted and exploited by McCormack. 'We soon realised that to make The Open a continued success we had to get bigger income,' Sir Michael adds. 'He made a lot of suggestions about how we could increase our returns. He would handle our television deals in America, which was the start of bringing in big money. Then there were television deals in Japan … and worldwide. Mark used to negotiate this for us, and with the BBC we had a deal that they didn't have to pay us very much but provide us with clean pictures which could then be sold around the world. The other broadcasters could put their own commentary on it if they wanted and this is when the big money started.'

With its growing popularity, The Open was able to attract sponsorship because companies wanted to be associated with an increasingly successful event. Players such as Palmer, Nicklaus, Player, Tom Watson, Lee Trevino, Tony Jacklin and an emerging kid from Spain called Severiano Ballesteros were sportsmen who made the game easy to sell. But the Championship also wanted to preserve traditions that stem from the game's roots and these principles remain in place today. 'The main thing is to keep the golf course clear and uncluttered,' says Sir Michael. 'You don't want too much commercialism, so everything has to be done fairly discreetly.'

Another important aspect was to enhance spectator experiences, so fans could get more than just world-class golf when they attended. 'We had this great big exhibition tent where you could go and buy anything,' Sir Michael recalls. 'Not just clothing but golf clubs, golf books, golf holidays. The tentage was rather different to what you have now; you had guy ropes and poles. It was very popular with the public and we wanted to give them the best time but also maintain it as a traditional golf championship. We were very careful in the sort of sponsors that we had.'

Like his predecessor, Sir Michael held the role of Secretary of The R&A for 16 years, giving way to Peter Dawson after the tumultuous Carnoustie Open of 1999. 'Peter and I were members of the same club,

Thorpe Hall,' Sir Michael points out. 'Peter was a junior member and we used to play a lot together. It was incredible that a small club like that in Essex produced consecutive Secretaries of The R&A.'

When Sir Michael left the job he became Captain of The R&A in 1999 and in 2000 presented Tiger Woods with his first Claret Jug. Woods romped to victory in the same manner he had at the US Open the previous month. Golf had its newest and most potent superstar and Sir Michael was not in the least surprised.

'Presenting the trophy to Tiger Woods was an amazing moment,' he says. 'I'd been out to the US Open at Pebble Beach and I walked the last two rounds as an observer with Tiger. I came back and said, "If Tiger Woods doesn't win The Open then there ought to be a stewards' inquiry." That got into the press. His arrival was the next step up.'

Dawson was the boss who sought to make the most of a new era. The first £1 million prize fund arrived in 1993 and seven years later Woods took home £500,000 for his St Andrews triumph from an overall £2.75 million purse.

That Open was preceded by a 'Champions Challenge' to mark the turning of the millennium. It was Dawson's idea to bring back as many Open winners as possible to play an exhibition event on the eve of the Championship. 'Michael actually didn't think it would work!' Dawson admits with a chuckle. 'He didn't think the players would come but I said we should try, and thank God it did work.'

Although Palmer was unable to attend, legends such as Sam Snead and Nicklaus took part, as did popular British champions including Jacklin, Nick Faldo and Sandy Lyle, along with the great Ballesteros.

'He got the biggest cheer,' Dawson recalls. 'That was a terrific thing to start the week.'

And then the Championship proper was under way and Woods started to do his stuff, in a way that only he could. He finished eight strokes clear of Ernie Els and Thomas Bjorn. 'The Tiger era began for The Open Championship and he just demolished the field that year. Tiger became the man of my time at The R&A,' Dawson adds.

'It was very important with Tiger to have a good relationship with his management team. We had that because The R&A was very close to IMG and his agent, Mark Steinberg, was IMG at the time so that helped.'

Dawson felt able to run ideas past Woods and believes the combination of the world's best player and his manager worked well for the game. 'I never found them difficult at all,' he says. 'I was able to say to Mark, "I wonder if I could get Tiger's opinion on something?" and that would be arranged. I think Tiger appreciated being asked. It was an occasional thing, I didn't overplay it.'

Dawson knew the importance of Woods to the sport in general and The Open in particular. 'The ratings on television are massive when he's playing,' adds the former Secretary, who also served for 16 years. 'The Championship every year has grown commercially and it is still doing so, which is great to see. In my time we started a commercial committee and everything grew, in particular television revenues in the UK and in America. Tiger was a big driving force, especially in the US. TV contract after TV contract we got good inflation so The R&A was able to carry on its governance role and have money for golf development.'

While Woods was important, so were other leading players. Dawson witnessed first hand the grumbles that surrounded the penal course set up at Carnoustie in 1999. He understudied Sir Michael at that Open ahead of taking over as R&A Secretary. 'If the players don't like the golf course and the set-up you don't

have a good Open,' Dawson concedes. 'So I always concentrated a lot on courses and set-up, making sure they were as right as we could get them. It was a good lesson to learn.'

During his tenure Dawson enjoyed getting to know players and forming relationships with them. He would keep possession of a supply of spare tickets to ensure competitors would speak to him personally with their requests. 'I got to know the players because they would stop for a chat,' he recalls. 'Sergio Garcia was always a great character. I would say: "Okay Sergio, which auntie is it this year?"

'One time a player came in and asked me why all the tees on the practice ground were white that year because they'd always been lots of different colours. I said I would check and find out. The people on the range said: "We don't do the coloured ones anymore because the player concerned used to steal them all and then use them for the rest of the season!"'

Dawson's business acumen came to the fore as he oversaw the separation of The Royal and Ancient Golf Club with the creation of The R&A companies that now run The Open. 'It was a complicated process but I wouldn't say it was difficult,' he says. 'It wasn't actually my idea. It came out of the finance committee. The late Fred Gibson was Chairman and it was driven forward by the finance committee at that time.'

As Chief Executive of The R&A, Dawson was in charge of The Open, an event with which he developed a love affair ever since watching Jacklin's win on television in 1969. Taking over from Sir Michael Bonallack some three decades later had been something of a surprise for a man who captained the Cambridge University team in his formative years. 'It was a dream job. They wanted someone who knew a bit about golf and the commercial world,' Dawson says. 'One or two people suggested I should go for it when Michael's retirement came up. My wife wasn't all that keen on moving from Northumberland at that time and my son said, "Oh, let him apply, he'll

LEADER BOARD

HOLES	+PAR-		PLAYER	SCORE	100TH OPEN GOLF
*72	14	UNDER	TREVINO	278	CHAMPIONSHIP
72	13	UNDER	LU	27	1971 AT
72	12	UNDER	JACKLIN	28	ROYAL BIRKDALE
72	11	UNDER	DEFOY	28	
72	9	UNDER	NICKLAUS		
72	9	UNDER	COODY		
72	8	UNDER	PLAYER		
72	8	UNDER	CASPER		
			HOMSON		

never get it." When I eventually got it he then wanted to know if the job was hereditary!'

Dawson handed over the first seven-figure winner's cheque when Zach Johnson collected £1.15 million for his 2015 victory at St Andrews. The following year golf returned to the Olympics after a successful campaign spearheaded by the leading golf authorities, with The R&A at the forefront. It was one of many highlights from his tenure because it helped to globally promote the game.

The death of Arnold Palmer in September 2016 was the most traumatic experience in Dawson's time at the top of the golfing world. It is a mark of the closeness between The R&A and this great and hugely influential Champion that the then retired Chief Executive was asked to speak at his funeral. 'I didn't want to mess that one up, for sure,' Dawson admits. 'I had come across him in his role as a member of The R&A and that's

where I got to know him. The Open Championship owes him an enormous debt because if you think of that post-war period there wasn't much of an American presence. Palmer really started that going.'

Palmer passed a baton to Nicklaus who handed it on to Ballesteros, Greg Norman and British stars such as Faldo and Lyle. Then Woods came onto the scene and he has spawned a modern generation of golfing athletes who dominate the game today.

The numbers that tell the tale of Lee Trevino's landmark 1971 triumph.

Building for the Future

The Open has ridden the wave and grown exponentially. Martin Slumbers, a two-handicap city banker, took over as Chief Executive in September 2015 and is now steering the Championship to the next level. 'I was hired to build on the success of many, many decades but to take it into a more modern world,' he says.

'My job is to try to find a way to reflect history in a modern way. When you first have the responsibility for staging The Open you have no idea how big it is until it kicks off. I thought this is going to be great because I love golf, but when you start to see people arrive, the sheer scale of it gets you.'

One of the biggest changes Slumbers has overseen is all-ticket crowds. Previously The Open reflected its name. It was always open. If you fancied seeing a day's play you could buy a ticket at the gate. But the current boss insists the Championship has outgrown that model. 'By having it all-ticket we are trying to move people to saying, "The third week in July, that's where I want to be." That way you get more loyalty to the golf and I think you get a better experience.'

Implementing this policy has many benefits. It provides crucial information about the people who want to attend the world's oldest golf championship and reinforces its contemporary relevance. 'If you haven't got data on your clients you are not going to be around for very long,' Slumbers states. 'You need to know who these people are, what they like and what they don't like. The opportunities to continually engage are huge. Historically, The Open is a one-week-a-year event, but if we can find a way of it being in the consciousness of our fans for 40 weeks a year that's good for The R&A, good for The Open and it's also good for our sport.'

Max Faulkner won in 1951 at Royal Portrush and 12,271 tickets were sold. When the Championship next returned to Northern Ireland in 2019, it coincided with the first all-ticket running of the event. The attendance was 237,750, and The 148th Open was watched by the biggest crowds of any staged outside St Andrews. Shane Lowry received a winner's cheque paid in American dollars rather than UK pounds, a switch made in 2017, and he took home $1.935 million. Faulkner's winnings 68 years earlier were £300.

The Open Is the One

While the golfing test remains the same, to beat the world's best players by overcoming the original challenges of links golf, the Championship fosters a genuinely modern feel and look.

'A sea change for us was the brand strategy work done prior to the 2015 Open,' says Johnnie Cole-Hamilton. Since that St Andrews Championship, spectators have been greeted by smart navy blue grandstands and hoardings; the tented village is decorated with unmistakably Open branding, whether in refreshment areas or the vast merchandise tents.

Fans can join 'The One Club', which provides year-round online access to The Open, including archive films and videos as well as the latest ticket information. 'We were really keen to make sure that the world knew we were staging the oldest and most prestigious golf championship,' Cole-Hamilton adds. 'That's why we have come up with the brand strategy; that we believe that golf only has one real true test and we want it to be the one to watch and the one to win. It was that work that really drove The Open going into a different space.'

It is an ongoing journey and every Championship occupies a continuously expanding footprint, meaning only a few venues are capable of staging it. Work to ensure a course is ready to hold the event can start seven or eight years in advance. 'We have to ensure that we have the land rentals in place,' Cole-Hamilton explains. 'We have to ensure that we have the accommodation requirement and if there are any major infrastructural works. Take Royal St George's, for example [the most recent Open]. There's been major work done on the railway station which has

involved cooperation and collaboration with Network Rail, local authorities within Kent and the UK government with enterprise partnerships.'

All of these sort of negotiations must start well before The R&A announce where a particular Open will be held. There is a bewildering level of infrastructure involved.

Around 30 miles of fibre optic cabling is buried at each venue and this delivers the event's data, TV pictures, internet and phone capability. It also feeds the vast media centre's colossal appetite for information while fans are kept up to date by 17 on-course LED scoreboards.

LEFT Inside the press tent at Royal Lytham in 1979.

OPPOSITE Reporters from around the world cover the action in The Open media centre, Royal Birkdale, in 2017.

Not everything has to rely on cutting-edge technology, though. The giant bright yellow leaderboards that sit above grandstands surrounding the 18th green are manually operated and remain much loved by fans and players for the way they convey the drama of every Open.

'We do see those as an iconic part of The Open Championship,' says Cole-Hamilton. 'When the Champion Golfer of the Year walks up the 72nd hole that it is the greatest walk in golf. Despite working so closely in this wonderful Championship for so many years, when I'm standing there it's like when I was watching as a 14-year-old. I still feel the same tingle when the Champion walks up to great acclaim, surrounded by thousands of people in a wrapped-around arena with those two iconic yellow boards standing proud. They are absolutely an iconic part of the Championship.'

Cole-Hamilton lives and breathes The Open. His team builds and takes down the mobile town that is the Championship as it continues an ever developing journey, delivering sporting drama on an annual basis around the United Kingdom.

No one saw the scale of the event's development more than Peter Alliss. His first visit was back in 1947 and he spent every subsequent summer bar one at The Open with either club or microphone in hand. 'I think The R&A have done remarkably well in this very hard commercial world and remember it is all run from a little town in Scotland,' Alliss said.

From his St Andrews office, Cole-Hamilton administers plans for one of the world's biggest events. It is a constant cycle, disrupted only by the coronavirus pandemic which delayed for a year the 149th Championship at Sandwich. Cancelling the 2020 running of the Championship was his 'worst day' but there was no alternative.

It means that 2022 is the year of the 150th Championship, a landmark well worth celebrating. 'The 150th has two faces,' says chief executive Martin Slumbers. 'It is a golf tournament and we will run The Open and we will do everything that is great about The Open, but we will have the ability to use the landmark to increase our reach.

'In 1860 eight competitive golfers got together to create something. I've said to my team, the 150th

should be about what is our gift for the next 150 years. We have to think about it like that and our gift has to be to young people.'

Cole-Hamilton is particularly proud of The Open's policy of welcoming a youthful generation. 'We've been letting in under 16s to The Open free of charge since 2004 – not many major sports do that,' he says. 'We must be nearing nearly half a million people who have come in that guise and we've also done a lot of work around removing barriers for our under 25s with discounted pricing, and if you are under 25 you get a free berth in the campsite which is paid for by The Open.

'That has hugely increased the number of young people. We think that's a really good direction to be going in. It's a real cornerstone; we want the young to touch The Open and be touched by The Open and therefore inspired.'

And that is what drives a relentless rhythm to deliver, grow and maintain the journey of the greatest of golf championships. 'We start building it around the start of April and continue right up to the Saturday prior to The Open starting in July,' Cole-Hamilton says. 'Then on the Sunday night the event finishes and we start taking it down. It probably takes until the third week in August to remove.

'That gives you six months before you start building it again … somewhere else.'

145TH ROYAL TROON

GLORIES AND STORIES: THE OPEN MOMENTS

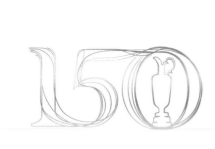

GLORIES AND STORIES: THE OPEN MOMENTS

Opens are lost as much as they are won.

There are occasions when it is simply the last man standing who becomes the Champion Golfer of the Year. Rivals fall away, sometimes in spectacular and memorable fashion. There are also supreme victories when winners seize the greatest of golfing moments to grab a chance to put their hands on the Claret Jug. It may be a shot of 72nd-hole brilliance or it might come from sheer relentless quality throughout a dominant Open week. Perhaps the Champion emerges from an epic duel, with the rest of the field long since consigned to the status of also-rans.

It all happens in the high-pressure atmosphere of elite sport, which means there is plenty of scope for controversy, intrigue and breaking news. Whenever an Open is played it becomes an occasion capable of generating moments that become permanently etched in sporting history.

Here are some of the biggest stories from the 149 Opens so far completed. Some are glorious while others inevitably come from the opposite end of the spectrum.

The 'Duel in the Sun'

TURNBERRY, 1977

A new venue was added to The Open rota for The 106th Championship and it proved an instant hit. As the sun beat down on a parched Turnberry links, it yielded one of the greatest Championships when Tom Watson overcame Jack Nicklaus in what will forever be remembered as the 'Duel in the Sun'.

These two great champions played the final 36 holes in each other's company. Watson finished 12 under par, with his American rival a single stroke behind. Hubert Green, the only other golfer to break par, was at one under.

Those are the bare facts from that extraordinary week in 1977. It was unforgettable for anyone who witnessed the drama unfold. Among then record crowds for an Open in Scotland was avid golf fan Alan Mackay. 'There was a bit of mystique about a new course coming onto the rota,' says the former journalist who was a huge Nicklaus supporter. 'I couldn't wait to see it.'

Mackay crossed the Firth of Clyde from a holiday on the Isle of Arran to make sure he was part of the first Open to be played on the spectacular Turnberry course. It boasted narrow fairways and proved no pushover despite a record-breaking second-round 63 by US pro Mark Hayes. Only three players were below par by the end of the week.

Mackay arrived in time for Friday's third round, when the iconic and enduring narrative began to take shape. 'To me it was all about trying to see every shot, if I could, and that involved quite a bit of running,' he says.

Nicklaus was the man he wanted to see and he was in the plum pairing with Watson, the Champion on debut two years earlier at Carnoustie. Storms were forecast and the distinctive Christmas pudding-shaped Ailsa Craig was shrouded in morning mist as it sat in the Irish Sea.

Watching every blow, Mackay saw Nicklaus and Watson both move to four under par, five holes into the third round. They joined Roger Maltbie at the top of the leaderboard. One hole later Nicklaus's birdie putt tumbled in the side door while Watson bogeyed from a tricky greenside bunker. The man they called the 'Golden Bear' led by two strokes, but progress was soon interrupted.

'I was out at the lighthouse at the ninth hole,' Mackay recalls. 'It got really humid and hot and looking back at the hotel I remember seeing an amazing streak of forked lightning right above its red roof. It was truly spectacular.'

Inevitably play was suspended. The two lead protagonists, who went on to thoroughly dominate the event, took shelter on the beach close by. 'Many of the crowds headed back to the tented village,' Mackay continues. 'I just sat on the banks by the ninth tee. I had a hunch that the few of us that decided to stay out there were going to get a really good view for the next few holes.'

Those brave souls were duly rewarded. Upon the resumption, they saw Watson draw level with his rival at six-under on the 15th before Nicklaus struck an imperious 2-iron to near tap-in range at the par-5 17th. Watson hit a 3-iron to set up a birdie before Nicklaus squandered his short eagle chance by misjudging a cruel left-to-right borrow.

Both men then parred the last, Nicklaus thanks to a sensational chip that nearly fell into the cup. They were each round in 65 after both had scored 68 and 70 in the first two rounds. With nothing between them at seven under par, they led Ben Crenshaw by three shots heading into what proved an even more extraordinary closing round.

'On that final day the galleries were amazing,' says Mackay. 'To see Opens played in that era was like a football World Cup final between Brazil and Italy being played in Scotland every other summer.'

Spectators charged around the fairways. Despite the Friday storms, clouds of dust mixed with the Saturday heat haze in their wake. And as the day went on there was a growing recognition that everyone present was experiencing something truly remarkable.

Nicklaus made the better start and the then two-time Champion leaped three strokes clear by holing a lengthy birdie putt at the par-3 fourth. Watson missed a significantly shorter attempt, but bounced back with a birdie at the next and a gutsy par save at the sixth. Then he dispatched a driver off the fairway to find the par-5 seventh green in two mighty blows. He was on a charge and the resulting birdie and another at the next brought him level with Nicklaus at nine under par. The pair were four clear of Crenshaw at this stage.

Watson dropped a shot at the next and simultaneously Hubert Green set a somewhat academic clubhouse lead at one under. Nicklaus surged further clear with a 25-footer for birdie at the 12th only for Watson to birdie two of the next three to draw level. The second of those, perhaps the most dramatic, came from a putt from wispy rough to the left of the par-3 15th green, the ball travelling a monstrous journey before disappearing.

Both players were locked at 10-under when they arrived at the long 17th. Watson found the green with two lusty blows, whilst Nicklaus's approach was a tad heavy and came up short. He chipped like the great champion he is to give himself a four-foot birdie chance. The crowd sensed these were key moments. Amid palpable tension, Watson putted close and Nicklaus settled over his crucial birdie attempt. Agonisingly, he tapped it left of the hole. 'I was very close to the green when Nicklaus missed and everyone just thought that was that,' Mackay recalls.

Watson made no mistake with his tiddler to take a one-stroke lead to the 72nd tee. It was the first time he had been in front in the entire Championship. He dispatched a judicious 1-iron that obediently bounced into the middle of the fairway. Nicklaus went for broke. Out came the driver and he gave his ball a fearful smack, imparting maximum effort. It flew off to the right towards potentially ruinous gorse bushes. The then 37-year-old thudded the grip of his errant driver into the turf of the tee as he trudged after his ball.

The younger protagonist by a decade, Watson played first to the green from the perfect position. It was a magnificent 7-iron that came to rest within two feet of the hole. Nicklaus, meanwhile, was left to work out whether he could fashion a shot from the trouble he had found to the right of the hole. Alan Mackay was among the hordes who sprinted to gain a vantage point to see the shot. 'He was very, very close to being under the gorse bush,' Mackay says. 'He might have been able to see his ball with half an eye, I don't know, but I think it was just his vast experience that kicked in. He thought I've got to do this, especially as he knew Watson's ball was so close to the hole.'

Somehow Nicklaus managed to muscle an 8-iron onto the front-right portion of the putting surface. 'I had no idea other than from the roars that the ball had even reached the green,' says Mackay, who then dashed to the green to watch the denouement on tiptoes.

'I remember Nicklaus studying the putt far more closely than earlier in the round. He was in the last-chance saloon. But there was no semblance of any nerves whatsoever in the way that he hit the putt; it was almost as though he knew it was going to go in.'

Watson watched on; most people – including the man closest to him – were convinced he was about to be handed the Claret Jug for the second time. 'My caddie Alfie Fyles said, "You've got him now, mister."' Watson recalled. 'I said, "No, he's going to make that putt." Ten feet from the hole I knew it was going in dead centre and it went in – geometric dead centre of the hole. And the crowd went absolutely ballistic; I mean it was a jet engine roar.'

Alan Mackay says, 'It was like a roar I have never heard before or since', and it went on and on and on. 'It was a great putt on 18, but the ovation for Jack was

really about the 36 holes of the duel. Everyone who walked Turnberry with the players over those amazing two days wanted Nicklaus to know, "You are much, much more than just the runner-up here."'

And Watson still needed to hole out for the closing birdie that assured him of victory. 'I'm waiting there, waiting for them to slow down but the crowd just kept on cheering the mightiest cheer you have ever heard in your life. And so I said, "The heck with this" and I bent over, put the ball down and as I bent over and picked up the coin I see in the corner of my eye Jack going like this.'

His opponent in his bright yellow sweater was raising his arms, calling for calm and decorum. 'Only in the game of golf would this happen,' Watson continued. 'That crowd went silent in three seconds. It was unbelievable. That's what the game is all about, respect for other people, respect for playing the game the way it should be played.'

Nervelessly Watson tapped in and the man in mint green raised both arms in triumph before Nicklaus congratulated him, putting his arm around the Champion as they departed the final green as one. It was an iconic moment in which two of the greatest ever Champions were able to epitomise the very best of the game of golf. 'He said, "I'm proud of you, congratulations, I'm happy for you,"' Watson recalled. 'And I thought, "Yes, maybe I can play with the big boys."'

At the presentation ceremony Nicklaus, the man who has won more Majors than any other, told Watson: 'I gave you my best shot and it wasn't good enough, you were better. Well played.' The Champion informed the watching spectators: 'This is probably the greatest thrill of my life in golf, beating Jack Nicklaus like this.'

And for the fans who had roamed and at times stampeded Turnberry's first Open, there was a genuine sense of delight at having witnessed great sporting theatre which built to such a dramatic climax. As Alan Mackay says: 'It was a rare privilege to be there, even though I had to wear out quite a bit of shoe leather in the process.'

Jean Van de Velde dries off after visiting the Barry Burn in 1999.

Jean van de Velde

CARNOUSTIE, 1999

'I have never seen a more dramatic and sad end,' said Peter Alliss, who was commentating for BBC Television in 1999 when Jean van de Velde took a triple-bogey-7 at the last, knowing a closing 6 would have made him Open Champion. 'This went on for 45 to 50 minutes and I honestly did not know what to say because it was all so ridiculous. The whole thing was ridiculous.'

Van de Velde was on the verge of becoming only the second man from France to win The Open after Arnaud Massy in 1907. He had battled a Carnoustie course set up with severe, penal rough and buffeted by strong winds throughout much of the 128th Championship. Van de Velde coped magnificently over the first 54 holes and held a five-stroke lead, with Australia's Craig Parry and American Justin Leonard his closest rivals. Despite his healthy advantage the unfamiliar leader rather prophetically raised the prospect of golfing disaster. 'Maybe I'm going to blow it tomorrow,' he told reporters on the Saturday evening. 'It's my first time ever there, what do you expect?'

By the time they reached the 12th tee the next day, the lead was gone. Indeed, Parry had gone ahead but promptly and fatally surrendered the initiative with a triple-bogey. Back in front, Van de Velde suddenly assumed the calm of a champion. A composed two-putt from the back of the 71st green meant he took his three-stroke advantage to the closing hole.

Parry was out of contention while up ahead Leonard, the Champion two years earlier, put his second shot into the Barry Burn. He finished six over par alongside clubhouse leader Paul Lawrie, the local man from nearby Aberdeen. At that stage both players thought their chances of victory were, at best, remote.

Van de Velde prepared to unleash his final tee shot. 'I was commentating with Alex Hay,' Alliss recalled.

Jean van de Velde led the 1999 Open by three shots before taking a triple-bogey-7 on the final hole.

'We saw him take his driver out the bag on the 18th tee and we thought, "Oh, crikey, I daren't look!" He missed the burn on the right and he was okay. He had surely won The Open. We thought he would knock an 8-iron down the fairway, chip it on and he could have three putts and still win by one.'

Van de Velde was fully aware of the potential safe play. 'The option was, do you hit a wedge down the left side and then pitch it on and two-putt it or three-putt it, whatever, and walk off with it. Or do you hit a shot over there and try to move forward with it.'

Fatefully the 33-year-old chose the latter and went for the green. As rain started to fall, his second shot flew towards spectators sitting on the banked green seats located to the right of the hole. 'He was unlucky when his ball hit the stand and came backwards,' Alliss continued. 'And then it was just a series of the most ridiculous things.'

Van de Velde's ball ricocheted into thick rough. He still had an option to pitch out sideways with his third shot but chose to go for the green. His attempt came up woefully short and to the collective gasps of the galleries it plunged into the Barry Burn.

Next, he considered playing from the water hazard, removing his shoes and socks before rolling up his trouser legs and wading in. The water level was relentlessly rising as the tide came in and his ball became ever more submerged. After lengthy deliberation, Van de Velde conceded that a penalty drop was his only option. 'And, of course, he had a very young caddie who didn't give him any support and his wife was getting hysterical,' Alliss recalled. 'They kept showing her on our television screens with her friends and it was hysteria, it wasn't humour. I tried to make that point. Some people wrote and said I had taken the mickey, I had no intention of doing that.'

What seemed a foregone conclusion was now the exact opposite. Van de Velde took his penalty drop in the rough and was playing his fifth shot needing to get up and down to win.

'He was such a nice guy, and we'd done a big interview with him and he was just absolutely charming,' remembers John Inverdale, who was on that 18th hole for BBC Radio. 'I watched the drama unfold with my bare eyes and I was just thinking, "Please don't mess this up," but when he did mess it up the journalistic bit inside you says this is irrefutably an "I was there moment". While it was happening I remember thinking this is something that people will talk about for years and years and years to come.'

That fifth shot did not find the green. It landed in the same bunker as playing partner Parry's ball. To add to the drama the diminutive Aussie proceeded to hole out, perhaps offering hope to the Frenchman that he could do the same and snatch the title in the most dramatic way possible. Instead Van de Velde managed to hit it to around eight feet and then bravely hole out to grab a place in the play-off with Lawrie and Leonard.

'I thought to hole the putt to get in the play-off was wonderful,' Alliss said.

The four-hole shoot-out was dramatically won by the Scotsman, who birdied the last two holes thanks to a pair of brilliant 4-iron approaches. Lawrie started that day 10 strokes behind and emerged as the Champion Golfer of the Year. 'Jean had the tournament in his pocket. I feel sorry for him,' Lawrie immediately admitted. 'He really should have won; thankfully for me he didn't.'

More than two decades later sports fans vividly recall the events of that crazy final hour on the north-east coast of Scotland. Writing in *The Times* in 2020, columnist Matt Dickinson stated: 'For a sense of sheer disbelief, Jean van de Velde's collapse at The Open still gives me shivers like no event I have seen first-hand … when asked by the boss to pick the most jaw-dropping day of sport I have covered, I found myself back standing on the 18th hole at Carnoustie in 1999, watching one of the most compelling, excruciating, unmissable yet also unbearable chokes of all time.'

Peter Alliss spoke of the regret he felt that Van de Velde failed to cross the finish line ahead and fell so spectacularly at the final hurdle. 'That was one of the saddest sporting moments, I think, of all time,' said the veteran commentator. 'I'm looking at it now as an old stager. I think from a golf point of view, a Frenchman winning The Open for the first time since 1907 could have meant so much … Van de Velde had charm and personality but he just made the most awful mess of it.'

The player himself has always spoken with grace and perspective about what was perhaps The Open's most extraordinary collapse. His message has never wavered from the one he issued at the time. 'There's worse things in life. I read the newspapers in the morning and some terrible things are happening to other people.' He went on to ruefully tell a stunned gathering of reporters: 'Next time I will hit a wedge, okay. You all forgive me.'

Bobby Locke

ST ANDREWS, 1957

The spirit of the game was also in evidence when South Africa's Bobby Locke won in unusual circumstances after the 86th Championship in 1957 had been switched from Muirfield to St Andrews because of fuel shortages due to the Suez crisis. Locke ended Peter Thomson's run of three successive titles to claim his fourth and final Claret Jug. But he might have been thrown out of the Championship after a curious incident on the 72nd green.

Having hit his second shot to within a couple of feet of the pin, the South African picked up his ball before placing his marker a putter head away from its original spot. Locke forgot to replace his ball in the correct position and no one noticed the error, including his playing partner Bruce Crampton.

The mistake was picked up on television and having signed his card the Champion was liable to disqualification. Following an investigation it was decided no action should be taken.

Chairman Bobby Selway later wrote to Locke to reassure him that in exceptional circumstances the committee had the power to waive disqualifications. He said: 'The committee considers that when a competitor has three for The Open Championship from two feet and then commits a technical error which brings him no advantage, exceptional circumstances then exist and the decision should be given in the spirit of the game.'

Doug Sanders

ST ANDREWS, 1970

Even greater sporting drama played out on that famous Old Course 18th green in 1970, the year of the 99th Championship when the flamboyant American Doug Sanders squandered a golden opportunity to win The Open.

This was one of the most dramatic Championships from start to finish. Title holder Tony Jacklin, who also held the US Open crown, raced to the turn in 29 on the first day by holing his pitch for eagle at the ninth. 'That was a dream start,' Jacklin says. 'I don't think I've ever had one like it before or since and especially when you are defending. Holing the shot on the ninth was a fluke. Hitting into one of those thick wooden pins, the ball hit halfway up and somehow went straight down.'

But the English favourite was then scuppered by storms that curtailed the action while he played the 14th. 'It became a nightmare when the rain came in,' he ruefully recalls. Jacklin never quite recovered the poise and panache of his spectacular start. In increasingly difficult weather his scores rose by three strokes each day; 67, 70, 73 and 76 and he finished fifth but only three shots back.

Sanders's Open started in an inauspicious manner as he found the Swilcan Burn to score a double-bogey-six on the very first hole, but the tall American quickly found his stride. At the end of the third round he coaxed in a tricky birdie putt for a 66 that took him to six-under and into the final pairing for the last day, two behind Lee Trevino.

On the closing day the third-round leader faded from contention and the destiny of The Open came down to a battle between Sanders and 1966 Champion Jack Nicklaus. The former showed prophetic frailty with a short missed putt for birdie on the par-5 14th, while Nicklaus remained secure. Sanders then played a wonderful recovery from the 'Road Hole' bunker on the 17th to stay six-under. It would be a score good enough to win because Nicklaus failed to birdie the last after three-putting from off the front of the green.

Needing par for victory, Sanders dispatched a sound drive, leaving a short pitch to the green.

But then things started to go wrong. This tall, charismatic figure, popular with fans on both sides of the Atlantic, abandoned the instinctive approach which had put him in this tantalising position. 'I knew I'd made a mistake coming up the 18th hole,' Sanders later told US broadcaster Peter Kessler. 'I was 76 yards from the pin after my tee shot.'

Sanders then paced out the remaining shot, strolling all the way up to the hole. 'Instead of playing it by feel, by eying, I walked up there. I don't know, maybe I was showboating a little bit,' he admitted.

'When I walked back I knew I could hit this club 80 yards and I was pumped up a little bit. Instead of playing it by feel, as I had done all week long, I played it by the yardage and I put it about 35 feet past the hole. Today, I know I would have put that ball closer.'

Sanders had two for the title and his first attempt came up three and a half feet short. He was left with a short putt, with a hint of left to right, for glory. His playing partner, Trevino, stood arms folded, watching and no doubt wondering what might have been.

The leader was on the threshold of greatness on this 72nd green. Clad in lilac, he crouched over the ball. 'I looked down on that green and I thought I saw a little pebble but it was where the sun had made one of those little spots brown,' Sanders recalled. 'And I started to pick it up and I realised it wasn't anything and I never got myself back in the right stance.'

With hindsight he knows he should have reset his position. 'That's another mistake I made – I didn't back away,' he admitted. It was a fatal error and the crowd knew it. A loud murmur spread around the gallery. Trevino raised his right hand to call for order. Sanders slotted the putter-head back behind the ball and then seemed to freeze. 'You don't win until you win. I was thinking about which side of the gallery I was going to bow to … that was a time where I was not a champion. There I was putting all the other stuff in front of me before I won the Championship.' Eventually he jabbed at the ball, his stroke lacking authority. His ball miserably dribbled to the right of the hole. Nicklaus, who thought he had blown his own chances moments earlier, was reprieved and the title went to an 18-hole play-off the following day.

Sanders manfully tried to bounce back from the disappointment of the previous evening. He fought tenaciously to narrow a four-shot deficit until it was just a single stroke at the last. With a strong wind at their backs both men dispatched long drives, Nicklaus charging his through the back of the green. Sanders put his second shot to within five feet of the flag, meaning Nicklaus needed to get up and down from the bank at the rear of the putting surface.

The blond-haired maestro from Ohio was left with a 10-footer for the title. His putter had been cold all day and he nudged forward his attempt at glory. The hole grabbed his ball, just as it threatened to slide by, and it disappeared. Fulfilled by triumphing at the 'Home of Golf', Nicklaus hurled his putter high into the air in wild celebration. Sanders needed to duck to avoid being struck before the two men embraced.

The beaten man then nonchalantly knocked in a birdie putt that had zero significance. If only he could have adopted a similar approach a day earlier.

Both men left the stage arm in arm in another extraordinary display of sportsmanship. As Nicklaus made his victory speech, Sanders could not resist a rueful stroke of the side of the Claret Jug. He knew it did not belong to him, but that it really should.

The man they called the 'Peacock of the Fairways' died aged 86 in April 2020. He spent decades recalling his missed opportunity at St Andrews, saying that there were some times when he could go five minutes without thinking about it. He was only half joking.

Costantino Rocca
ST ANDREWS, 1995

Thanks to one of the most astonishing Open finishes, Italy might have celebrated its first winner 23 years before Francesco Molinari was eventually crowned Champion in 2018. The genial Costantino Rocca forced his way into a play-off at St Andrews against John Daly with one of the most outrageous and famous putts the Championship has ever seen. Ultimately, Rocca's extraordinary feat only delayed Daly's name being engraved on the Claret Jug, but it remains one of the iconic moments in Open history.

It occurred during a stirring finish to that windswept 124th Championship in 1995. Daly set the target at six under par as Rocca toiled with the punishing 17th, where his second shot finished on the road. The Italian opted to putt, his ball jumping off a stone into the air and onto the green. Rocca calmly holed out, meaning a birdie at the last would take him into a four-hole shoot-out with the American clubhouse leader.

'I remember on the 18th tee I said to my caddie if I put it on the green I will make two,' Rocca recalls. 'In my mind there is no four, only two or three.' Rocca's drive came up short of the putting surface and the packed grandstands held their breath as he prepared to chip. They were hoping to hear the distinct click that accompanies a cleanly hit pitch. Instead there was a foreboding clunk as turf was struck before ball. As a result it lamely hopped forward into the infamous 'Valley of Sin'. 'Could there have been a more devastating let-down, with the whole world watching?' wondered the esteemed sports columnist Ian Wooldridge afterwards.

Now Rocca was 60 feet from the hole, with Daly surely about to celebrate his second Major title. This putt had to drop, but it was extremely unlikely not just because of the distance that needed to be covered but because of the undulations of the depression from where he was putting. But holing it was his only objective. 'In that moment I was so concentrated, I didn't see or hear anything,' he said.

Rocca struck the putt and it never deviated from its destination – a target four and quarter inches in diameter, cut out of the most famous green in golf. His ball disappeared and the stands erupted. The then 38-year-old fell to his knees looking skywards, shaking his fists. Next he tumbled forwards onto the upslope of the 'Valley of Sin', beating the turf with both hands in celebration.

The cheers were long and loud as Daly turned to his wife and said: 'I gotta go.' There was now a four-hole play-off to be negotiated but at this precise time it was Rocca's moment. 'When you see it on TV, you feel what you had around you and I think it was fantastic,' he said. 'To see people jumping on the terrace and the right side of 18 and jumping everywhere, that was a nice moment.'

The Italian went on to play on the winning Ryder Cup team later that year and in 1997 beat Tiger Woods during Europe's victorious defence of the trophy at Valderrama. While those were memorable successes, that putt at St Andrews will stay with him and all those present forever – even though he ultimately lost the play-off. As Rocca says: 'I became more famous for that putt than if I won the tournament.'

Farewell to the Greats

Few sporting events are better at ensuring an appropriate send-off for their greatest stars. When time was called on their distinguished Open careers, Arnold Palmer, Jack Nicklaus and Tom Watson all received fitting farewells on the home green of St Andrews' Old Course. Adoring fans shared in emotional goodbyes that involved the players posing for photographs on the Swilcan Bridge to create iconic images worthy of their elevated places in Open history.

In many respects, the end of Watson's Open career was the most extraordinary because it happened so late at night after weather interruptions. 'We had been toying with the darkness falling,' recalls former R&A Chief Executive, Peter Dawson. He credits Watson's South African playing partner for making sure it was the memorable occasion it became. 'The Rule of Golf was that if play is stopped and one player hits off, the others can follow. We persuaded Ernie Els that he was going to hit off the 18th because we didn't want them coming back at six o'clock the next morning. It was terrific. Amazing, because it

was about twenty to ten at night and you couldn't have played anymore.'

Watson struck the final putt of his 40-year career as an Open competitor at six minutes before ten on Friday 17 July 2015. It concluded his 129th round in the Championship and ended a glittering association which brought five Claret Jugs. There is little wonder that the people of St Andrews emerged from their homes and hung from windows to greet him as he strode up the famous 18th fairway, flickering flashguns burning bright in the night-time gloom. 'The way St Andrews came out of their houses I thought was just stunning,' Dawson adds.

It did not matter that the 65-year-old Watson scored 80 and finished 12 over par. His past glories ensured that those with genuine appreciation would say a proper farewell to one of their favourite Champions. The player soaked up unbridled adulation on that 18th fairway, prompting him to think of another great Champion. 'About halfway up, just across the road, I'm looking all the way up the right side and then to the back and the road was all jammed with people,' Watson remembered. 'When Bobby Jones won the

Grand Slam, he came back and played a friendly here. I'm not putting myself in the same shoes as Bobby Jones, but walking up that 18th fairway, as the legend goes, he was engulfed by thousands of people who had come out and heard that he was on the golf course. When I was going up there, I think I had an inkling of what Bobby Jones probably felt.'

Watson might have gleaned some idea of the sort of acclaim he would receive a decade earlier when he accompanied Nicklaus's final competitive round at the 2005 Championship. 'It's been a long walk, a long time, a lot of years, a lot of great things,' Jack said. 'I just felt like this was the place I wanted to end my golfing career, here at St Andrews.'

Nicklaus was finishing in an era when pretty much every player dons well-remunerated headgear, but not on this occasion. 'We persuaded him in advance not to wear a baseball cap,' Dawson recalls. 'We said, the British public want to see the blond-haired Jack Nicklaus like they used to and he readily agreed to that.'

Packed galleries accompanied and cheered the then 65-year-old on his every step, culminating in a deafening climax on the Friday evening. 'People were fantastic as I was coming down those last few holes,' Nicklaus said. 'I think these people are wonderful. They gave me a lot more than I deserved.' This great Champion was being overly modest. Throughout a glittering career he thrilled millions of fans all around the world, winning three Opens among 18 Majors.

Nicklaus signed off in typically classy style and Dawson is not surprised. 'Three months prior to the Championship, I'd been interviewed by one of the golf magazines in the UK,' he says. 'I told them that

I thought Jack would rather be remembered as a competitor than a monument.'

Needing a birdie for a level-par 72 Nicklaus curled home a downhill left-to-right 10-footer to ensure his career finished on a tumultuous exclamation mark. Of all the moments I have commentated on for BBC Radio, this was among the very best. It had no material effect on the Championship but it meant so much to everyone present and beyond. The cheers were as loud and heartfelt as any that have greeted the winner of an Open. St Andrews fans saluted the greatest of champions with extraordinary scenes of adulation.

'I always make it on 18,' Nicklaus joked. 'It always happens, so I figured it'll go in. I just hit it and it went in. No, I wanted to putt that one, obviously.' Dawson was watching while standing on the Clubhouse steps when Nicklaus made his emotional exit. The former boss reveals: 'As he walked by he said, "Hmm, competitor rather than a monument? I like that," and walked on. For him to do that at that time, I thought was astonishing.'

Similar scenes greeted the departure of Arnold Palmer in 1995. He was 66 years old and thanks to a tweaking of the age eligibility rules for that year was able to choose the 'Home of Golf' as the venue for his 23rd and final Open appearance. 'This is going to be a very special tournament for me,' he said prior to teeing off. 'One that will bring back a lot of memories … and they are all good memories.'

Earlier in the week Palmer closed the Champions Dinner held in the Royal and Ancient Clubhouse. In his speech he told fellow Open winners: 'To have come here in 1960 and played this Championship and to see what I saw then and to see what I have seen over the years has been a fantastic pleasure. The Championship is one that I came to because I thought it was the most revered Championship in the world. I still think that.'

On the following Friday, off the final tee Palmer dispatched his drive in typically muscular style. Then he took the visor from his head, paused briefly on the Swilcan Bridge and waved to thousands gathered around the closing hole. They rose as one to applaud someone who did more than any other to promote the international standing of the Championship. He tapped in from around four feet at the last to take his final bow. 'I guess it's over and that's significant to me,' he told reporters, exhaling with emotional feeling. 'But I can't help but remember all the years that I've had and enjoyed and that is most important … I guess I'm not going to play again. That bothers me, but there is also a happy note on that in that it's been good through the years.'

My predecessor as BBC golf correspondent, Tony Adamson, commentated on the end of Palmer's Open career. 'I will always remember interviewing Arnold after that last round,' Adamson says. 'He gave me everything, he talked all about The Open. I was trying to capture what Arnold Palmer meant to The Open but what I got was how much it meant to him. I remember him saying that his proudest moment was being associated so closely with The Open. I didn't need to ask him more than two or three questions. He was just unbelievably nice, such a modest and self-effacing guy, a terrific bloke.'

It is little wonder that Palmer set a precedent with the glorious send-off he generated and that it was replicated so memorably for fellow greats such as Nicklaus and Watson.

Tony Jacklin

ROYAL LYTHAM & ST ANNES, 1969

**'What a corker,' is one of the great commentary
lines and it was about one of the greatest drives ever
hit. Commentator Henry Longhurst delivered it for
BBC Television viewers as they watched an Open in
glorious technicolour for the very first time. He was
describing Tony Jacklin's drive off the 72nd tee while
anticipation reached fever pitch for a first British
winner in 18 years.**

Ahead of that tee shot there was considerable tension
because Jacklin bogeyed the penultimate hole and a
comfortable three-stroke advantage had slipped to a
more perilous two. Playing partner Bob Charles, the New
Zealander who was looking to repeat his success of
1963 on the same Lytham course, was his closest rival.

'I was very much aware The Open had been lost a
couple of times by British players in the years before,'
Jacklin recalls. He needed to summon composure and
execution for that final drive at the 98th Championship.
Playing safe was not an option because he knew his
1-iron would not be long enough to carry cross-
bunkers. He therefore needed to go for broke with
his driver.

'It's a very difficult driving hole because the
bunkers are deep and you know very well that if
you go in one you are not going to get on the green,'
Jacklin says. 'I remember thinking, "This is what
you've worked for and just keep doing the same thing.
Keep it wide and smooth," and as I was saying it to
myself I was doing it. I looked up and there it was
flying down the middle of the fairway.'

The normally understated Longhurst was sent
into raptures by this nervelessly brilliant blow. 'My
word, that was a fine drive. Look at it, miles up the
fairway.' The Champion was left with a mere 145 yards
to the pin, which was a comforting 7-iron, the club
he had practised with more than any other. Jacklin
found the heart of the green and very nearly holed
his birdie attempt. His ball hung on the edge of the
hole and, amid rapturous scenes, the Englishman
tapped in. 'There is the shortest shot that ever
won a Championship,' Longhurst commented.

For Jacklin it was a crowning moment made all the more special because he was on home soil. The son of a Scunthorpe lorry driver, he had based himself in the United States and so revelled in the chance to compete in front of British fans. 'Playing in America was a lonely business,' Jacklin remembers. 'Palmer and Nicklaus took all the big galleries and coming back home there was an anticipation among the public. To be followed every day by the biggest support was a turn-on, and when you are on the top of your game like that you've got to be a bit of showman. There's nothing better when you get the applause and it was very, very special.'

Jacklin was mobbed by the crowds as he came up the 18th fairway, losing his golf shoe as he battled through the crowds before finishing off the

Championship and becoming the first Briton to lift the Claret Jug since Max Faulkner in 1951. 'It's all the build-up of the pressure,' he says. 'The night before I took a pill to help me sleep and then there was the wait all morning before teeing off at 2.30 in the afternoon. It's such a test of nerve and patience so there was a real element of relief when it was over and I'd come out victorious.'

All eyes on Jacklin as he closes in on Britain's first Open win for 18 years.

David Duval confounded by the 'Road Hole Bunker'.

Tommy Nakajima and David Duval

ST ANDREWS, 1978 & 2000

Tsuneyuki Nakajima, better known as 'Tommy', was a highly promising youngster when he arrived at the Old Course for The 107th Open in 1978. At 23 he was the youngest Japanese PGA champion but was also known for taking an unfortunate 13 at the par-5 13th at Augusta during his Masters debut earlier that year.

Further infamy awaited after Nakajima climbed the leaderboard on the third day at St Andrews. He arrived at the 'Road Hole' within a shot of Tom Weiskopf's lead and had seemingly done the hard part by reaching the green in two on the treacherous par 4.

Then it all went wrong. The Japanese putted from the front but his aim was too far to the left. His ball found contours that swung it into the sheer-faced 'Road Hole' bunker. Playing his fourth shot, Nakajima's ball failed to emerge. The same happened with his next attempt. His third effort crept out of the hazard, only to fall back into the sand. A last desperate swipe resulted in his ball eventually finding the green and he two-putted for a quintuple-bogey-9.

That famous bunker became known as the 'Sands of Nakajima', although it was almost renamed after David Duval fell foul of its brutality in 2000. The American was in a share of second place, nine strokes behind Tiger Woods, when he found the bunker in two during the final round. Duval's first two attempts at escaping hit the face. After the second attempt, his position was so hopeless he needed to play a one-handed back-flick to knock his ball into the middle of the hazard.

From there he escaped, somewhat fortunately as his sixth shot of the hole hammered into the side face of the bunker before emerging on the green. Duval took a quadruple-bogey-8 and tumbled to a share of 11th place.

The former world number one went on to suffer worse in 2019 at Royal Portrush. On the seventh he played most of the hole with the wrong ball and ran up a 14 on the par 5, en route to a first round 91 – his worst score as a professional. 'It's just one of those god-awful, nightmare scenarios that happened today,' he reflected after his round.

RIGHT Tony Jacklin and Lee Trevino chatting at the 1972 presentation ceremony.

OPPOSITE Jacklin congratulates Trevino on the final green at Muirfield.

Lee Trevino

MUIRFIELD, 1972

Championship week did not begin well for Lee Trevino's title defence in 1972. The man known as 'Merry Mex' arrived at the wrong airport, flying to Prestwick on Scotland's west coast when the event was being held in the east at Muirfield. But pretty much every break went his way thereafter, especially when the Championship built to its memorable climax.

Trevino was bemused by the lack of interest when he touched down. As defending Champion he was sure media and fans would greet his arrival into Scotland. By flying to the wrong airport he avoided anticipated attention and, anyway, most of that was directed at Jack Nicklaus. The 'Golden Bear' was on a charge. He had won the Masters and US Open, and arrived at the scene of his 1966 triumph looking to preserve hopes of winning every Major that year.

Nicklaus played in the only rain that week. It fell on the afternoon of the first round when he scored a one-under-par 70. He was a shot better than Trevino, one behind Tony Jacklin and two adrift of unheralded leader Peter Tupling from Yorkshire. Glorious weather accompanied the rest of a Championship played on fast, firm, baked-out fairways – ideal links conditions.

For the final 36 holes of this 101st Open, Trevino was paired with Jacklin. On the 16th hole of the third round the talkative American holed out from a bunker. On its second bounce his ball slammed into the cup

for the most unlikely birdie and it gave him share of the lead. At the par 5 next he collected his fourth birdie in a row.

Interrupting his singing of The Beatles classic 'Yesterday' when he strolled off the 18th tee, Trevino called over his legendary caddie Willie Aitchison and said to him: 'If I could make a birdie here, I've never had five in a row in Great Britain, I'm sorry, I mean Scotland.'

It looked unlikely when his approach raced through the back of the green, but Trevino's touch was magnificent and a deft chip tumbled into the hole. 'Five in a row!' he exclaimed before signing for a score of 66 and a share of the lead with Jacklin at six under par.

Nicklaus seemed out of it, languishing at level par, but the 'Golden Bear' was about to roar. He put together a typical charge to set the tone for a truly dramatic final day. As the leaders faltered over the early holes, Nicklaus surged to the turn in 32, four under par. As Trevino was distracted by a dashing hare when he bogeyed the seventh, the reigning Masters and US Open champion was capitalising and thrillingly shared the lead well into the final day of The Open.

If he won and then claimed the upcoming PGA, Nicklaus would make an unprecedented clean sweep of Major titles in a single year. At this stage hopes of a Grand Slam were in decent health, especially when he then birdied the 10th and 11th holes. For the second of those he was forced to back off his putt and regain his composure because of the loud cheers that greeted eagles for both Trevino and Jacklin at the par-5 ninth.

Crucially, Nicklaus could not maintain the momentum. He lipped out for a birdie on the 15th and bogeyed the short 16th before failing to birdie the penultimate hole, an inviting par 5 that would soon after witness an extraordinary turnaround in fortunes.

Nicklaus set the clubhouse lead at five under par as Trevino and Jacklin came to the 17th tee sharing the lead at six-under. While Jacklin hit a good tee shot, Trevino was distracted by photographers and hooked

his drive under the lip of a fairway bunker. He tumbled over in the process of escaping the trap before dispatching a desperate fairway wood into thick rough left and short of the putting surface. Jacklin was just short in two. Trevino then blasted his pitch through the green in four. It was surely over. 'I'm through, it's all yours,' a resigned Trevino told his playing partner.

'I just wanted to get the hole over with and I think Jacklin was about 18 feet away for a birdie,' Trevino later told the PGA Tour. 'I was pretty frustrated at how I had played the hole.'

Then it all changed.

'I grabbed the 9-iron quickly, glanced at the hole and then pitched it in for a par. I think it stunned Tony and he was overly aggressive with his first putt and then missed a short one coming back. Suddenly I had a one-stroke lead.'

It was the fourth time Trevino had chipped in that week. He went on to par the last and a shell-shocked Jacklin, who admitted he was never the same again, bogeyed to finish third. Trevino successfully defended his crown and ended Nicklaus's Grand Slam dream. At the presentation, the Champion struggled to lower the microphone. 'Hey, I'm a little short guy,' he joked. 'I really don't know what to say. All the words of encouragement that Jack has given me in the past couple of years seem to be paying off, although he probably wishes he kept his mouth shut.'

Trevino, meanwhile, was simply delighted to have made the most of his trip to Muirfield, even if he had taken a somewhat circuitous route to get there.

Sir Henry Cotton
ROYAL ST GEORGE'S, 1934

Three-time Open Champion Sir Henry Cotton always said: 'To be a Champion, you must act like one.' He was one of golf's great ambassadors and took the game to a new level with practice regimes and fitness work which concentrated on strengthening arms and legs.

It helped the influential Englishman enjoy a distinguished career which will always be remembered for a stunning 65 on his way to the first of his Open titles, achieved at the 69th running of the event. Cotton's score, compiled in the second round of the 1934 Championship at Royal St George's, was at the time the lowest in Open history. It came after an opening 67, and he also set the 36-hole record at 132.

Yet Sir Henry had arrived at Sandwich low on confidence, with four sets of clubs and, as Henry Longhurst observed, 'unable to hit his hat with any of them'. Uncharacteristically the eventual Champion gave himself a day off in the build-up, choosing to caddie for someone else instead. Refreshed, he shot 66 in his first qualifying round at Royal St George's and followed it up with a 75 at Royal Cinque Ports to take his place in the field.

Once the Championship was under way the name of Cotton was quickly posted at the top of the leaderboard. He was three strokes ahead going into that glorious second round. There was only one dropped shot, which came after he was cruelly bunkered, with his ball a long way above his feet for his second shot at the short eighth. Cotton compiled a brilliant finish with scores of 4, 4, 3, 3 and 3 over the closing five holes. His lead stretched to nine strokes and he could afford closing rounds of 72 and 79 and still win by five.

The triumph will always be remembered for his exploits in the second round. It was immortalised with the naming of the best-selling Dunlop 65 ball. To be a Champion you also had to play like one and Cotton did that better than anyone had done before during a stunning victory.

Thomas Bjorn

ROYAL ST GEORGE'S, 2003

Thomas Bjorn hit fewer shots than anyone else during The Open of 2003 at Sandwich, but he failed to win. The Dane found sand on the 17th hole of his first round and in the process of taking two strokes to escape he slammed the sand in anger, which earned him a two-shot penalty. He ultimately lost by a single stroke to the 750–1 outsider Ben Curtis. Despite its numerical impact, it is not that bunker mishap for which Bjorn is best remembered.

Even though he suffered that early frustration the then 32-year-old rose to the top of the leaderboard with scores of 73, 70 and 69, and a first Major title moved within touching distance on the final day. After 54 holes he was the only player under par, one clear of Davis Love III. By the 15th Bjorn had stretched three strokes ahead and looked pretty comfortable when he made a composed bogey after driving into a bunker on the difficult 15th.

Then came calamity. This was the 13th time Royal St George's had staged the Championship and we know for whom it was most unlucky despite diligent homework early on the morning of the final round. Bjorn's caddie, the experienced Billy Foster,

walked the course and noticed the pin position on the right side of the 163-yard par-3 16th. He also saw deep sand in the bunker guarding that portion of the green. 'I've still got the notes to prove it. On the 16th I put a big cross in the middle of the green, for Thomas to aim 15 yards left of the hole,' Foster recalled. 'There was more sand in it than any other bunker on the course. It just had nightmare written all over it.'

Before striking his 6-iron tee shot, Bjorn's bagman told him to aim for a television tower, which would mean he would find the centre of the green. But as soon as it left the clubface the ball tracked straight for the pin. It was too far right. 'I just got one there that got caught on the wind and just leaked off right into the bunker,' Bjorn remembers. 'A couple of yards left and it's to within three feet.'

A first attempt flew onto the putting surface but not quite far enough. The ball trundled back into the sand. The same thing happened with the next try and it finally took three shots to escape the bunker. Bjorn did well to make a double-bogey.

Simultaneously, Curtis bravely holed for par on the final green. The unheralded American completed a 69 to move to one under par. It proved a winning score as a shell-shocked Bjorn bogeyed the 17th. 'I stood on the 15th tee with one hand on that trophy, and I let it go,' he ruefully recalled. 'That's the way Open golf is. I had my good breaks but I had a bad one there. You live with it and you move on.'

Shane Lowry
ROYAL PORTRUSH, 2019

Was there ever a more eagerly anticipated Open than the 148th Championship held at Royal Portrush in 2019?

The glorious Antrim links fell from the rota after staging the 1951 event won by Max Faulkner. It took a lengthy, concerted and determined effort to bring it back some 68 years later. And this inspired decision to return was rewarded with an astonishing week that yielded a hugely popular Irish winner in what was only the second Open to be staged on the island of Ireland.

Shane Lowry's triumph, his first in a Major, was completed amid vociferous scenes. It was due reward for some of the best golf ever played in the Championship. 'No doubt about it, there was only one deserving winner, which was Shane,' commented his closest rival, Tommy Fleetwood. 'He played the best golf all week.'

From the moment the gates opened early on Thursday 18 July, the event felt truly special. Northern Ireland's Darren Clarke had the honour of hitting the first tee shot. 'I was totally cool with it, until I walked down the steps,' he said. 'The stands were completely full.'

Rarely, if ever, have so many people arrived in time for the very first shot of an Open, such was the sense of anticipation. Those early-bird fans were rewarded with the local hero making a beautiful opening birdie. Clarke's original plan was to hit a 2-iron off the tee, but given the nerves he felt he decided the bigger head of a driver would give him a more comforting margin for error. It was a superb tee shot that set up a 9-iron approach and a comfortable 10-footer to complete the perfect start.

While Clarke, the 2011 Champion, was a popular figure, the biggest sense of expectation surrounded Rory McIlroy, who was seeking his second Claret Jug. He had won twice on the PGA Tour in 2019 and was in justifiably confident mood when The Open came around. It was his first chance to compete for a Major in his native Northern Ireland, but this unique scenario sadly inhibited rather than inspired him.

'I felt it was a good opportunity for me to get my name on that Claret Jug for the second time,' said the man who fired a course record 61 on the Dunluce Links when he was a teenager.

This time he made a shocking start. 'I remember putting my ball on the tee and, you know, I felt nervous,' he later admitted. McIlroy's opening tee shot flew left. 'I turned it too much with the wind and it kept going.' Fatefully it ignored the player's pleas to 'sit' and bounced out of bounds.

This four-time Major champion faced the ignominy of hitting three off the tee before dispatching his uphill approach to the green into tangly ferns that sat treacherously to the left of the green. His lie was unplayable. Another penalty shot. By the time McIlroy missed a short putt after pitching onto the green, he had racked up a dreadfully anti-climactic quadruple-bogey-8.

Although he battled for much of the round, having set himself the target of trying to get back to level par, McIlroy suffered a finish every bit as horrific as his miserable start. A careless three-putt cost him a deflating double-bogey at the par-3 16th, the appropriately named 'Calamity Corner'. Then, on the closing hole, he ran up a shell-shocked seven

to complete an eight-over-par 79. 'It's golf, right? Some days these things happen,' he reasoned. 'It just so happened that I had one of my worst days at a time when I wanted to produce something close to my best.'

It was not what the home crowds had expected nor what they wanted to see. But at least they were able to cheer another Irishman, Shane Lowry. The man from Clara in the county of Offaly, in the centre of the island, scored 67 despite anxiety the night before. He had missed the cut in four previous Opens and it took a calming coffee with his coach Neil Manchip and caddie Brian 'Bo' Martin on the eve of the Championship to settle his nerves. By the end of the first day he trailed only American J.B. Holmes, who was round in 66 blows.

Despite a bogey at the last, Lowry matched his first-round score on day two. Ironically, though, this particular Friday belonged to McIlroy as he strived manfully to try to make the cut. His inspired and inspiring 65 was one stroke short of booking a place at the weekend. He was raucously cheered every step of

the way. 'One of the most enjoyable rounds of golf I've ever played,' said McIlroy, who at times struggled to keep emotions in check. 'I'll look back at Portrush with nothing but fond memories because it was a great experience for me.' That was some statement from one of the world's best players having missed the cut at an Open.

Lowry shared the halfway lead with Holmes at eight under par, one shot ahead of a pair of Englishmen, Fleetwood and the veteran Lee Westwood. Lowry then put together one of the all-time great Open rounds.

The catalyst proved to be the 10th hole, where the Irishman was faced with a tricky approach from the left rough. He was torn between an 8- and 7-iron. Fearing the 8 might fly left, he chose to chop his 7, ensuring he kept the clubface open through impact. 'The shot worked out pretty much as we called it,' caddie Martin remembered. By intelligently using the contours guarding the green, he set up the first of five birdies on the inward half. He came home in 30 for a breathtaking 63.

An Irish winner as The Open
returned to the island of Ireland:
the perfect script.

'Shane Lowry and his caddie Bo walked up the 18th together and I actually switched off my microphone,' says Ewen Murray of Sky Sports. 'I thought there's nothing I can say that can improve this. You had them standing up in the grandstands and you had Shane with his arm round Bo. This was Ireland for me. I just didn't think there was anything I could say that would improve it.'

Lowry called it 'a very special round of golf', adding: 'I felt like I was going to birdie every hole.' By the end he had opened a four-stroke advantage, the same margin he had held and squandered after 54 holes of the 2016 US Open at Oakmont. Reporters were quick to raise that disappointment as Lowry conducted his post-round news conference but the player was ready for it. 'I'm a different golfer,' he explained.

They were brave words and Lowry was still aware those demons could easily resurface. It took immense fortitude to hold them at bay on the first hole of a closing round that started two hours early because of forecast storms. His four-shot lead was in immediate danger of slipping to just a single stroke. Playing partner Fleetwood surveyed a seven-footer for birdie, with Lowry six feet away having already played four shots. But the Englishman's putter was cold and Lowry's held firm.

Ireland's favourite clenched his fist to celebrate dropping only one stroke. Yes, his lead had narrowed to three shots, but it could have been so much worse. Short of momentum, Fleetwood bogeyed the third and Lowry birdied the next to go five clear. He went on to produce a magnificent exhibition of front-running golf in windy, sometimes ferociously torrential conditions. The mood among the crowds, the biggest for any Open outside St Andrews, reached fever pitch.

When he holed for birdie at the 15th, Lowry knew the Claret Jug was destined for his mantelpiece. He could enjoy a champion's stroll to the finish and capped an astonishingly convincing win with a tap-in to triumph by six strokes.

'Playing in front of your home crowd is a very, very difficult thing to do because you want to do so well,' says 2014 Ryder Cup captain Paul McGinley, who tipped Lowry at the start of the week. 'Shane had shown us a glimpse when he won the Irish Open as an amateur. The home crowd is something that propels him, excites him and empowers him.'

McGinley adds that it was Saturday's 63 that effectively won the Championship for his Irish compatriot. He was then assisted by the wild conditions of the final day. 'God looked down on him as well with the weather conditions that we got on the Sunday, they played right into his hands. He's a heavy, robust guy. He likes the wind, he likes the gnarly conditions, having grown up in them. He won the Irish Open playing in waterproofs – those conditions suited him and he delivered.'

It was no cliffhanger but it was a spectacle of epic proportions. The Irish tricolour flew proudly and to universal acclaim in Northern Ireland, emphatically demonstrating sport's capacity to be a genuine force for good. 'To be able to knock that putt in, raise my hands, hug Bo and my family, is just incredible,' the Champion said in his interview for The R&A's *Chronicles of a Champion Golfer* documentary. 'If you put down on a piece of paper which tournament you'd really, really, really like to win, that'd be it. How lucky am I to be able to do that?'

Well, we were astonishingly fortunate to be mere witnesses. Returning to Portrush was more than worth the 68-year wait.

Ian Woosnam

ROYAL LYTHAM & ST ANNES, 2001

A survey carried out at the 1935 US Open showed that on average competitors were carrying 18 clubs in their bags. There was no limit and players would often take advantage of options afforded by different shafts, traditional hickory and new-fangled steel. Others would even carry right- and left-handed implements, just in case. Eventually The R&A and the United States Golf Association decided this was an abuse of the spirit of golf and, to the relief of many a caddie, a limit of 14 clubs was introduced in 1938.

Most infamously in Open history, the former world number one, Ian Woosnam, fell foul of this rule when he led The 130th Open at Royal Lytham & St Annes in 2001. The popular Welshman experimented with a different driver when he warmed up for the final round. This followed scores of 72-68-67 which had given him a share of the lead with eventual winner David Duval, Bernhard Langer and Alex Cejka.

Woosnam was aged 43 at the time and his tilt at a first Open title excited home fans, who swarmed around the first green. They saw him brilliantly birdie the only par-3 opener on the Championship rota. It was then that the 1991 Masters winner discovered his caddie Myles Byrne had failed to discard one of the drivers before the round.

Woosnam was liable to a two-stroke penalty and informed the referee on the second tee, where he ruefully tossed away the extra club. 'I felt like I had been kicked in the teeth,' Woosnam said at the time. 'It's hard enough playing against the best players in the world without giving them a two-shot advantage.' He struggled to cope with the setback and dropped two shots in the next three holes before battling to a 71 that left him in a six-way share of third place.

Without the penalty he would have finished in outright second and taken home an extra £218,333 prize money. Who knows, he might have gone on to win a second Major without the derailing effects of the mistake. 'I've been asked about it so many times,' Woosnam reflects. 'If he hadn't put that driver in, would I have won The Open? I did feel good at the time, I'd made a birdie at the first even though I don't usually get off to a good start. I felt that it might have been my time. But that's what happens and yes it was disappointing.

'What's more difficult is still getting people going on about it all the time. When you're playing tournaments, I'm always asked, "How many clubs have you got in the bag?" To me it's gone, but when people keep reminding you it's just annoying.' And with good reason. It was perhaps Woosnam's best chance to win the Championship he has always put above any other. 'It was always the ultimate thing I wanted to win,' he says. 'I had my opportunities, I just couldn't put all my game together at the right time to get that one, which was a shame.'

Hale Irwin

ROYAL BIRKDALE, 1983

Leaderboard operators during The 112th Open at Royal Birkdale in 1983 spent the entire week displaying familiar names, including Champion Tom Watson, Lee Trevino, Craig Stadler, Nick Faldo and Hale Irwin. The US Open winner in 1974, 1979 and 1990, Irwin was at the height of his powers and 38 years old when he arrived at the Championship.

After opening rounds of 69 and 68 he was within three strokes of the lead and remained in contention deep into the third round. At the 14th he struck a beautiful approach putt that hung on the edge of the hole. Walking up to his ball, the American flicked his putter to nonchalantly tap it in. He missed the ball completely. The extra stroke counted in a third-round 72. A day later Irwin fired a closing 67 to finish eight under par, agonisingly a single stroke behind the winner.

Players Nearly Strike

ROYAL ST GEORGE'S, 1899

One of the most worrying moments in The Open's history occurred ahead of the 39th Championship at Royal St George's, in 1899. It was the first to be staged in England and there was a record entry of 98, but the event was threatened by a potential players' strike over prize money. The rebels' cause was undermined by the greats of the time: defending Champion and eventual winner Harry Vardon, J.H. Taylor, James Braid and

Willie Park Jr. These were players fans would turn up to watch and crucially they refused to lend support to the dissidents. According to *A Course for Heroes*, the official history of Royal St George's, Championship delegates were persuaded to increase the prize fund by £30, but issued a statement to say they would never bow to threats.

Hale Irwin, who missed the shortest putt imaginable before losing the 1983 Open by a single stroke.

Seve Ballesteros

ST ANDREWS, 1984

The 113th Open, held at St Andrews in 1984, was a landmark Championship for several reasons. More than 193,000 people flocked to the 'Home of Golf', smashing the record attendance by over 50,000 spectators. Ticket sales broke the £1 million barrier for the first time and prize money rose to an unprecedented £451,000. In a sun-kissed week of records, it would have been appropriate for Tom Watson to match Harry Vardon's unequalled haul of six Claret Jugs. But Severiano Ballesteros, the swashbuckling Spaniard, had other ideas and produced one of the most memorable and iconic Open finishes ever witnessed.

Throughout it was a thrilling Championship, led at halfway by Australia's Ian Baker-Finch after he covered the first 36 holes in a superb 10 under par. He added a 71 and was joined at the top by Watson, who scored a fabulous 66 in the penultimate round. After 54 holes this pair were two clear of Ballesteros and Germany's Bernhard Langer. The rest were also rans, the leading quartet being five strokes clear of the remainder of the field.

Ballesteros had won his first Open in 1979 and felt very positive about his chances of collecting a second title, even though he was now up against the defending Champion, Watson. The previous evening the Spanish matador told journalists that he would be returning to the media tent at the end of the Championship. 'It was obvious I didn't mean I was going to be there as runner-up,' Ballesteros later wrote in *Seve*, his official autobiography. 'I'd beaten Watson in the Masters the year before; and, though I thought Langer was very good, I didn't think he was ready to win a Major yet.'

Seve's final round began in frustrating fashion when he lipped out for a birdie on the opening green. He made amends at the long fifth with a glorious up and down that involved holing a treacherous left-to-right birdie putt that took him to ten under par. One hole behind, Watson bogeyed, and so they were tied at the top. Ballesteros then took the outright lead after a superb tee shot on the short eighth, but handed back

the initiative at the 11th, where his first shot came up short of that par 3's elevated green.

Watson, meanwhile, drove onto the putting surface on the par-4 10th and comfortably two-putted. With Baker-Finch having tumbled off the leaderboard, the five-times Champion was back ahead. But his advantage lasted only until the 12th, where his curious choice of driver led to his tee shot finding bushes and a dropped shot.

Over the closing stages the drama proved unrelenting and the vast galleries were enraptured. Watson birdied the 13th; up ahead Ballesteros did the same at the 14th. Both were locked at 11 under par, two ahead of the dogged Langer, determinedly hoping to pounce on any errors that might come from the leaders on the homeward stretch.

Cooler weather blew in and on the 15th Ballesteros 'dressed for the kill', selecting the same navy blue sweater he wore for his Lytham triumph five years

earlier. Maybe his choice of clothes emboldened him for the crucial challenge which was soon to be posed by the infamous 'Road Hole'.

Up to that point Ballesteros had suffered only five bogeys and three of them came on the devilish 17th hole. As on previous days, he drove into the left rough but his ball sat nicely. From there he fired an inspired 6-iron around 200 yards, avoiding the dangerous pot bunker behind which the pin tantalisingly stood. It was a pragmatic approach that paid huge dividends. Two putts later Ballesteros banked a precious four. 'I relished the par as if it was a birdie,' he later wrote.

Behind, Watson was fretful. His drive flew further right than he wanted, skirting the grounds of the Old Course Hotel. He feared he may be out of bounds and was relieved to receive a signal that his ball was safe. Indeed, it was now ideally positioned for the American to attack the flag. But for his second shot he hesitated over his club selection. 'I took the 2-iron off the

LEFT Seve walking to the presentation with R&A Secretary Michael Bonallack.

OPPOSITE The pitch that set up that famous winning putt.

upslope and tried to hit it on to the green in the air,' Watson later recalled.

It was too much club. His ball bounded through the back, over the road and up against the unyielding wall, an intrinsic part of the course. Watson's grip on the trophy he had won five times in the previous nine years was loosening in dramatic fashion. He could only stab his third shot onto the green and leave a lengthy par putt.

Meanwhile, Ballesteros was finishing in style on the final hole. He hit a 3-wood tee shot and a delightful pitch to 16 feet to set up a closing birdie. 'The putt had a clear borrow to the left, but as I struck the ball I felt I had overdone it,' Seve recalled in his autobiography. 'I hadn't. It rolled sweetly towards the hole, then seemed to hover on the edge of the cup, before finally going in as if in slow motion, perhaps impelled by my powers of mental suggestion, so strong was my desire that it should drop in.'

Former BBC golf correspondent Tony Adamson was beside the green. 'St Andrews almost exploded, the place nearly took off,' he says. 'It was as if the hole grabbed it. I've never known a celebration like it from Seve. It's the only time in sport that I've failed to hold back tears; it was the most emotional thing. I adored the man, a wonderful golfer to watch.'

Amid the pandemonium echoing down the closing fairway, Watson surveyed his long par attempt on the penultimate green. It failed to drop and the resulting bogey, he said, was 'my most disappointing memory'. He ruefully added: 'You just don't mess with the Road.'

Watson needed an eagle at the last to force a play-off and when he sent his approach to the back of the home green it meant Ballesteros was Champion for the second time. 'This was the happiest moment of my whole sporting life,' the five-time Major winner later wrote. 'My moment of glory, my most fantastic shot.'

Muirfield Storm

2002

'It was truly extraordinary; you could see it coming,' BBC Radio's John Inverdale recalls. 'I've never seen a tidal wave but this was a tidal wave in the sky.' The presenter was on the course during third-round day at the 2002 Open when Muirfield was struck by one of the most severe storms ever witnessed at the Championship. 'There was an inevitability about it that was absolutely certain and so it was, with that cloud and sky coming towards us. You just knew it was coming.'

Tiger Woods was on the first tee as the deluge arrived. He had the third leg of a Grand Slam within his sights. That year's Masters and US Open champion scored 70 and 68 in the opening rounds and was only a couple of shots off the lead. 'We were just about ready to go out, and it just hit,' Woods said. 'You could see this wall of rain coming in.'

It wasn't just the wind and rain; temperatures plummeted. 'No one had forecast for the wind chill to be in the 30s,' Woods said. 'It just got so cold that nothing was working, and no one was prepared for that. No one had enough clothes. Everything was soaked. It got to the point where the umbrella was useless. It was raining too hard, and it was too windy.' He went to the turn in 42 shots and came home in 39. His only birdie came at the par-5 17th and the American's chances of a third successive Major perished in the wind and rain.

Eventual Champion Ernie Els fared better with a one-over-par 72. 'We were fortunate in a way,' recalled his caddie Ricci Roberts. 'We only had to play 14 or 15 holes in the monsoon, but I have to say it's probably right up there with one of the hardest days ever on a links golf course. I mean, the weather was brutal.'

Inverdale sought help from his listeners. 'I put out an appeal on air for a new pair of socks because I was walking around in a pair of galoshes effectively,' he recalls.

'But there is something manifestly appealing to the handicapper of seeing great golfers struggling and taking the kind of shots we regard as the norm ... I do think The Open Championship is the greatest of all the Majors because the weather plays a bigger part than it does in the other three Majors. There are occasions it tests these guys to the limit.'

This was undoubtedly one of them.

OPPOSITE Taking cover at Muirfield in 2002.

ABOVE Tiger Woods was one of the biggest victims when the storm blew through.

Gary Evans
MUIRFIELD, 2002

Gary Evans played more than 350 tournaments on the European Tour without winning any of them. His biggest brush with glory came at The 131st Open at Muirfield, where he missed a play-off by a single stroke, one of the most bizarre finishes completed by any Open contender.

'Be strong like a bull' was his mantra for that week in Scotland. The line was given to him by his bank manager's wife and it served him well. The little-known Englishman surged into contention. He collected eight birdies in 10 holes, including sinking an 80-foot putt on the 10th, before taking the outright lead at the 11th. With two holes left he could have been forgiven for dreaming that he might be about to join immortal names such as Nicklaus, Player, Faldo, Cotton and Hagen by becoming an Open Champion at Muirfield.

Then at the par-5 17th, Evans's swing deserted him on his second shot, which flew wildly to the left of the green. Despite the presence of hundreds of spectators his ball was never found, and he was forced to take a penalty stroke and trudge back to the original spot. 'I thought at that point it was pretty much over,' he recalled. 'I couldn't believe I had hit it into a crowd of about 150 people and no one saw it, no one heard it.'

The 33-year-old's second attempt, his fourth shot, was much better and found the putting surface to leave a 40-footer for an unlikely par. 'The putter head was moving like you cannot believe when I was standing over that putt,' Evans revealed. 'I thought, "Please God let me hole it."'

Whether it was divine intervention or sheer skill, his prayers were answered and his ball disappeared in spectacular style. Evans raced off in animated celebration. He found a television camera and leaned onto the lens, yelling: 'That was for you, Mum.' He knew his mother, Betty, would be watching at home.

Alas, there was not much more for her to celebrate. Her son, who first played The Open as an amateur in 1989, could not maintain his composure on the closing hole. The resulting bogey meant he failed by the narrowest margin to join eventual Champion Ernie Els, Thomas Levet, Stuart Appleby and Steve Elkington in a four-hole play-off for the Claret Jug.

LEFT Gary Evans's title charge halted by a lost ball at the 17th.

OPPOSITE Evans sinks a monster putt to save par and keep hopes alive.

Jordan Spieth

ROYAL BIRKDALE, 2017

Despite winning two Majors before his 22nd birthday, Jordan Spieth brought demons to The 146th Open at Royal Birkdale in 2017. Two years earlier the charismatic Texan arrived at St Andrews as reigning Masters and US Open champion. On the final day, when he rolled in a monster birdie putt at the 16th, Spieth was in a share of the lead. The third leg of a potential Grand Slam seemed within touching distance, but with a tentative bogey on the 71st hole the Claret Jug slipped from his grasp.

Zach Johnson went on to beat Louis Oosthuizen and Marc Leishman in a four-hole play-off which Spieth missed by a single stroke. It was a defeat that hurt a young player for whom so much had gone so well in a blistering start to his career. Then the following year he blew a five-stroke advantage on the back nine of the final round of his Masters defence. He had been cruelly reminded just how tough it is to win the biggest tournaments in golf.

So when he came to Birkdale, Spieth admitted: 'I was going to be dealing with some scar tissue.' And for this youthful American The Open was a genuinely special event. 'There is no greater history than The Open Championship,' he said in The R&A's *Chronicles of a Champion Golfer*. 'I fell in love with the tournament, I fell in love with the imagination that you needed over there for your tee to green play.'

'Pick that out of the hole':
Jordan Spieth charges to
his 2017 victory.

Rarely has that creativity been more needed than when he played an extraordinary 13th hole of the final round while tied for the lead with US Ryder Cup teammate Matt Kuchar. Spieth sprayed his drive so far off line it finished unplayable on the wrong side of the giant dunes down the right side of this fearsome par 4. 'This is catastrophic,' claimed the broadcasters.

'I remember seeing the slow mo of my driver on the ball and the face just kind of jerked open right when it hit it,' Spieth admitted. 'And I'm thinking to myself, that's not good.'

For European Tour Productions, on-course commentator Jamie Spence stated: 'I've got to tell you, this is absolutely carnage.'

Spieth found his ball in thick rough and the situation seemed dire. 'I was trying to decide the best route to make the best score from there,' he said. And this was the point at which Spieth summoned the composure and creativity of a champion. 'It took a lot of patience,' he said. 'What took the most amount of time was really the Rules officials, talking to each other, trying to figure out where that drop would actually have to take place. My decision on what I wanted to do was made relatively quickly.

The three drops took him among manufacturers' trucks parked adjacent to the range. With vast dunes obscuring his target, Spieth fired an incredible approach that finished just short of the green but leaving a tricky pitch. He executed it well and nervelessly holed his putt. Most bogeys are not good news but this one was a fabulous outcome.

'When I knocked that putt in I was walking off the green really thinking like I stole something, and to the next tee actually feeling more comfortable than I felt anytime during that day,' he said. 'And then I just struck the best iron shot I probably ever hit in my life.'

It came at the par-3 14th and it very nearly found the cup for a hole in one. Instead it set up a perfect bounce-back birdie. Better was to follow. A massive putt disappeared for an eagle at the long 15th and then came superb birdies at the next two holes. Spieth had accelerated away from his shell-shocked rival Kuchar, who had done nothing wrong during this devastating spell.

It enabled Spieth to tap in on the 72nd green for his third Major title and one that meant so much. 'For myself it was a great feeling that, hey, this is The Open Championship. Wow, this is the Claret Jug, the most sought-after trophy in our sport.'

Spieth had needed to defeat the frailties that had cost him in 2015 and at the following year's Masters before he could put his hands around this most precious prize. Those demons had resurfaced on that final day, when he threw away a commanding three-stroke overnight lead on the front nine. Then there was that potentially ruinous drive on the 13th. But he overcame them in spectacular style. 'There were times where I just didn't see myself holding it at the end of the day,' Spieth admitted. 'It was kind of overwhelming at that point.'

Branden Grace Shoots 62

ROYAL BIRKDALE, 2017

Until 22 July 2017 there had been 10 rounds of 63 but none lower in an Open Championship. This was a magic number, a barrier. Sixty-three was a figure the golfing gods decreed no man could go lower than in a Major. In all, 29 players had collected 31 rounds of 63 – Vijay Singh and Greg Norman did it twice – making it seemingly the lowest score possible at any of the four biggest events on the male calendar.

On the morning of what proved a historic Saturday, former caddie Jim 'Bones' McKay, who witnessed his old boss Phil Mickelson narrowly miss a putt for a 62 at Royal Troon 12 months earlier, told US television that a previously unattainable low score might prove to be possible. Conditions were calm and the course, softened by rain, would yield birdie opportunities. For his foresight Golf Channel referred to him as 'Bonestradamus' – an insightful and prescient Nostradamus of golf punditry.

On cue, up stepped the 29-year-old South African Branden Grace. Blissfully unaware of the history he was making, he serenely collected eight birdies with no dropped shots on a par-70 Royal Birkdale. 'I had no idea I was about to shoot the lowest round ever,'

South Africa's Branden Grace makes history with the first sub-63 round in men's Major Championship history.

he told BBC Radio listeners. His record score began with a birdie at the first and more followed at the fourth, fifth, eighth, ninth, 14th, 16th and 17th holes. He needed only a par at the last to make history. His drive found the first cut of rough and his approach came to rest 45 feet from the hole.

It was early afternoon and the third-round leaders had yet to tee off. Grace trundled his ball to around three feet, from where he made no mistake before becoming the first player to sign for a 62 on an Open scorecard. 'I was in the zone, trying to finish the round and it's never nice to finish with a bogey,' Grace said. 'After I made it, my caddie told me the situation and that made it even better.'

Watching from the commentary box, Colin Montgomerie stated: 'This is momentous. The day Grace broke the unbreakable record.' The South African's round started at four over par and he finished it four-under, seven shots behind leader Jordan Spieth, who went on to win. Grace scored a final-round 70 to finish in a share of sixth place.

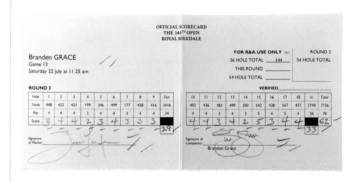

TOP Grace started the day four over par and finished it four-under.

ABOVE Eight birdies and no bogeys on a history-making scorecard.

Gene Sarazen failed to qualify for the 1923 Open after controversy surrounding his sand wedge.

Holes in Wedges

ROYAL TROON, 1923

American Gene Sarazen arrived on the Ayrshire coast as reigning US Open and PGA champion and among the favourites to win The 58th Open in 1923. But in the build-up he was mired in controversy. Sarazen, along with other US players, had holes punched deep into the faces of his irons. This alteration generated backspin and afforded extra control for shots played onto firm greens. But the clubs were declared illegal. Files were brought to Troon from Glasgow shipyards and were used to modify the clubs to make sure they conformed. Sarazen then failed to qualify in gale-force conditions. According to one account, it was so windy Aubrey Boomer hit a bunker shot which curled back over his head and dropped into his jacket pocket.

Nick Price

TURNBERRY, 1994

Nick Price came to the 123rd Open playing the best golf of his life. Twice a runner-up, after holding commanding positions at the 1982 and 1988 Championships, he arrived on the west coast of Scotland for the 1994 edition having already won four events that year. But for much of the final day, the Zimbabwean looked as though he may have to settle for yet another second-placed finish. Sweden's Jesper Parnevik had been setting a blistering pace with five birdies on the back nine. And then came a dramatic climax to cap another thrilling Turnberry Championship.

Price made a superbly judged bump and run for a vital up and down at the 14th to stay within touching distance of the leader, who was bidding to become the first Scandinavian man to win a Major. Parnevik, the eccentric Swede who always wore a distinctive upturned cap and had a curious liking for chewing volcanic dust, carried a two-stroke advantage to the final tee. Price, who birdied the 16th, was playing behind and found the left edge of the green on the par-5 17th with a 6-iron approach.

Then, after settling over a huge 75-foot putt for eagle, Price struck it briskly. 'I knew there wasn't much break in it,' he said. As it edged closer and closer to the cup it seemed to threaten to run out of steam. The player animatedly urged his ball to continue its journey. He knew the line was good, but did it have the length? The thunderous roar that greeted its disappearance left no doubt for anyone on the Ayrshire links that it had, in fact, been a perfectly paced putt. 'I couldn't believe it went in,' he admitted.

Price leapt towards his caddie in celebration. Out of the blue, he bolted into a winning position with only one hole to play. 'I nearly jumped out of my skin when it went in,' he said. 'My heart was pounding.'

Up ahead Parnevik had been ignoring leaderboards and, as the cheers for Price's putt echoed across the links, he was in the recorders' hut checking his scorecard. It showed a decisive bogey at the last because of a crucial tactical error. He went for the pin with his approach to the 18th when playing for the middle of the green would surely have been a better option. 'I thought I needed another birdie on 18 to win,' he said. The Swede missed his target and found tricky rough short and left of the green. It resulted in a difficult short-sided chip and he failed to get up and down. 'The way it turned out, maybe I should have taken a glimpse on 18,' Parnevik ruefully admitted.

After that sensational eagle putt on the penultimate green, Price knew a closing par would give him his second Major title. The 37-year-old duly obliged in regulation fashion. It was a victory that confirmed him as the world's best player of the time. He gleefully stated: 'It was back in 1982 I had my left hand on this trophy. In 1988, I had my right hand on this trophy. Now at last I finally got both hands on it … and does it feel good.'

At last Nick Price gets both hands on the Claret Jug.

Seve Ballesteros

ROYAL LYTHAM, 1979

When Seve Ballesteros won The 108th Open he became known as the 'car-park' Champion. The flamboyant Spaniard, who thrilled Birkdale crowds in 1976 when he was runner-up to Johnny Miller, secured the first of his three triumphs three years later with a characteristically unorthodox performance at Royal Lytham & St Annes. It was typified by the events of the 16th hole on the final day when his wild drive to the par 4 ended up next to a parked car. 'I was convinced that sooner or later I was going to become The Open Champion,' Ballesteros later revealed.

As he embarked on that blind tee shot on the 16th, the man who went on to win five Majors was at the top of the leaderboard. Ballesteros's brother Baldomero told his younger sibling that he was two strokes clear while he made his way to the tee. 'That was good information to have,' Seve said. He swung without restraint as he tried to send his drive close to the green. Instead his ball flew 70 yards wide, to the right of the fairway. 'I tried to hit a really hard tee shot but also I knew that the pin position was on the left, so I didn't want to miss the shot on the left side,' Ballesteros recalled. 'I pushed the shot a little bit to the right,' he added with a fair dose of understatement.

It finished up in an improvised car park that was needed to help cope with larger than anticipated crowds generated by the presence of the charismatic Spaniard's name on the leaderboard. His caddie was Dave Musgrove. He told ESPN: 'He hit it where he wanted to and it finished up perfect on a tractor path ... but it was under a motor car.' Spectators, police and Rules officials swarmed around the makeshift parking area, where Ballesteros's ball lay beneath the front right bumper of one of the vehicles.

He was allowed a free drop and 'line of sight' relief from the cars. Ballesteros dropped his ball onto hard-packed ground trodden down by the Lytham fans and it resulted in a pretty straightforward approach into the wind, with plenty of green with which to work.

'It was only 69 yards to the hole and it was a perfect distance and I was on the right with no bunkers, nothing,' Ballesteros admitted. 'I played it conservatively into the middle of the green because I knew I was two shots ahead and hit the sand wedge to maybe 25 feet.'

There are precious days when things seem to work out splendidly and this proved to be one of those. Seve rolled in the birdie putt which effectively secured his first Claret Jug. 'To be honest I didn't try to hole the putt, I was just trying to get it close but for some reason the ball went in,' the Champion admitted. 'When you win you are full of confidence, you feel like you are the King of the Earth.'

Henrik Stenson

ROYAL TROON, 2016

BOTTOM LEFT Henrik Stenson and Phil Mickelson separated themselves from the field in an epic duel at Royal Troon in 2016.

OPPOSITE At long last, Stenson becomes a Major Champion.

Henrik Stenson looked in a mirror that hung on the wall of his rented home. It was Sunday 17 July. At 40 years old he was one of the very best golfers in the world and had amassed seven top-four finishes in Majors without ever winning one.

It was his time.

'I just told myself, "You can do this, this is the way it is meant to be. Make this happen,"' the Swede recalled. But he had no idea that it would take such inspired, record-breaking golf to win an epic battle with Phil Mickelson to land The 145th Open at Royal Troon and secure that long-overdue first Major title.

This was the 'Duel of the Sons'. There must be something about the air on the west coast of Scotland or the spectacular views of Arran and Ailsa Craig that inspires the finest Open contests. This one instantly evoked memories of the great 'Duel in the Sun' of 1977 between Tom Watson and Jack Nicklaus at Turnberry, a little further to the south of the same glorious coastline.

After conversing with his reflection, Stenson headed to the golf course carrying a one-stroke advantage. He and Mickelson had stretched clear of the field with astonishing golf over the first three rounds.

The American came within a whisker of the first ever 62 at a Major on the opening day. 'I was fully aware what the last hole meant and how rare this opportunity is to break that record,' Mickelson remembered. When his ball was only six inches from the hole, he was convinced it would drop and prompt a rewriting of golfing history. Somehow it stayed above ground; never has a player been more disappointed to sign for a 63 in the first round of an Open.

In the second round, Stenson fired a 65 in wet conditions to move within a stroke of Mickelson's halfway lead and two ahead of the next closest players on the leaderboard: Keegan Bradley and Søren Kjeldsen at seven under par.

Paired together for the third round, Stenson fired a fine 68 to Mickelson's 70. Throughout they traded blows – Mickelson went two ahead with a birdie on the 13th but Stenson bounced back with a birdie at the next as his US rival buckled by missing a short par putt. 'I just lost focus,' Mickelson admitted. 'It sometimes happens, I hate it when it does.' He bounced back with

a birdie at the 16th but at the next Stenson fired a 'flat out 3-iron' onto the green to set up a crucial birdie on that long par 3.

It helped the man bidding to become Scandinavia's first male Major winner to move to 12 under par with one round to go. He was one ahead of his American challenger and six clear of the next best player, Bill Haas, also from the United States.

Mickelson had reassured Stenson at the previous month's US Open at Oakmont that he would one day win a Major. 'Something inside told me it would probably be at my expense, when I said that,' the US left-hander recalled. Of course, he did not want it to be this day and Mickelson came flying out of the blocks with a stunning approach to tap-in range at the first. Stenson was tentative, came up short, three-putted and an instant two-stroke swing propelled his rival to the top of the leaderboard. 'It was a great way to start,' Mickelson said.

Thereafter the drama and excellence of both players was unrelenting. Stenson birdied the next three holes while Mickelson collected an eagle at the fourth. They were locked at 14 under par, seven strokes clear of the rest. 'Then I knew it was just between he and I,' Mickelson said.

At the 'Postage Stamp' eighth, Mickelson hit a beautiful tee shot to within seven feet of the flag. His co-leader spun his ball back to around 15 feet but was relishing the one-on-one combat that had developed. 'I've always been good at match play,' the Swede recalled. 'I think that simplifies it for me.' He rolled in his birdie putt and Mickelson missed.

Stenson took a one-stroke advantage into the back nine. 'I was there on a mission,' he said. 'There was only one prize I was interested in.'

Both players birdied the 10th. Observers were agog at the way they were tearing up a course that for the rest of the field still presented a typically mighty challenge. It was a classic contest between the unflappable 'ice-man' Swede and the high-rolling

American playing on sheer guts and inspiration. 'You couldn't let up,' Mickelson said. 'You had to make birdies and eagles to gain ground and it wasn't over an easy golf course. Shot after shot Henrik just striped it.'

Both players were inspiring each other but Stenson bogeyed 'Railway', the tough par-4 11th, to slip back into a share of the lead at 16-under. Then, somehow, Mickelson fashioned an unlikely par at the next. 'He's very hard to get rid of,' Stenson commented later when recounting the glorious details of this extraordinary Championship.

Stenson knew that the title would not be handed to him, he would need to earn it. If it was his time, he knew that when he arrived on the 14th green it was the moment to make a decisive move. He did so in spectacular style. 'I had a 20-footer, and I just thought, how many chances coming in here am I going to have to try to pull away?' Stenson told reporters afterwards. 'Because I knew he was not going to make too many mistakes. So I just knew I had to take it.'

He grabbed his birdie and at the next, from around twice the distance, the Swede astonishingly fashioned another with his ball dying into the cup on its final revolution. 'The adrenalin when that thing found the bottom of the cup was amazing,' Stenson said.

Mickelson responded by alighting on the par-5 16th green with two mighty blows, while the leader found thick rough to the left of the putting surface. But from there he played a delightful pitch before Mickelson's gallant eagle attempt defied gravity, missing the hole by a fraction of an inch.

Stenson held a two-stroke lead with two holes to play. It had been exhilarating golf throughout and more followed with a superb tee shot to six feet on the tough par-3 17th. Mickelson looked beaten when his tee shot missed the green, but he came up with a brilliant up and down to save par. Stenson then failed with the birdie attempt that would surely have secured him the Claret Jug.

A two-shot lead with one to play is healthy but nowhere near as secure as a three-stroke advantage. Stenson was aware he could not let up on the 72nd hole as he fired his 3-wood tee shot. 'It came out like an absolute rocket,' he said. His ball bounded towards a fairway bunker and he feared it had reached a hazard he was convinced was out of reach with that club. He departed the tee fearing the worst, but as he emerged onto the fairway he caught sight of his ball lying less than a yard short of the bunker. With a huge sense of relief he was able to find the heart of the green with his approach, and for good measure he rolled home the birdie putt to seal an epic triumph.

Sixty-three, a magical number, was his score, setting a record for the lowest final round by a Champion. His 20-under-par score of 264 was the best in Open history, while Mickelson's tally of 267 was the lowest of any runner-up.

In the same way as Watson and Nicklaus had departed back in 1977, the two protagonists left the 18th green arm in arm. They had separated themselves from the rest of the world's best golfers to such an extent that J.B. Holmes, who was third, finished 11 shots behind the man who came second. On every other occasion that Mickelson had produced that high standard of golf he had left the Championship with the trophy. 'It's the first time I've played to that level and didn't win,' he said.

For Stenson it was the crowning moment. He was third in 2010, second to Mickelson in 2013, but now he was The Open Champion. 'The first thing that went into my mind was, "You did it!"' he recalled.

It was a victory that will always be remembered for the quality of golf it produced. Watson accepted that it eclipsed his historic Turnberry victory over Nicklaus, who wrote a hand-written note of congratulations to the new Champion. 'He thought it was the best round of golf he had ever seen,' Stenson revealed.

Echoes of the 1977 'Duel in the Sun' as the two protagonists depart arm in arm.

Tom Watson

TURNBERRY, 2009

The 59-year-old Tom Watson, so close to one of the greatest sporting stories of all time.

With so much shared history at Turnberry it was appropriate that one of the first people to call Tom Watson after the 138th Championship in 2009 was Jack Nicklaus. They duelled in the sunshine of 1977 when Watson emerged on top of the golfing world, but 32 years on this great Champion needed consolation. He had almost created arguably the greatest story in all of sport. It would have happened but for a missed eight-footer on the final green. Watson was aged 59. Twenty-six long and middle-aged years had passed since his last Open victory and yet, extraordinarily, a record-equalling sixth Claret Jug had been within touching distance.

All the American needed was a par at the last.

To that point he had beaten everyone in the modern game; players such as Tiger Woods, Phil Mickelson, Padraig Harrington and Lee Westwood, all of them in the prime of their careers.

Watson had done it with golfing guile, skill, knowledge, super-human levels of enduring talent and a quiet inner confidence. 'I was playing about my best golf from tee to green,' he said afterwards.

Brought into the media centre on the eve of the Championship, he met reporters wanting to discuss bygone glories. But Watson's eyes were on the immediate future. He had noticed forecasts saying the wind would switch on the Friday afternoon when he would be playing. The five-times Champion knew it would make golf more difficult when it blew from the north-west, but crucially he, unlike many in the field, would have the experience to cope.

'I still have a chance here,' he insisted. But he was also aware time was running out, acknowledging that he would soon be 60 and the following year's Open at the 'Home of Golf' would be his last. 'Unless I play well at St Andrews or play well here,' he said with a twinkle in his eye. 'And maybe have a sixth Championship under my belt after Sunday. Now, that would be a story, wouldn't it?' The interview room roared with laughter. Little did they know that Watson was not joking.

'It wasn't pompous or from an ego standpoint, it was a practical standpoint,' he later recalled. 'The golf course was not too long for me and the other thing in the back of my mind was that I knew what was going to happen to the winds.'

During an extraordinary week, those reporters who had giggled at the notion of Watson contending were rapidly forced to reappraise. The 59-year-old shot 65 and was one shot off the first-round lead. In the north-westerly winds of Friday afternoon he scored 70. At five under par he shared the halfway lead with unheralded American Steve Marino.

Then came a Saturday 71. Astonishingly, the veteran was out in front – one stroke ahead of England's Ross Fisher and Matthew Goggin of Australia. 'I was putting the best I've ever probably putted in my life,' Watson said. 'I made everything.'

Surely he had to falter, in the way the experienced Greg Norman had the previous year at Royal Birkdale. Watson was in no such mood and told his wife, Hilary, that he genuinely thought he could win. 'Who knows, it might happen,' he said.

Conditions remained tricky and Watson was more than a match for them. By the time he arrived at the final tee, golf was braced for its greatest story. The doubters had been silenced by enduring brilliance and one final par was all that was needed for him to become Open Champion, a massive 34 years on from his first triumph at Carnoustie in 1975.

One more par – that was all that was needed.

Watson's tee shot was unerring. The second shot was from an ideal position on the fairway. 'We chose an 8-iron from 187 yards,' he recalled. Then the blustery conditions took a capricious turn. In his interview for *Chronicles of a Champion Golfer*, Watson details what happened next. 'People told me that when that ball landed on the green there was a gust of wind that went with it,' he said. 'Maybe my ball caught that gust of wind and it took the spin off my ball. It landed right where I wanted it to and it just did not have enough spin on it to stop the ball. It was coming down right on the flag.' Watson's ball ran through the back of the green and nestled down in the rough.

'I wasn't thinking about the sense of history, I was just thinking about winning the golf tournament,' he remembered.

Now the question was: should he chip or should he putt? There was not much green to work with and he opted for the putter, thinking he could pop it out of its 'cuppy' lie and roll it up to the hole-side. The ball emerged with too much juice and ran eight or nine feet past the pin. A loud collective murmur rumbled through the galleries. Thousands upon thousands of people were desperate to witness a most extraordinary piece of sporting history achieved by already one of the most popular champions the sport had ever produced.

And that's when the magnitude of the moment seemed to hit Watson. 'I sensed the weight of what was going to happen right there,' he admitted. He tried to take himself back to his schooldays, to swing his putter with the freedom of youth and knock in the ball without a care in the world. This, though, was a putt for history, sporting immortality and a story that had generated laughter only a few days earlier.

'I decelerated on the putt and hit a terrible putt,' Watson confessed.

Yes, he was in a play-off with Stewart Cink, but everyone knew his chance was gone. Cink lifted the Claret Jug, he was the Champion Golfer of 2009. But the Championship of that year would be remembered more for the improbable charge of a smiling 59-year-old. It was one that inspired thousands of people from older generations and all walks of life, as proved by the thousands of messages Watson subsequently received.

That evening in Scotland he graciously conducted scores of post-round interviews. Tom returned to his hotel room and prepared to go to dinner with Hilary. They were about to leave the room and the phone rang.

It was Nicklaus.

First he reassured Watson that the choice of putter for the third shot on 18 was the right one. 'You gave yourself a chance,' said the record winner of Major championships, before adding: 'You hit the putt like the rest of us would have hit it!'

Now it was Watson who was roaring with laughter. 'That just cracked me up,' he said. 'It made you laugh; that's the type of friend Jack is to me. He knew how I was feeling.'

It was truly fitting that the man with whom Watson had triumphantly departed the same Turnberry 18th green, arm in arm after their epic duel in 1977, added the memorable final touch. It had been one of the most extraordinary final days in Open history. Back home in the United States, Nicklaus had watched his great friend and old rival every step of the way.

After the 'Duel in the Sun', Nicklaus was the man who produced a congratulatory hug. This time it was a consoling arm stretched from the other side of the Atlantic, and one that meant so much to Watson. These gestures epitomise the true and special spirit so frequently generated by The Open Championship, whether in triumph or despair.

OPPOSITE No one knew better than Tom Watson how to cope with Turnberry's changing wind patterns.

LEFT The galleries were desperate for Watson to make the closing par he needed for glory.

THE GREATS

THE GREATS

Galleries watching The Open have always enjoyed seeing the greats of the game. The event's stature as the ultimate Championship can be measured easily. It has been played by all of the best male golfers since 1860 and those leading players have earned elite status with their achievements in the Championship.

It is hard to think of a golfing great who has not been crowned the Champion Golfer of the Year. Special talent and temperament are required to earn such a prize. It is the preserve of the very best. From the early days of Old and Young Tom Morris and Willie Park through to the latest prodigy, Collin Morikawa – who won the 149th Championship on his debut in 2021 – only a relatively select few have proved themselves by winning The Open.

An even more select club are multiple Major champions, Open winners who have dominated other tournaments that help define the most significant careers.

These are the Greats.

PREVIOUS PAGE Tiger Woods winning his second Open title at St Andrews, 2005.

LEFT Jack Nicklaus tees off during his Open debut at Royal Troon in 1962.

OPPOSITE Nicklaus with the trophy after winning at St Andrews in 1978.

Jack Nicklaus

'He was the ultimate competitor, he was just absolutely supreme,' says former BBC golf correspondent Tony Adamson of Jack Nicklaus, a man who boasts more Major titles than any other to have played the game. Nicknamed the 'Golden Bear', Nicklaus won 18 Majors, three of them Opens, with two secured at the 'Home of Golf' in 1970 and 1978.

Despite evolving into the game's most successful, popular and influential player, Nicklaus struggled to attract supporters in the early part of his career. Born in Columbus, Ohio in 1940, he won the US Amateur in 1959 and 1961 and finished second to Arnold Palmer in the 1960 US Open. He was regarded as a chubby upstart and a threat to the charismatic Palmer. American golf fans were not keen. 'Jack took a bit of time to get under their skin, it wasn't until he got a new hairdresser and lost about 30 pounds,' said Peter Alliss. One of Nicklaus's great rivals, Tony Jacklin, adds: 'He had to battle to win acclaim above Palmer. He was the imposter, if you like. That toughened him up.'

Nicklaus's first score at an Open was a disappointing 80 at Royal Troon in 1962. Nevertheless he battled back to play all four rounds. He was third and second in the next two Championships and by the time he arrived at Muirfield in 1966, Nicklaus had won three Masters, the 1962 US Open and the PGA Championship of 1963. All that was missing was a Claret Jug for a career Grand Slam of Major trophies, something that had only previously been achieved by Gene Sarazen, Ben Hogan and Gary Player. Nicklaus triumphed on the East Lothian links by beating Doug Sanders and Dave Thomas by a single stroke.

During his winner's speech, the Champion famously paused to take in the scale of his achievement. 'When the moment came to accept the trophy,' Nicklaus said, 'the tears began welling up and I couldn't get any words out. Being about to receive something that even I, never much of a self-doubter, had genuinely doubted would ever be mine, was extremely emotional. Finally, I asked the people to excuse me and to let me just stand there and enjoy myself for a moment. It's a moment I still enjoy recalling as much as any in my career.'

Nicklaus was the most formidable of golfers. 'He had a great swing,' says Jacklin. 'He did everything the way it was supposed to be. His lower body was very powerful and he overpowered golf courses. But his mind was so good; the way he focused on Majors, his whole schedule was about arriving at every Major prepared physically and mentally and I think he was the first one to do that. We didn't focus on Majors like he did. His ability under pressure to think clearly was another great strength.'

He was massively influential in the growth of The Open on an international scale. 'Nicklaus was terrific for the game, not only because of what he did on the course but the way he played,' remembered veteran writer and broadcaster Renton Laidlaw. 'When Jack Nicklaus started coming, the American golf writers would come and the media tents got bigger. He wasn't just the biggest golfer, he was the biggest sports star in the world. When he was coming down the 18th, if I was commentating for the radio, I had to stand up for Nicklaus.'

Inevitably he became one of the most influential figures in the game, whether as a player, manufacturer, golf course designer or ambassador. 'In my lifetime I've seen three Jack Nicklauses,' Alliss contended. 'The original, the handsome one – there was a time for a few years when he was very, very striking – and then the elder statesman, who I think is very worthwhile to listen to. Nowadays he talks about how he did things, and it is so sensible.'

Others may have won more Opens but his record in the Championship was still phenomenal. Along with three victories, he amassed seven runner-up cheques in a period between 1963 and 1982 when he only twice finished outside the top 10. 'The tournament was never over until it was over and that was Jack's great creed,' Adamson says. 'And he was a great one for the galleries. It was like watching a royal procession going out with Jack and watching him walk through the crowds. He was wonderful for the game of golf.'

Tom Watson

'On his day, over four rounds, you couldn't beat him,' says Ken Brown of Tom Watson. 'He was just an exceptional performer at links golf.' Brown played with Watson for the final 18 holes of the 1983 Championship at Royal Birkdale when the American, born in Kansas City, Missouri in 1949, won his fifth Open title.

From pretty much the first moment Watson arrived at an Open it became clear he was destined for greatness at the Championship. This was in 1975 when he went to Carnoustie with two PGA Tour wins under his belt but with a reputation for fading from contention when the biggest prizes were at stake. Indeed, when the 54-hole leader Bobby Cole was asked about the chasing pack he merely highlighted the threats of Jack Nicklaus, Hale Irwin and Johnny Miller. 'If I was Bobby Cole, I wouldn't have mentioned Tom Watson as a threat either!' Watson laughed in The Open Conversation podcast when recalling his debut.

OPPOSITE Tom Watson putting en route to victory at Muirfield in 1980.

TOP Watson is always a fan favourite, especially in Scotland.

Events on the final day did not play out as expected. Watson birdied the closing hole to force an 18-hole play-off with Jack Newton. The following day he outscored the Australian 71 to 72. In the post-war era Ben Hogan (1953), Tony Lema (1964) and latterly Ben Curtis (2003) and Collin Morikawa (2021) are the only other players to win the Claret Jug at the very first attempt.

Two years later Watson triumphed in the great 'Duel in the Sun' with Jack Nicklaus at Turnberry. 'It was a win that told me I could play with the big boys,' the winner said. But, remarkably, he still did not enjoy the demands of links golf. 'I didn't like the way you had to play short,' Watson says. 'I played golf the American way – I hit the ball high through the air and I expected the ball to stop. On links golf courses it didn't stop; I had to go back to my childhood and play the roll.'

Doing that meant living with bad bounces and Watson's view of British seaside golf did not markedly improve until he played a friendly game at Royal Dornoch in pouring rain in 1981. 'That's when I had the epiphany – this is the way golf should be played,'

Watson adds. 'If you hit the ball solidly you can hit the ball the right distance and that's the key, get it flag high and put it where you must put it.'

Watson had been imperious in beating Lee Trevino by four shots to win at Muirfield in 1980, the first Open to finish on a Sunday, and two years later he outlasted the field to triumph again at Royal Troon. By this time Watson was considered an honorary Scotsman because all four of his titles had been won in the country. His final victory, the following year, was the only one he achieved on an English course. A nine-under-par total of 275 was a record for Royal Birkdale at the time. 'He hit the ball high but he didn't hit it high with spin,' Brown recalls. 'He swept it off the top and had that ability to hit it so that it went through the air and did not stall. It was much harder to do in the eighties because the balls were not so good and he was exceptional.'

The former Ryder Cup player and television commentator also praises Watson's resilience as a defining quality. 'He took everything in his stride and that was a tremendous skill. Of that era no one holed more putts and he missed nothing from short range and holed a bonanza full of 15- to 18-footers. His strategy was good as well.'

Watson missed out on equalling Harry Vardon's record of six Open titles the following year when he bogeyed the 71st hole at St Andrews after Severiano Ballesteros birdied the last to win. Thereafter he posted only three more top tens, the most sensational of which came in 2009 when, aged 59, he cruised to within a par putt of another Turnberry victory. Watson's approach inexplicably bounced through the green, forcing him to putt from a collar of rough just off the putting surface. That left an eight-footer for glory, which proved a putt too far. 'Watson's second shot to the last at Turnberry should have been the shot of the year,' says Sky Sports' Ewen Murray. 'I've no idea how it finished over the green; he landed it on a sixpence.'

Watson's five Open titles were among eight Major victories that all came between 1975 and 1983. His final Open was played at St Andrews in 2015, when the Championship bade an emotional farewell to not only a great Champion but a superb ambassador for the game. 'He was always courteous, always sporting,' says Ken Brown. 'He got on with his game in a very businesslike way. A legend of the game for how he played, how he handled himself and a complete gentleman.'

Peter Thomson overcame the top American players to win his fifth Open title at Royal Birkdale in 1965.

Peter Thomson

'Peter Thomson had a simple way of playing the game and was a very smart man and a very, very capable golfer,' says Ian Baker-Finch. The 1991 champion's fellow Australian dominated The Open throughout much of the 1950s before winning his fifth and final Claret Jug at Royal Birkdale in 1965. 'Links was his speciality,' adds Baker-Finch. 'He had strategy and out-thought his fellow competitors, but also possessed a great swing and great self-belief.'

Born in Brunswick, Victoria in 1929, Thomson was the only golfer to win three Opens in a row in the twentieth century. His first victory also came at Birkdale, in 1954, when he edged out Bobby Locke, Dai Rees and Syd Scott by a single stroke. He was Australia's first Open winner and it was only the second time the country had celebrated a Major victory after Jim Ferrier's PGA win seven years earlier. Thomson's Birkdale triumph was far from unexpected. He had already finished sixth on his Open debut at Portrush in 1951 and runner-up in the next two Championships.

Thomson credited an extraordinary escape on the 16th hole of his final round for his breakthrough victory. His ball was on the steep slope of a bunker 25 yards from the hole. Despite an awkward stance, with his feet together, the 24-year-old gave the ball a mighty thump and it flew high in the air before landing and stopping within inches of its target. 'That won it for me, no doubt,' he said. 'Had I made a mess of that one, I'd have been a goner.'

At St Andrews the following year Thomson beat Johnny Fallon by two strokes before enjoying a three-shot triumph at Hoylake in 1956. A year later the Old Course again played host and Thomson was runner-up to Locke before winning his fourth Open at Royal Lytham, where he beat the young Welshman Dave Thomas in a play-off. Both players set a new record score of 278, with Thomson opening the week with a brilliant 66. Thomson won the 36-hole play-off by four strokes, meaning he went an astonishing seven straight years without finishing outside the top two at an Open.

'Peter Thomson was wonderful, a very interesting, bright fellow who had his own ideas about a lot of things,' remembered his great friend Peter Alliss.

'He was an elegant, easy, jaunty golfer. He would come over in May time and it was all about preparation for The Open. Peter had this ability to click in when the ball was running. He could manoeuvre it and he had a sharp brain and used wonderful caddies.

'He did some extraordinary things. When it was pouring with rain he would never wear a zip-up jacket. He never wore a glove; he'd have his hands in his pockets, the caddie would hold the umbrella and Thomson would have two cashmeres on. In those days it was proper cashmere, almost bulletproof. And he would just play.'

A winner of 95 professional tournaments, Thomson died in his native Victoria in June 2018, aged 88. He was a true pioneer for Australian golf and an inspiration for the likes of Kel Nagle, Greg Norman and Ian Baker-Finch, his only other compatriots to win an Open.

'He was such a generous person with young players with the help and advice he provided,' says Baker-Finch. 'He was a great example to follow.'

Tiger Woods

Among his 15 Major wins, Tiger Woods has three Open titles. 'They were all emphatic victories and they were all achieved in very linksy conditions,' says Colin Montgomerie, who played with Woods when he was runner-up to the American at St Andrews in 2005. 'The beauty of Tiger is that he could adapt to different conditions and that's why he's won all four Majors. He could adapt to the situation better than anyone else.'

Having made his Open debut on the Old Course in 1995 as a raw 19-year-old, he returned the following year to Royal Lytham and was the only amateur to make the cut. After opening with a ragged 75, Woods fired a superb 66 and a pair of 70s to finish in a share of 22nd place to claim the Silver Medal for finishing low amateur.

By the time he returned to his next Open, 12 months later, Woods was already the Masters champion and a sporting phenomenon. 'I have stood ten yards from Tiger Woods when he has been hitting and, in his pomp, he just exuded an aura unlike anything else I've ever experienced at such close quarters,' says former BBC Radio presenter John Inverdale. 'I haven't received a serve from Roger Federer on Centre Court and I imagine if I did I would probably feel the same way.'

Woods's name first appeared on an Open leaderboard in 1998 when he was third to his good friend Mark O'Meara. Two years later, fresh from a record-breaking US Open triumph at Pebble Beach, the Californian superstar landed his first Claret Jug with an emphatic eight-shot win at St Andrews.

Tiger Woods about to land his first Open title at St Andrews in 2000.

By then he was indisputably the biggest name in sport. Inverdale adds: 'When he walked onto a tee box and acknowledged the crowd, you just sensed something that you'd get with very, very few practitioners – maybe opera singers or the occasional rock star. It felt like you were in the presence of genuine greatness.'

Woods's next Open triumph came when he returned to the Old Course in 2005. 'It's fitting his best performances have come at St Andrews because the greatest champions win there,' notes television commentator Andrew Cotter. On that occasion Woods won by five strokes. Runner-up Montgomerie admits the destiny of the title was always in the hands of the man who famously wears an intimidating red shirt for final rounds.

'Playing with him, there was an aura about the guy,' says the Scottish Ryder Cup star. 'He was by far the best of our generation, by a mile. When his first-round score came up in 2005, 66, somehow you felt you were playing for second place. Anyone else scoring 66 you'd still have hope.'

Montgomerie says he was proud to have been a part of Woods's triumph and admits he knew he was playing for the runners-up spot. 'When I was lying second, if I was honest with you, I was trying to keep José María Olazábal and Retief Goosen at bay behind me,' he says. 'To be realistic, Tiger would have to do something really silly and he never did in Majors. Tiger never gave a Major away.'

Woods dominated the following year at Hoylake even though his eventual winning margin over Chris DiMarco was a mere two strokes. The Champion used his driver only once on a dry, fiery, fast Royal Liverpool layout and went to the top of the leaderboard with a second-round 65. It included an eagle, holed out with a 4-iron from 191 yards on the par-4 14th. This was a position from which he was never toppled despite a high-quality chasing pack that included Ernie Els and Sergio Garcia. It was a highly emotional victory, Woods's first Major triumph following the death earlier that year of his father Earl, a man he credits for being the biggest influence on his extraordinary life.

The latter part of his career was blighted by injuries, which cost him places in the fields for the 2008, 2011, 2016 and 2017 Championships. At Carnoustie in 2018 he stirred the galleries once again with a seemingly improbable charge that finished in a share of sixth place.

It also indicated he was ready to contend for the biggest prizes once again and within a year he won a fifth Masters green jacket.

Woods has also endured plenty of Open frustration, with five winless finishes in the top six and three missed cuts. 'Sometimes the tale of Tiger at The Open has been one of dramatic disappointment,' Cotter contends. 'Some wild shots and hunting for balls and getting frustrated. And not necessarily being able to cope with the vagaries of an Open Championship in terms of the weather or the luck of the draw. Think of Muirfield in 2002 where he was the greatest player in the game by a country mile but the weather got to him. The Open Championship can do that. It can frustrate the very best. But Tiger at The Open has provided some amazing moments, great drama and great victories.'

And from a player's perspective, Woods has always been the man to beat. As Montgomerie comments: 'When that red shirt went on and he was leading, it was very, very difficult for the rest of us.'

Lee Trevino

BOTTOM Lee Trevino about to win in 1971 after Li Liang-Huan (Mr Lu) misses at Royal Birkdale.

OPPOSITE Trevino lifts the trophy he would hold for two years running.

'Lee Trevino was a tremendous ball striker, as good as you will ever see and he loved links golf,' says Tony Jacklin, who finished third in both of the wise-cracking American's Open triumphs. The son of a gravedigger, Trevino was born in Dallas, Texas in 1939 and left school at 14 to become a caddie. Despite serving a four-year stint in the US Marines between the ages of 17 and 21, he developed into one of the biggest and most charismatic golf stars ever known.

Nicknamed 'The Merry Mex' and 'SuperMex' because of his Mexican heritage and an overt sense of humour, he won six Major titles, claiming two US Opens and two PGAs along with his successes in lifting the Claret Jug. 'You could hear him before you could see him,' Jacklin recalls, laughing. 'He did it to get rid of the nerves, I think, but I'm not taking anything away from him as a player; he was one of the greats of golf.'

Trevino was the reigning US Open champion, having beaten Jack Nicklaus in a play-off at Merion, when he arrived at Royal Birkdale in 1971 for The 100th Open. He had finished third the year before at St Andrews, in only his second appearance in the Championship, and his relentless hitting, low ball flight and unerring accuracy meant he was made for golf on coastal courses of the UK. 'He was best suited to links golf – it suited him down to the ground,' Jacklin says. 'He was a great driver; he didn't have any shortcomings. He was self-taught, the club stayed on line for a long while and he had a good short game.'

Rounds of 69, 70, 69 and 70 illustrated the solidity of Trevino's form as he edged out another great character, the pork-pie-hat-wearing Liang Huan Lu of Taiwan – known as Mr Lu – by a single shot, with Jacklin a further stroke back. Trevino extravagantly hurled his cap into the crowd in celebration after securing the win, despite recording an uncharacteristic seven at the penultimate hole.

A year later Trevino eclipsed a charging Nicklaus and faltering Jacklin to retain the trophy. This was courtesy of an outrageous chip in at the 17th to save par before his English rival three-putted, squandering a share of the lead.

Trevino's triumph ended Nicklaus's run at a Grand Slam of Major titles that year. 'I have always loved links courses,' Trevino later told PGATour.com. 'They are right down my alley and I was thrilled to win the British Open [sic] twice. I will always have a soft spot in my heart for the Old Course at St Andrews and I would put Muirfield second.'

Sir Nick Faldo

**Winning The Open was Nick Faldo's 'lifetime goal'
and he was able to do it on three occasions among
his six Major titles. He became the first British golfer
to land a hat-trick of titles since Sir Henry Cotton
in 1948 and Faldo's triumph at Muirfield in 1987
was the first by an Englishman since Tony Jacklin
18 years earlier.**

To become capable of being crowned Champion
Golfer, Faldo needed to reassemble a previously
flowing but flawed swing. It had been good enough
to contend for big titles but would break down under
pressure when Major trophies were at stake. Five times
Faldo had finished in the top eight of an Open before
he could finally and triumphantly put his hands on the
Claret Jug. It only happened after intense rebuilding
of his technique under the tutelage of coach David
Leadbetter. The process took up two potentially
prime years in his career.

However, Faldo knew the work had been
successful in May 1987 when he won the Spanish
Open. Arriving at Muirfield that summer he felt a
deep inner confidence and visualised his name sitting
at the top of the distinctive yellow Open leaderboards.

On the Saturday of the third round he turned 30,
but any celebrations were tainted by a bogey at the last,
which cost him a share of the lead with Paul Azinger.
The following day, the American swept to a three-
stroke advantage by the turn. Faldo, meanwhile, was
relentlessly picking up par after par. The home player
holed from 30 feet after finding a bunker at the seventh
and there were two more sand saves but otherwise
it was regulation golf.

He famously collected 18 straight pars while, in the group behind, Azinger started to falter.

After signing his card Faldo could not bring himself to watch the rest of the Championship. So he did not see his rival collect a fourth back-nine bogey on the closing hole, which meant the man from Welwyn Garden City in Hertfordshire, who was hiding in the recorder's hut, was at last a Major Champion.

Faldo played arguably his best golf three years later when he won on the Old Course by five strokes, having arrived in St Andrews as the reigning Masters champion. Rounds of 67, 65, 67 and 71 included an eagle and 20 birdies and on the third day he outscored his main challenger Greg Norman by nine shots. The triumph generated treasured memories, which were fuelled by an unexpected call from former US tour player Ed Snead while Faldo was driving to the Golf Channel's studios in Florida during the coronavirus lockdown of 2020.

Thirty years earlier Snead had played in that Open and his then 15-year-old daughter worked the scoreboard overlooking the 18th green. Snead informed Faldo that she had been allowed to take home a name and score as a souvenir after the Championship finished. 'She kept "Faldo, 18 under",' Faldo revealed in an interview for BBC Sport. 'I nearly crashed the car. I said, "You're kidding me?" and he asked, "Do you want it?"

'So I have got from 1990 the "Faldo 18 under" from the leaderboard and I'm so chuffed with it. I'm actually going to build an R&A leaderboard and I'll do it with the slots where you can slide in the names and I'll get the official R&A yellow paint colour of the scoreboards. I couldn't thank him enough ... I love it, I think it's really cool.' Thirty years earlier he had said to the galleries, while cradling the Claret Jug like a babe in arms, 'I've got to tell you it's wonderful to win at St Andrews.'

LEFT Faldo tees off on the 18th at the Old Course in 1990.

OPPOSITE The Red Arrows help Nick celebrate in style at the 'Home of Golf'.

The English golfer, who was knighted in 2009, was reunited with the trophy in 1992 when he surged from two shots behind by playing 'the best four holes of my life' to pip another American, John Cook. Again, Muirfield was the scene of his success and Nick has said that the 18th hole of the East Lothian course is his favourite golfing location because of the victories he completed on that green.

Faldo played 37 Opens, the last coming at St Andrews in 2015, when he nearly pulled out with a finger injury but persevered to score a creditable second-round 71 after a miserable opening 83. It included a remarkable birdie on the fearsome 'Road Hole'. Moments later he donned the famous yellow Pringle sweater that he wore when he won the first of his Claret Jugs. He looked skywards as he posed for photographers on the Swilcan Bridge before completing the final hole. 'I was just trying to say, thank you, St Andrews,' Faldo later told reporters. 'That's why I looked at the gods, the St Andrews golfing gods at 17. I thought, thank you very much for that. I felt beat up yesterday, but that was one of my great moments ... making a three there and walking the walk. That won't get any better.'

Greg Norman

'Greg Norman was idolised through the 1980s and 1990s,' says Ian Baker-Finch, a fellow Australian, who won the Claret Jug in 1991. 'The blond hair and shark logo, those broad shoulders encapsulated a compelling athlete to watch and to root for.'

Norman was a dominant figure, spending 331 weeks as world number one, and among 88 professional wins he claimed The Open on two occasions. They were his only Major triumphs. 'He was a tough competitor who always wanted to win; he wasn't happy with second,' Baker-Finch adds.

Norman was born in Mount Isa, Queensland in 1955. He discovered a love for the game through his mother, Toini, who was club champion at Virginia GC. He went on to become the first player to earn more than $10 million on the PGA Tour, where he won on 20 occasions.

Norman was a charismatic, global force and is known as the 'Great White Shark'. 'He was aggressive like Arnold Palmer and was always going for it,' Baker-Finch says. 'He was a great driver of the ball, strong with a fast swing speed and that brought length

and power to his game. He became a very rounded player and was one of the best putters on the tour.'

Eleven years after his Open debut, Norman romped to a five-stroke victory at Turnberry in 1986. His second-round 63 was one of the great Open performances because only 15 players broke par that day. Tom Watson described it as 'the greatest round ever played in a tournament in which I was a competitor'.

Norman was victorious despite recording scores of 74 in the first and third rounds. 'Outside of Australia, Britain was the first place that accepted me as a professional golfer,' he said afterwards. 'To win my first Open here in front of that gallery was the best feeling ever.' Norman made sure no one touched the trophy before his mother when he took it home. It was Australia's first Claret Jug since Peter Thomson in 1965. 'His win at Turnberry was extra special,' adds Baker-Finch.

Seven years later Norman put together an even greater performance to defeat a star-studded leaderboard at Royal St George's. His closing round of 64 made him the first Champion to shoot all four

rounds in the 60s and his total of 267 set the lowest aggregate in Open history. Norman left in his wake a string of great names: runner-up Sir Nick Faldo, Bernhard Langer, Corey Pavin, Ernie Els, Paul Lawrie, Nick Price, Fred Couples, Wayne Grady, Scott Simpson and Payne Stewart. Of the top dozen finishers, only fellow Aussie Peter Senior did not claim a Major title.

It was a breathtaking performance from Norman, who is widely regarded as having under-achieved in terms of Major wins. He was runner-up in all four of the Grand Slam events and became a 'nearly man' despite the immense overall success of his career. 'Greg Norman has been underrated in the same way as Ernie Els has been underrated,' said veteran commentator Peter Alliss. 'On balance they should have each won about eight Majors. Greg Norman it was even suggested didn't have the nerve for it, but I watched Norman win big events all round the world and he was flamboyant and he looked the part and he did a lot for the game.'

Norman charged into a play-off with a closing 64 at Royal Troon in 1989 but lost to Mark Calcavecchia after finding two bunkers and out of bounds on the closing hole of the shoot-out. It was one of ten top 10s in 27 Open appearances, which included a share of third place at Royal Birkdale in 2008 when he was 53 years old.

Norman dressed for the part as he outlasted a high-quality leaderboard to win at Sandwich in 1993.

Ernie Els

**Cast from the traditional mould of globe-trotting
South African golfers, Ernie Els became a dominant
force all over the world. Swinging with elegance
and apparent ease, he has been a fan favourite ever
since landing his first Major title as a 24-year-old
at the 1994 US Open. Els added a second victory
in that championship when he edged out Colin
Montgomerie at Congressional three years later.**

More Major successes were predicted but he needed
to wait until 2002 to make his winning breakthrough
at The Open. He had posted five top-six finishes before
claiming the 131st Championship on a tortuously tense
and dramatic final day.

Els was seemingly in charge, three shots clear, when
he played a remarkable bunker escape at the 13th that
was later voted shot of the year. He then bogeyed the
next hole and dropped two strokes at the 16th. A vital
birdie at the next meant he was able to tie with three
other players for the lowest 72-hole total.

Eventually he won on the first hole of sudden death,
beating Frenchman Thomas Levet after both men
emerged from the initial play-off over four holes.

Australians Steve Elkington and Stuart Appleby
bowed out and then Els produced another superb
up and down from an awkward stance in a greenside
bunker to land his first Claret Jug. 'It's hard work,' he
later admitted. 'I guess I've really earned it and you
really feel good after that. It would have been nicer
for my health to do it a little bit easier. But Major
Championships are the most important tournaments
that we play, and so I guess we put a lot more pressure
on ourselves.'

Two years later Els was involved in another play-
off, losing to American Todd Hamilton at Royal Troon.
The Johannesburg-born golfer remained remarkably
consistent – third in 2006, fourth a year later and then
posted top-eight finishes in the next two Opens. But
there was a feeling time was running out for Els to
add to his Major tally by the time he arrived at Royal
Lytham in 2012. He had suffered his first missed cuts
since his debut in 1989 at the previous two
Championships and was now 42 years old.

Nevertheless, he became Champion Golfer of
the Year for the second time with a stunning Sunday
back-nine 32, which was capped by a brilliant birdie

at the last that prompted one of the loudest roars ever heard from an Open gallery. It was enough to pip Australia's Adam Scott, who headed into the closing holes with a four-stroke advantage. 'I really feel for my buddy, Scottie, I really do,' Els sportingly told reporters. 'I've blown Majors before and golf tournaments before, and I just hope he doesn't take it as hard as I did.'

The South African's career, much of which coincided with the huge dominance of Tiger Woods, did include several near misses among 35 Major top tens. But he enjoyed more than 70 worldwide wins and led the European Tour money lists of 2002 and 2003. Like his compatriot forerunners Bobby Locke and Gary Player, Els was one of the greats of his era.

Padraig Harrington

'I don't think there is any question that The Open was the one he most wanted to win,' says RTE's Greg Allen, who – as the Irish radio station's golf reporter – has interviewed Padraig Harrington more times than any other journalist. The player had to wait until he was nearly 37 years old before realising his dream with victory in a play-off against Sergio Garcia in the 2007 Championship at Carnoustie.

A decade earlier, just 18 months into his professional career, Harrington showed his Open potential by finishing in a share of fifth place at Royal Troon. 'I remember meeting Padraig as he came off the 18th,' Allen recalls. 'I thought fifth at The Open, he'd be delighted, but he looked kind of disappointed. I said to him it was a great performance and he said, "Nah, doesn't mean anything, there was no pressure on." You'd think a guy who'd only been professional a year and half would have been thrilled with fifth in The Open but he wasn't.'

Harrington did not join the paid ranks until he was 24 after a long and distinguished amateur career. It was during that time he honed the skills that made him a two-time Open Champion. 'He once told me that as an amateur on links courses in Ireland there wasn't a single position that he couldn't see himself getting up and down,' Allen says. 'Back then he often missed greens and found himself in loads of positions around the humps and hollows surrounding links greens where his imagination was stimulated by the challenge.'

The Dubliner came close in 2002 at Muirfield when he was only one stroke out of a four-man play-off after bogeying the last, where he used a driver and found a ruinous bunker off the tee. It was another week that showed he was capable of challenging for the biggest prize in the game and proof arrived five years later with his Carnoustie triumph.

On the closing hole Harrington needed to get up and down for a double-bogey after finding the burn with his drive and his approach to the green. 'I hit a lovely pitch,' Harrington told reporters. 'Holing the putt, that was probably the most pressure-filled putt I had of the day. If I missed it, it was the end of it, and to hole it was a great boost to me. That was a moment that I thought, now maybe things are going to go my way.'

It was a lot less stressful 12 months later at Royal Birkdale where Harrington emulated Tiger Woods's feat of two years earlier by successfully defending the Claret Jug. On the final day the Irishman struck an imperious 5-wood from a tricky downhill lie to set up a Championship-clinching eagle on the 71st hole. 'Once I hit it, it was perfect,' Harrington said. 'It's one of the few times I think I've ever heard my caddie say good shot to me before the ball is finished.' The player took no chances with the three-footer that gave him a four-stroke advantage on the final tee. 'It helped me enjoy the last hole. Obviously I was cautious. I wanted to get my tee shot away, and I hit a beautiful 3-wood. Once I did that, I knew I had won The Open.'

That summer Harrington was playing the golf of his life and in August he went to Oakland Hills where he won the PGA Championship to claim a third Major title. 'He did want to win an American Major,' Allen recalls. 'That was to show that he could win in America, but The Open is the one that catches the attention on this side of the Atlantic. The Open is magical for him.'

Harrington successfully defended his title at Royal Birkdale in 2008 despite a wrist injury.

Gary Player

Feeling overwhelmed when he arrived at Royal Liverpool for his first Open in 1956, Gary Player thought Hoylake seemed 'bleak'. The entire experience of embarking on his first Major Championship was 'strange'. Little did he know, but he was taking his first steps on a glorious path that would make him one of the true greats of the game.

Player recorded an astonishing 163 victories in his professional career during an incredible 43-year period that started with his first triumph on home soil at the East Rand Open in 1955. A year later he was a wide-eyed innocent ready to compete in the world's oldest and most prestigious Championship. 'Of course for a young boy from South Africa it was the Holy Grail to play in The Open,' he says. 'I was honoured, frightened and lonely. Fortunately, the club and several members were very kind to me and made me feel welcome.'

Player finished fourth in that first Open, five strokes behind Peter Thomson, but within three years he collected his first Claret Jug at Muirfield. Player started the final round four strokes behind but fought his way to the top of the leaderboard only to double-bogey the closing hole. He thought he had blown his chances. 'I actually broke down crying afterwards with my wife Vivienne, thinking I had thrown it away with my poor finish,' he says. 'She scolded me and told me to remain positive as the tournament was not over yet.'

Gary Player during play prior to his 1968 triumph at Carnoustie.

LEFT The 'Big Three': Nicklaus, Palmer and Player at St Andrews in 1970.

OPPOSITE Player lifts the Claret Jug for the first time in 1959 at Muirfield and goes on to win The Open in three separate decades.

Player had time to change into a suit and tie before the presentation of the first of his nine Major trophies. 'It meant everything,' he says. 'I was 23, had no money, a growing family and commitments I did not know how to manage. Now, I was a Major champion, the youngest ever, in the modern era, a player to be recognised with and my life changed immediately and dramatically almost overnight.'

Player became a world force and part of the 'Big Three' alongside Jack Nicklaus and Arnold Palmer. He won two more Opens; in 1968 at Carnoustie and then six years later at Royal Lytham & St Annes. He remains tremendously fulfilled by his achievements at the Championship. 'To win once is a dream,' he says.

'Twice means you prove it was not luck, but three times over three decades is unreal. The satisfaction is hard to explain but vindicated all my sacrifice, hard work, practice and dedication over a long period of time. I remain very proud to this day.'

Having made his debut in the mid-1950s, the South African legend played in every Open until his last in 2001, which he played just three months shy of his 66th birthday. 'The Open really seems to get better and better over time,' he insists. 'The course conditions, the organisation, the fans' appreciation, the global television audience, the players, the prize money, the commercial activities. It is a truly remarkable tournament that is respected all around the world.'

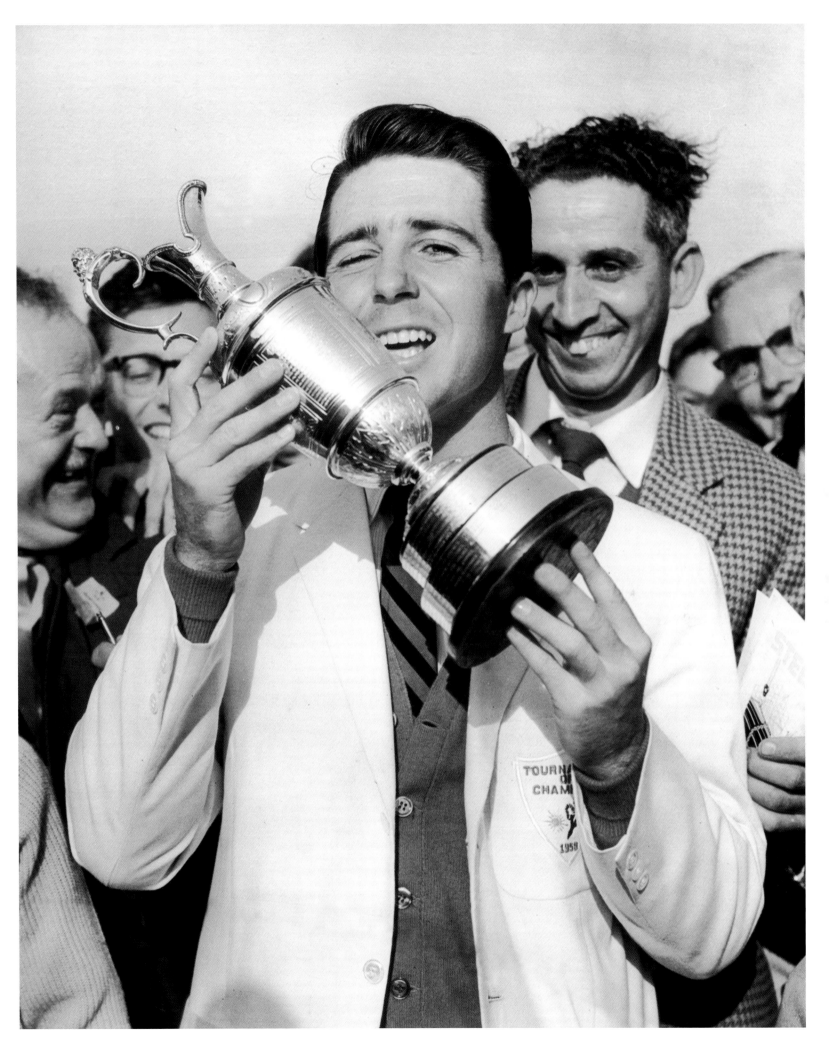

Harry Vardon

Every player who has competed in The Open since the start of the twentieth century has lived in the shadow of Harry Vardon, the legendary golfer from Jersey who won six Championships between 1896 and 1914.

According to the World Golf Hall of Fame, Vardon was 'golf's first superstar'. His reputation was forged on both sides of the Atlantic and his methods became a blueprint for the way the game should be played for every generation that has followed.

It is an extraordinary legacy for someone who had no great golfing ambition in his formative years. One of eight children, he was born in the town of Grouville and standing five feet nine inches tall, taught himself how to play the game. Initially an apprentice gardener, Vardon only embarked on a competitive career when he saw his brother, Tom, turn professional and do well in tournaments.

Despite never taking a lesson, he fashioned an upright and easy swing. 'Relaxation,' he said, 'added to a few necessary fundamental principles, is the basis of this great game.' Unusually for the time, Vardon swung with both hands touching each other. His right little finger rested on the index finger of his left hand. This 'Vardon Grip' is still taught to and used by the majority of worldwide golfers today.

With sound technique he was capable of relentless consistency. Harry's initial Open triumph came in a play-off against the great J.H. Taylor at Muirfield and it was the first of three Claret Jugs in four years. 'A greater genius is inconceivable,' wrote the distinguished Bernard Darwin of Vardon's ability when he was at his very best. He won the US Open in 1900 at Chicago Golf Club and in The Open he was runner-up three times in a row before a fourth title was added at Prestwick in 1903. On that occasion Harry beat brother Tom, the runner-up, by six strokes.

But in the wake of that victory the Champion contracted tuberculosis and spent months in a sanatorium as he suffered a long and debilitating period of ill health. Vardon's golf suffered and his shot-making did not seem as potent with the wound rubber Haskell ball.

Nevertheless, his success was not only founded in technique, he possessed tenacity aplenty and eventually it brought him back to prominence at The Open. In 1911 at Royal St George's he won a play-off against Frenchman Arnaud Massy and his familiar name was engraved on the trophy for a fifth time. The following year Vardon was second to Ted Ray but in 1914 he went to Prestwick to claim, to date, an unsurpassed sixth title, beating Taylor by three strokes.

JOHN HENRY TAYLOR
& Open Champion
1894.1895.1900.1909.1913.TIED 1896.

JAMES BRAID
Open Champion
1901.1905.1906.1908.1910.

HARRY VARDON
Open Champion
1896.1898.1899.1903.1911.1914.

CLEMENT
FLOWER
1913

Walter Hagen

**Only Jack Nicklaus (18) and Tiger Woods (15) have
won more Majors than Walter Hagen's 11. Among
them he claimed four Opens in a seven-year period
when he never finished outside the top three.
This American, born in Rochester, New York in
1892, was one of golf's most influential figures.
He was the original full-time golf professional and
is thought to have been sport's first millionaire.**

Hagen bridled at the way he and fellow pros were
treated in the early twentieth century and successfully
campaigned for better rewards and more respect for
his peers, who were often excluded from clubhouses
and changing facilities. On his Open debut at Royal
Cinque Ports in 1920, he pointedly changed his shoes
in a Daimler in the car park after being told he could
not enter the clubhouse. At a dinner in Hagen's honour,
the great Arnold Palmer commented: 'If not for you,
Walter, this dinner tonight would be downstairs in
the pro shop, not in the ballroom.'

Hagen's playing prowess helped ensure that his
was a voice that would command attention. By the
time he won his first Open at Royal St George's in 1922,
this charismatic figure had already claimed two US Opens
and the previous year's PGA Championship. He was
the first American-born player to lift the Claret Jug.

Known as 'Sir Walter' or simply 'The Haig',
according to the World Golf Hall of Fame, he was
'the most colourful character' the game has ever seen,
often overshadowing 'what a supreme player he was'.
He employed a sense of perspective to ensure rounds
would not be derailed by an error. Hagen reasoned
that he would invariably make seven mistakes during
18 holes. 'Therefore, when I make a bad shot, it's just
one of the seven.'

The fact that he never complained about bad luck
stood him in good stead for the vagaries of links golf,
which no doubt helped him in his quest for Open
successes. After edging out George Duncan and
Jim Barnes at Sandwich in 1922, he won again at
Royal Liverpool two years later by beating Ernest
Whitcombe by a single shot after holing from six
feet on the final green.

Hagen was the trailblazer for Americans at The
Open and needed to fight off compatriots to collect
successive titles in 1928 and 1929. First, back at Royal

St George's, he defeated Gene Sarazen and then he left Johnny Farrell trailing in his wake with a six-stroke triumph at Muirfield. During that Championship he became the first player to score a 67 in The Open.

Having come to the game as a caddie, this son of a blacksmith, who died in 1969, played countless exhibition matches to supplement handsome tournament winnings. Famously he said: 'I never wanted to be a millionaire, I just wanted to live like one.'

Gene Sarazen

Gene Sarazen tees off at
Royal Troon in 1973, aged 71.

**Among his seven Major titles, Gene Sarazen
became Champion Golfer of the Year in 1932 when
he dominated the Championship held at Prince's in
Kent. Known as 'The Squire', the New Yorker born
of Sicilian parents had promised his wife he would
return with the Claret Jug and duly obliged thanks
to a five-stroke victory.**

This win came a decade after his first Major success,
victory at the US Open. In 1935 when he won what
was then known as the Augusta National Invitational
(soon after rebranded as the Masters), Sarazen became
the first golfer to complete the career Grand Slam.
In the course of that victory he holed his 225-yard
second shot for an albatross on the par-5 15th hole.
It was known as 'the shot heard around the world'.

For two decades he was a dominant figure and
became a genuine global superstar, winning 48
professional events. He claimed to have invented
the modern sand wedge and after keeping it secret
during practice rounds he introduced it during
his triumphant week at Prince's.

At the age of 71 he completed a famous hole
in one at Royal Troon's 'Postage Stamp' par 3
during the 1973 Open. He retired soon after and
died in 1999, aged 97.

Bobby Jones

'It is clear he had a swing that could be described as a work of art,' Jack Nicklaus wrote of Bobby Jones in his foreword to Steven Reid's book *Bobby's Open*. 'Just as important as his technique was his ability to compete and win under the immense pressure he imposed on himself.'

Jones was one of the giants of the game and indisputably the finest amateur player golf has ever known. Between winning the 1923 US Open and securing the US Amateur at Merion in 1930, the Atlanta-born player won 13 championships out of the 20 he entered.

Three of those were Opens, but his debut in the Championship did not suggest he was a candidate for success in the seaside links form of the game. At St Andrews in 1921 he ripped up his third-round scorecard after taking four strokes to escape a bunker on the 11th hole. It was hardly an action that suggested he would become not only one of the game's great players but also a most influential figure, widely regarded as the epitome of golfing sportsmanship.

Jones first became Open Champion in 1926 at Royal Lytham thanks to one of the greatest shots ever played. He was the first amateur winner for 29 years and the key was a miracle shot from 175 yards on the 17th hole of the final round. Tied with playing partner Al Watrous, Jones hit his tee shot left into unpromising sand dunes while his rival was well placed on the fairway. Somehow the celebrated amateur fashioned an approach that found the putting surface. Watrous ended up further away after his more prosaic second shot and then three-putted to give Jones a decisive lead. The Champion covered the formidable five closing holes in only 19 shots to secure his first Claret Jug.

By successfully defending the trophy the following year, Jones earned redemption at St Andrews, banishing memories of his embarrassment six years earlier. He won again in 1930 at Royal Liverpool, the last time an amateur has won The Open. This was the second leg of what was the Grand Slam of its time. That year he also won the US Open, US Amateur and The Amateur Championship, a victory achieved at the Old Course. By this time he had forged a loving relationship with St Andrews and was later made a 'Freeman of the City'.

Renowned for his sense of fair play, Jones famously called a penalty on himself at the 1925 US Open after his club brushed grass which caused his ball to move by a fraction of an inch. No one else saw the incident and the subsequent penalty stroke cost him outright victory. Jones dismissed widespread acclaim for his honesty, stating: 'You might as well praise me for not robbing banks.'

Jones retired from competing after his clean sweep of the Major honours in 1930. He was only 28 but was also a dedicated academic, devoting no more than three months of any year to competitive golf. He studied mechanical engineering at Georgia Tech, received a degree in English Literature from Harvard and studied law at Emory University, going on to pass the bar.

With Clifford Roberts he co-founded the Augusta National Golf Club in his native Georgia and was the driving force behind the establishment of the Masters, which was first played in 1934. Jones competed on several occasions but never finished better than the 13th place he secured in the inaugural tournament. Later life was marked by ill health as he developed a debilitating spinal condition which ultimately left him wheelchair bound until his death aged 69 in 1971.

Bobby Locke

By finishing low amateur as an 18-year-old debutant in the 1936 Open at Royal Liverpool, Bobby Locke provided the first indication that he would enjoy a glorious career in the Championship. Rounds of 75, 73, 72 and 74 left the young South African at two under par and in a share of eighth place. It was one of a dozen top tens, including four victories, in 29 Open appearances.

After serving as a pilot in the South African Air Force during the Second World War, Locke claimed his first Open title by beating Irishman Harry Bradshaw in a play-off at Royal St George's in 1949. He won the 36-hole shoot-out by 12 strokes to become the first South African to lift the Claret Jug. In regulation play, Locke needed a birdie on the 71st hole to force a tie. He converted from 8 feet after a superb 7-iron approach. In the play-off Locke's form was scintillating as he recorded scores of 67 and 68, including an eagle-3 at the 14th in the morning round following a 200-yard 4-iron approach to a couple of feet.

Locke, who was renowned for his authoritative putting stroke and unerring accuracy on the greens,

defended his title at Troon the following year by beating Roberto de Vicenzo by two strokes with a new Championship record score of 279. He was the first player to retain the trophy since Walter Hagen in 1929. Taking full advantage of benign scoring conditions on the Ayrshire links, Locke showed extraordinary accuracy from the tee and missed only two fairways throughout the four rounds. He also putted brilliantly on the smooth surfaces and from then onwards he sent a Christmas card to the Troon members which always included the same message: 'Best wishes for this year and the future. Still the best greens in the world.'

A third Claret Jug in four years came Locke's way in 1952 but only after surviving a scare on the final morning of the Championship, which was held at Royal Lytham & St Annes. He left his clubs in the boot of his car, which he discovered was locked in the garage of the Blackpool house where was staying. With panic rising, it took the help of a passing milkman, who gave Locke a lift to where the home owner was staying, to locate the missing key. The player arrived at the course with only enough

time to change his shoes and walk to the first tee. He scored a 73, which left him a stroke ahead of Australia's Peter Thomson.

Five years later Locke beat Thomson again, this time by three strokes at St Andrews, to claim his fourth and final Open title. By then his legacy was in place, having inspired the next South African superstar, Gary Player. 'Bobby Locke was a hugely positive influence on my life and career,' says Player, who won the first of his three Claret Jugs two years later. 'He really explained to me the importance of The Open and how to prepare, practise and create the correct mindset to win.' Locke's Open wins were his only Major victories, but he enjoyed huge global success with 73 professional wins, 41 of them in his native South Africa.

Ben Hogan

OPPOSITE Played one, won one. It was mission accomplished for Ben Hogan in his only Open appearance, at Carnoustie in 1953.

NEXT PAGE Hogan was the talk of the town as he sought to complete a full set of Major titles.

Only the most exceptional of players could boast a one hundred per cent winning record at The Open and there are few more special golfers than Ben Hogan. The legendary Texan played the Championship only once and, thanks to his 1953 victory at Carnoustie, is one of only five players who have completed the career Grand Slam of all four Major titles. With a total of nine Major victories, Hogan trails only Jack Nicklaus, Tiger Woods and Walter Hagen for wins in the biggest four championships in the world.

Hogan's first Major victory came at the 1946 PGA Championship. Two years later he won his first US Open and collected a second PGA crown. Then came a life-threatening car crash when he drove home in February fog from a play-off loss at the 1949 Phoenix Open. His vehicle crashed head-on with a Greyhound bus. Hogan threw himself across his wife Valerie to protect her, and the move saved both of them because his car's steering column ended up puncturing the driver's seat. He was aged 36 and in the prime of his career. He suffered a double fracture of his pelvis, fractured collar bone, a left ankle fracture and rib damage. There were complications with blood clots and doctors wondered whether he would ever walk again.

Astonishingly, after spending 59 days in hospital, Hogan returned to competition the following January, losing an 18-hole play-off to Sam Snead at the Los Angeles Open in his first tournament back. Thereafter he played sparingly, but a year later Hogan won his first Masters green jacket. It meant the only Major trophy missing from his mantelpiece was a Claret Jug.

In 1953 he won for the second time at Augusta to start the most successful year of his career. Hogan then clinched a fourth US Open crown before deciding to miss the PGA. Its dates overlapped with those of The Open, so he could not play both, and to complete his set of Majors he needed to head to Carnoustie.

'There was great excitement around Hogan – "Hogan's coming, Hogan's coming",' recalled Peter Alliss. 'We stayed at a hotel that's now a block of flats, a couple of hundred yards from the then clubhouse. He was still recovering from that bad car smash and he was staying at the same hotel but his room didn't have a bathroom.' He needed to soak his legs every evening to ease the pain he still felt after the crash.

Suddenly Hogan's participation seemed under threat. 'He was about to go home,' Alliss claimed. 'Fred Pignon, who then wrote for the *Daily Mail*, said to me: "Have you heard about Hogan? He's going home. He can't deal with the accommodation here." But there was a big American company in Dundee and they had a house for visiting dignitaries from the company, and the boss was a golfer and he offered Hogan a suite in the accommodation and he stayed there.'

Other accounts state he transferred to a guest house; either way, moving accommodation averted potential crisis. An early departure by the reigning Masters and US Open champion would have been a big blow for The Open at a time when fewer Americans were coming over to compete. Instead the Championship received a huge boost because the best player in the world was making it a priority. 'Most certainly Ben Hogan put The Open on the map in the USA,' says Gary Player. 'And no doubt his victory ensured the likes of Nicklaus, Palmer, Trevino and Watson followed.'

Hogan had arrived a week early and used the time to familiarise himself with the smaller ball used on this side of the Atlantic as well as the unique demands of links golf. During the competition he grew stronger and stronger with rounds of 73, 71, 70 and 68 to complete a four-stroke victory. Vast crowds followed his every move, including the great entertainer Frank Sinatra, who was performing in nearby Dundee. 'All America is rooting for Hogan,' the singer informed reporters. The locals christened him the 'Wee Ice Mon' for his unflappable display.

Hogan's performance was more creditable because he was still inconvenienced by the injuries suffered in his car crash and was battling flu and chills. His brilliance on the par-5 sixth, where he repeatedly drove down the narrow stretch of fairway between bunkers and out of bounds, led to that stretch of Carnoustie being known as 'Hogan's Alley'. There are some fanciful claims that he hit from the divot left by his second shot in the morning when he played his final round that afternoon. What is not disputed is that his closing 68 was a course record. He claimed his third Major of the year, a feat unmatched until Woods equalled it 47 years later in 2000.

'He was very stoic and very quiet,' said Alliss, who also remembered Hogan as a stylish and immaculate figure. 'Very elegant and he wore the most beautiful clothes. He wore the most wonderful shoes, beautiful handmade shoes. He wore cashmere, light grey trousers, dark grey cashmere sweater, white shirt and cap. Quietly elegant.

'When he hit the ball he had a very quick swing. It wasn't so elegant but it was exciting. And the noise off the club face of proper, seasoned persimmon – the crack and the sound really was something to behold.'

Hogan's Carnoustie triumph was his last Major success. Although he suggested he might return to The Open, he never did. He departed the UK, along with his wife Valerie, on the SS *United States*, returning to New York, where he received a ticker-tape parade down Broadway. Aged 40, with victory in The 82nd Open, his place in golfing history as a global superstar was even more secure.

Arnold Palmer

When you consider the size and scale of a modern Open you have to remember the influence of two-time Champion Arnold Palmer. Today the Championship is so huge because every golfer in the world wants to compete in it. This was not always the case, especially in the austere years that followed the Second World War. But then came Palmer, who emphatically showed just how important is The Open. No single player was more significant in making sure that the Championship prospered and he did it with the strength of his uniquely charismatic personality.

Palmer was the reigning Masters and US Open champion when he made his first appearance in the Championship in 1960. The powerful hitter from Latrobe, Pennsylvania was runner-up on the Old Course. 'He came over for the centenary Open, which Kel Nagle won,' recalled veteran golf journalist and broadcaster Renton Laidlaw. 'That was what really brought players back to The Open.'

Arnie had an army of support and was always centre of attention. 'Whoever he was playing with was sort of lost in the crowd when Palmer came through,' Laidlaw adds. 'He looked absolutely fantastic, bronzed and tanned. It was everything you would expect him to be. Whenever Palmer came, other American golfers said well if Arnold Palmer's coming it must be really important.'

A year after finishing just short at St Andrews, Palmer edged out Dai Rees at Royal Birkdale by a single shot. He then romped to a six-stroke victory to defend his title at Royal Troon in 1962. His was a voice that commanded attention and he successfully argued that the most established players should not be forced to go through local qualifying competitions in order to compete at future Opens. From 1963 exemptions were introduced which initially meant leading players, including the past 10 Open Champions, were allowed straight into the Championship field.

'They called him "The King",' remembered Peter Alliss. 'He had an aeroplane and he had the crowd. He was the blue-collar favourite and he looked the part. He smoked when smoking was okay. And when he started winning big money he became powerful within the game. Someone realised here was a hero, and by God the press treated him like a hero. He took reporters up in his plane and he flattered them and no one ever wrote a negative word about him.'

Not that Palmer gave them cause, winning seven Majors among 95 professional victories. Until his death shortly after his 87th birthday in 2016, he exerted huge influence on the game as a successful businessman and a figure who transcended his sport. Palmer set up the Golf Channel television station in the United States and had an iced tea drink named after him. And for The Open he was a vital figure. To carry such sway he did not need to do much more than turn up. His force of personality did the rest.

Seve Ballesteros

The week of The 136th Open began in sombre mood. On the Monday afternoon Severiano Ballesteros, the most celebrated European to have ever played the game, arrived in the media centre to tell reporters he would never play again. The Spaniard was just 50 years old. He was a three-time Open Champion, among five Major victories. The driving force, as a player and captain, behind his continent's mounting successes in the Ryder Cup, he had done more to popularise golf in Europe than any other player.

Ballesteros played in 28 Opens and it was at Carnoustie in 2007 that he decided to tell the world of his retirement. His Open career had begun at the same course 32 years earlier, albeit in inauspicious fashion. He suffered a cut foot in the build-up to his Open debut and hobbled to scores of 79 and 80 to miss the final two rounds by a distance. At that stage there was little to suggest he would end his playing days referring to The Open as 'the best tournament in the world'.

But it all changed the following year when we first saw the flamboyant, daring and dashing flair of a Spanish matador unafraid of any golfing challenge.

At Royal Birkdale he was still only a teenager but he set a blistering pace with successive rounds of 69 to take the halfway lead. Ballesteros was eventually chased down by Johnny Miller's closing 66, but the sporting world knew that this joint runner-up with Jack Nicklaus was destined for greatness.

More than three decades later, sitting in the booths at the back of the Carnoustie media centre after announcing his retirement, Ballesteros told BBC Radio listeners that his Birkdale experience in 1976 remained his abiding Open memory. 'That's one picture very much in my mind,' he said, eyes watering with emotion. 'When I was 19 at Royal Birkdale, I mean I can visualise myself. I was with my brother Manuel and I can really visualise where I was, what I was doing, how I was feeling and it is a fantastic memory.'

For golf fans worldwide Ballesteros generated so many enduring recollections. Winning from the car park at Royal Lytham & St Annes in 1979 and holing for birdie five years later when he overtly willed his ball to disappear on the home green at St Andrews. Then celebrating the moment with his uniquely exuberant repeated fist pump. It told everyone just how much it meant.

His infectious smile lit up Lytham again in 1988 when he held off the formidable challenge of Nick Price and Nick Faldo for the Spanish star's third Claret Jug.

'He meant more to The Open than The Open meant to him,' reveals Ballesteros's former Ryder Cup teammate Ken Brown. But Seve's modest view goes the other way. 'Golf gave me so much over the years that it's really hard to give back even 25 per cent of how much I got,' he said on the day of his retirement.

At The Open Seve's unique skill set was most apparent. 'His ability was made for links golf,' Brown adds. The former player turned commentator knew just how special Ballesteros would be when he saw his famous chip between the bunkers on the 72nd green at Royal Birkdale, which helped secure a share of second place in 1976. 'There's not another player in the world who would have tried that. He had creative genius. He trusted his game; brilliant chipper, the heart of an absolute lion, he loved the battle, loved to win, beating the others,' says Brown.

'Even if you played better than him he would probably beat you. What he brought to our Open was being a sort of honorary home player. We had someone to nail our mast to if you followed golf from Britain. We had someone who could match up to the Americans. He was exciting to watch, dynamic to play with and you never knew what was going to happen. Was he about to say something? What might he do?

'I played with him hundreds of times and if you played with him you'd watch him. I played with Jerry Pate and Seve for the first two rounds at St Andrews in 1978. It was just a joy to watch. Walking down the 15th on the Friday I said to Jerry, "I don't think I've ever seen golf played better than this. It's unbelievable."

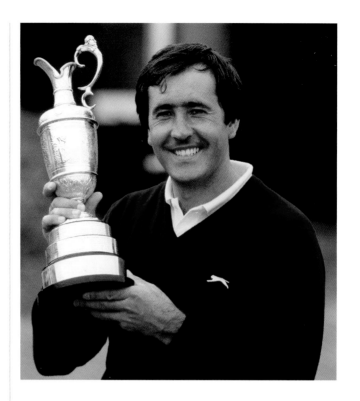

St Andrews as a course was just right up his bag. He could hit a few wild ones here and there and chip and putt from everywhere. He was special in every aspect.'

Renton Laidlaw remembered covering Ballesteros's exploits with huge fondness. Coming up the 18th on the Old Course in 1984, Laidlaw watched as he broadcast from the commentary box and was physically moved. 'Seve's victory at St Andrews was an iconic moment when he beat Watson and Langer.'

Less than four years after his retirement, Ballesteros succumbed to a brain tumour in May 2011 and died at the age of 54. He had enjoyed 90 professional wins, 50 of them on the European Tour. He played in eight Ryder Cups, three times on the winning side, and skippered Europe to victory in his native Spain in 1997. There were two Masters victories as well, but it was the triumphs that yielded Claret Jugs that meant most. 'I have great memories from The Open,' Ballesteros told us. 'I hit so many good shots and so many good things that happened that it's hard to describe how good it felt. It was great.' And 'great' is the most apt word to describe this legendary figure.

Rory McIlroy

'The Open Championship was the one you really wanted growing up, and the one you holed so many putts on the putting green to win; to beat Tiger Woods, Sergio Garcia and Ernie Els,' Rory McIlroy remembered soon after being handed the Claret Jug for the first time. 'The more I keep looking at this trophy and seeing my name on it, the more it will start sinking in.'

Triumphing at Royal Liverpool in 2014 gave McIlroy his third Major title. That summer the Northern Irishman played the golf of his life, maintaining the momentum found at Hoylake in the weeks that immediately followed. He won the World Golf Championships Invitational at Firestone and then a second US PGA crown for his fourth Major title. At just 25 years old his emphatic Open win gave him the third leg of the career Grand Slam, having already won the US Open in 2011 and the 2012 PGA Championship, both by the astonishing margin of eight strokes. Only Jack Nicklaus (23 years, 181 days) and Tiger Woods (24 years, 171 days) had reached this career landmark at younger ages.

McIlroy dominated throughout his Open victory, from the moment he scored 66 in the first round. He led after every day but needed to remain composed in the final round when Garcia and Rickie Fowler mounted stirring charges. The Champion held firm with a closing 71, giving him a two-stroke win that was more commanding than the margin suggested.

Open victory was achieved at the seventh attempt for McIlroy, but he had signalled his potential in a stunning debut as a teenage amateur at Carnoustie in 2007. 'He came out in the first round and shot a 68 without a bogey – it was extraordinary,' remembers RTE golf reporter Greg Allen. 'What an incredible way to announce your talent. It was totally a "hello world" moment.'

McIlroy was 18 years old and turned professional the following September after playing for Great Britain and Ireland in the Walker Cup. He quickly established himself as one of the best players in the world, although his high ball flight did not always favour traditional links conditions. At St Andrews in 2010 he scored 63 in the first round before being blown away by sweeping winds that led to a ruinous 80.

The youngster from Holywood near Belfast went on to share third place behind Louis Oosthuizen. It was his best finish until Hoylake in 2014.

McIlroy's title defence at the Old Course was ruined by a freak injury suffered playing football the week before the Championship. He missed the event and unwittingly embarked on the longest Major-less run of his career. The rest of the decade proved fruitless for him at the biggest tournaments. 'I'm a big believer that twisted ankle in 2015 stopped his momentum,' Allen contends. 'I thought that was something that was hugely significant.'

Without genuinely contending, McIlroy added top-five finishes in his next two Opens before settling for a share of second behind Francesco Molinari in 2018. He produced four sub-par rounds to finish two strokes behind the Italian Champion on a parched, running golf course. It was a performance to suggest more Open glories may come McIlroy's way. 'Carnoustie in 2018 was a real illustration that he does have a chance of winning an Open Championship even in hard and firm conditions,' Allen says. 'I think Rory has worked so hard to make himself a better firm turf player.'

There has been a feeling that McIlroy is yet to fulfil his vast potential. 'I get how frustrated people are, because the talent level is through the roof,' Allen contends. 'Rory was given almost everything Tiger Woods was given in talent and ball-striking ability. He has the capacity to be the dominant figure in golf.'

In his first 10 Opens McIlroy amassed five top-five placings including his 2014 victory. He is surely destined for further glory in the event he most wanted to win when, like so many other greats, he was learning the game on the practice putting green.

Famed for his driving prowess, McIlroy is also an accomplished shotmaker from the fairway.

What The Open Means to Me

IAN BAKER-FINCH (AUSTRALIA)
1991, ROYAL BIRKDALE

Growing up as a young man in Australia it was all about The Open. It was the one I wanted to win but, realistically, just to play in it was my main ambition. In my mind I would be playing Nicklaus, Player and Palmer to win the tournament. The Championship brought to life what I always wanted to be. It was always presented to us in magazines, books and on television as the Major of all Majors, where all the best players congregated to play the best links courses for the Claret Jug.

MARK CALCAVECCHIA (UNITED STATES)
1989, ROYAL TROON

The Open provided me with my greatest career accomplishment. It is the greatest golf tournament in the world in my opinion. Everything from the fans to the golf courses, to the atmosphere of the event. It is just the coolest event and it is my favourite golf tournament ever.

SIR BOB CHARLES (NEW ZEALAND)
1963, ROYAL LYTHAM & ST ANNES

Every tournament golfer aspires to win a Major and my Open in 1963 was the pinnacle of my 60 years in competitive golf. I have great memories and pride in claiming the title at Royal Lytham & St Annes to be called Champion Golfer of the Year. Following three days of Championship golf I found myself in a play-off with Phil Rodgers. At that time a play-off was over 36 holes. It was the final year of this format and was demanding both physically and mentally but I was fortunate to score 69 and 71 to win by eight strokes. In my third year as a professional golfer I felt my future was secured.

STEWART CINK (UNITED STATES)
2009, TURNBERRY

Playing The Open Championship is truly one of the most special experiences of each year. It's like travelling back in time. The type of golf that's played on the seaside links is so pure. It tests different aspects of your game more than any other type of course set up in the world. You really have to have it all to play well in that environment.

DARREN CLARKE (NORTHERN IRELAND)
2011, ROYAL ST GEORGE'S

The Open is the oldest, biggest, best tournament in golf. I'm extremely proud that I was able to win the tournament I dreamt of winning as a young boy. To have my name on the Claret Jug with all of the greats of our game is very humbling.

BEN CURTIS (UNITED STATES)
2003, ROYAL ST GEORGE'S

The Open Championship is the most historic and greatest event in golf. Obviously my win at Royal St George's was a life-changer. Every time I hold or look at the Claret Jug and see all the greatest names in golf history, it leaves me speechless. For someone who grew up in a small American town of under a thousand people and learned the game on a golf course that my grandfather built, to then win on one of the greatest courses in the world is a dream come true. It was a week that I will never forget. The greatest memories of my career took place playing in The Open.

JOHN DALY (UNITED STATES)
1995, ST ANDREWS

To me The Open is the hardest Major to win. It is played on the oldest and most challenging courses ever. It requires talent and imagination, while navigating the ultimate test of conditions.

DAVID DUVAL (UNITED STATES)
2001, ROYAL LYTHAM & ST ANNES

The Open is the most unique event in the world in that the fan is the most educated and the golf courses ask basically everything of you. They ask for power, precision, imagination and distance control. Sometimes that control is through trajectory through the air and sometimes it is on the ground and trying to figure out how to get the golf ball to slow down. At Carnoustie a few years ago the fairways were faster than the greens. Trying to figure that out makes it a magical event to play in. The way they set up the golf courses and present them to the players and then, depending on weather, that determines the score. The R&A is really good at presenting the test and then letting Mother Nature dictate what the scores are.

ERNIE ELS (SOUTH AFRICA)
2002, MUIRFIELD;
2012, ROYAL LYTHAM & ST ANNES

The Open will be my favourite tournament for as long as I'm playing. I grew up watching it on TV back home in South Africa. In '89 I made my debut at Royal Troon as just a skinny kid with a mop of blond hair! Honestly, I felt pretty comfortable on links courses right from the get-go. Muirfield in '92 was a big turning point for me, it marked the start of my international playing career. I had a strong week, finished fifth, and that really opened some doors. It was quite fitting that Muirfield was where I finally got my hands on the Claret Jug. I'd never wanted to touch that beautiful old trophy until that point. I didn't want to jinx myself! Jeez, that win was almost like an out-of-body experience.

All the courses on The Open rota are special. I love the unique shots that you have to play and how you have to adapt your game to suit whatever the conditions give you. I always liked my chances when things got tough and that happens quite often in The Open. Hats off to The R&A. No one sets up courses better than they do. And I love the atmosphere at The Open. Not taking anything away from the other Majors, but these are the greatest fans in the world. You feel the energy from them. At times it's as though the roar is coming out of the earth and, when you get something going, it's incredible. When I holed my birdie putt on 18 at Royal Lytham to win in 2012, that's the biggest roar I ever heard. The hairs on my arms were standing up. That's what you dream about, that's what you play for. That's what The Open has given me. It's given me some of the greatest moments of my career and some of my biggest heartbreaks.

SIR NICK FALDO (ENGLAND)
1987, MUIRFIELD; 1990, ST ANDREWS; 1992, MUIRFIELD

It's very hard to put into words. It was a lifetime goal: you start as a kid on the putting green, 'This to win The Open,' and you slowly progress. In 1978 when I finished four back I said to myself, 'I can win The Open' and it took me nine more years. There was my swing change and all sorts of things to get there. To be part of our game's history going all the way back to the Morrises and the Vardons and all those guys, to win at St Andrews in such a historic sport and the fact that your name is on the trophy and in the history books, it's a pretty cool achievement.

TODD HAMILTON (UNITED STATES)
2004, ROYAL TROON

When trying to win a golf tournament, many times we fall into the trap of focusing only on our closest competitors. At The Open Championship that may be the least of your troubles. Deep bunkers, wispy rough and the always unpredictable Mother Nature are just some of the pitfalls one must be aware of when fighting to win the Championship. For the winners it may seem easy as they are pushing toward their victory, but when they look back they will realise what they did was nowhere near easy. This is what sets them apart.

PADRAIG HARRINGTON (IRELAND)
2007, CARNOUSTIE; 2008, ROYAL BIRKDALE

For me The Open Championship is the spirit of golf. It is everything about what the competitive game of golf should be. It has it all. Everybody can enter, everybody can play. It is played in an environment that has such a great heritage but there are also the traditions of it now in a modern era. It is something that you grow up watching and always dreaming of being there – not just as a player, just being involved in it. For me it holds very much the spirit of all things good about golf.

TONY JACKLIN (ENGLAND)
1969, ROYAL LYTHAM & ST ANNES

It's my country's Major and the oldest championship. If I was dreaming and was asked which of the four Majors I would rather win, The Open would be top of my list because of the history and everything that goes with it: St Andrews, Tom Morris, the club and players. In my marquetry, the woodwork I still do, I focus a lot on Allan Robertson and his relationship with Old Tom. We are coming up to The 150th Open and wish more people were aware of the history. We wouldn't be here now but for everything that has happened before. I'm thrilled that my name will never be rubbed off that trophy. It's a wonderful feeling.

ZACH JOHNSON (UNITED STATES)
2015, ST ANDREWS

I'm not a great historian. I know the little things that probably most know, but I do know that this [St Andrews] is the birthplace of a great game and a place that has fantastic fans. For those that love the game, this needs to be on their bucket list and I love playing it. I've said it many, many, many times: this Championship … it's probably my most fun golf tournament inside the ropes. Ryder Cup is the Ryder Cup, Augusta is Augusta, I get that. But I just respect and appreciate what this tournament is all about and I could go on and on about that. It's the best.
(Press conference, St Andrews, 2015)

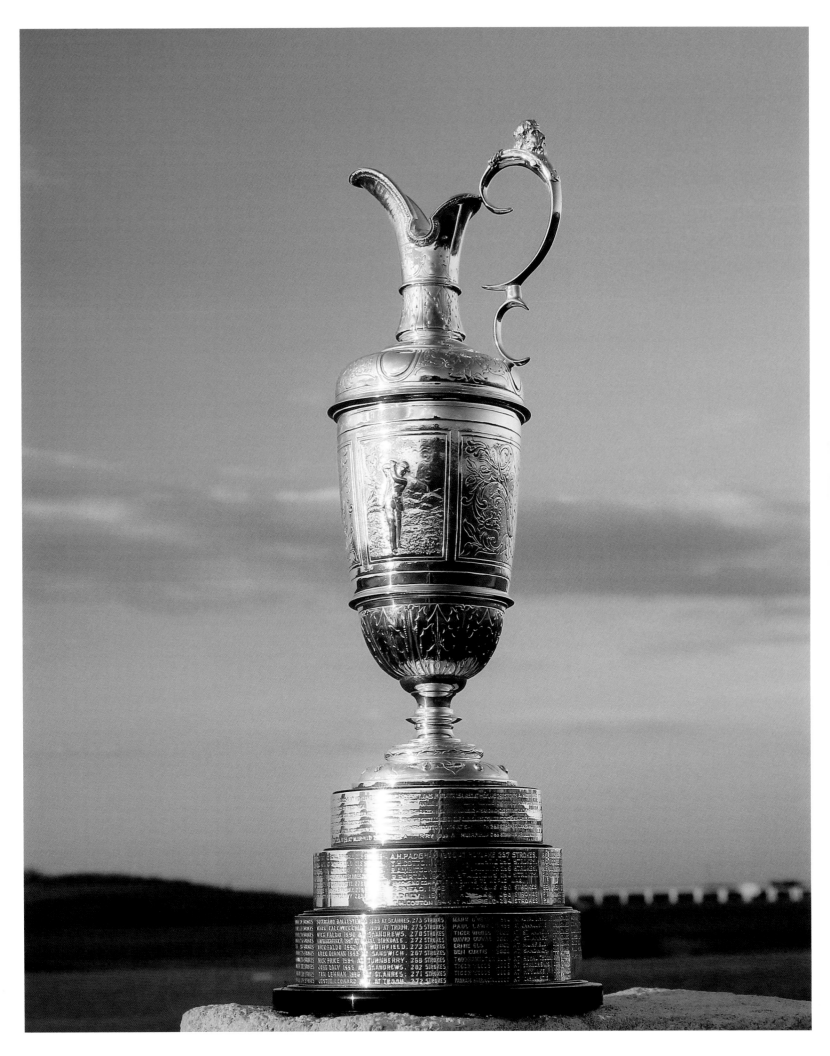

PAUL LAWRIE (SCOTLAND)
1999, CARNOUSTIE

_____

Like a lot of little boys when they start playing golf, I was always on the putting green. There would be two or three balls and in my mind it would always be Seve or Watson or Nicklaus and myself and it was always for The Open. To me, it has always been the biggest event in the world. If I was only allowed to win one tournament as a pro it would be the one. When I turned pro I never thought I'd get the chance to play in an Open and so to have played in so many of them and to actually win it and have my name on the trophy is dream stuff. It is just a fairy tale. It has always been my favourite event of the year.

TOM LEHMAN (UNITED STATES)
1996, ROYAL LYTHAM & ST ANNES

_____

There is no golf championship anywhere that surpasses The Open Championship, and within this highest echelon of historic competitions, an Open at St Andrews is easily the greatest single golf championship in the world. To be a part of any Open is memorable and to become a Champion at Royal Lytham & St Annes is one of the most significant moments in my life. However, when it comes to purity of competition in the most significant and inspirational place in the golfing universe, competing at St Andrews is the ultimate fulfilment of any serious golfer's bucket list.

JUSTIN LEONARD (UNITED STATES)
1997, ROYAL TROON

_____

The opportunity to play the oldest championship on just truly historical golf courses is something I look back on with so much fun and excitement. Now to be able to go over and commentate is a thrill. If I wasn't able to do that I would probably still go over there and play, even if it was just that one week. To be there and still be involved is great. To be at Portrush in 2019 and see the work that went in to make that what it was, a spectacular venue and Championship as a whole, to be a part of that kind of history is maybe my crowning moment in the game.

SHANE LOWRY (IRELAND)
2019, ROYAL PORTRUSH

_____

I wasn't from a golfing family, so it probably would have taken a lot longer for me to realise what The Open actually is. That changed when I saw the magnitude of when Harrington won back in 2007 and 2008 and what it meant to the Irish people and how big it actually was. But even before that, when you start playing, and you realise how much you love golf, you start looking at golf on TV and you watch The Open every year. For us, where I grew up, it is the biggest tournament in the world. I'm just very grateful that I got to achieve something like that, that I actually have one of those Claret Jugs on my mantelpiece and my name will be on that trophy for ever.

SANDY LYLE (SCOTLAND)
1985, ROYAL ST GEORGE'S

_____

We still needed to get that one thing, The Open Championship. The Americans had dominated The Open since Tony Jacklin won in 1969. Britain was hungry for that one Major ... I think when you have won The Open you can never prepare yourself for it. It was a big boom in '85, it was huge. Even now it gets your emotions going. Winning The Open is a great moment and, even many years on, it can hit the old heart strings. (From _Chronicles of a Champion Golfer_)

RORY MCILROY (NORTHERN IRELAND)
2014, ROYAL LIVERPOOL

The Open means an awful lot. It was the first Major Championship that I ever attended. I played the junior Open Championship in 2004 and then went and watched The Open at Troon that year. Where we are from, it's the biggest golf tournament in the world. Whether you go and watch it in person or you watch it on TV, the big yellow leaderboards, the Claret Jug, everything that goes along with it, it's a huge sporting occasion every summer.

PHIL MICKELSON (UNITED STATES)
2013, MUIRFIELD

For me personally, The Open is the greatest accomplishment I could ever get in my career because of the shots that I had to learn and the challenge that it created for me over the course of my career. It was so difficult for me to play my best golf in The Open under those conditions, more than any other tournament ... Not having grown up here, I had to learn it during my professional years. And it was an obstacle to overcome, and that's why it brought out so much emotion. (*Press conference with British reporters, May 2014*)

JOHNNY MILLER (UNITED STATES)
1976, ROYAL BIRKDALE

After coming close in 1973 and 1975, I really wanted to win The Open Championship and I knew I had the game to get the job done. In 1976 at Royal Birkdale it was the Seve show on the first three days. In the final round I three-putted the first green and I thought, 'It's not going to be one of those days, is it?' But from the second hole on I played six under par to break the course record. I won by six shots over Seve and Jack Nicklaus. It was my second and last Major title and it meant so much to my career. It was 'the Seve Ballesteros coming-out party' to the world and I was so proud to be a part of it. This was the foundation for a lifelong friendship between us. Why did I win? My caddie was a local named Ted Halsall, a fine local golfer. He knew Royal Birkdale better than most. He convinced me to hit a 1-iron off every tee ... that low burner shot finding the fairway would roll and roll, while keeping me out of the rough and the sand hills. My other irons took care of the rest! I never missed a fairway in the tournament. Nothing can compete with the feeling of winning The Open. Breaking through the crowd walking up 18 is the most exciting emotion I ever experienced in my playing career. It is a cherished memory that I will have for the rest of my life.

FRANCESCO MOLINARI (ITALY)
2018, CARNOUSTIE

I grew up watching The Open on TV, dreaming of one day playing in it and, like so many young golfers, that I might one day manage to win it. Funnily enough, I did not find links golf at all easy but that didn't mean I didn't love the experience and challenge of it. The atmosphere is always so amazing at The Open and the crowds are always huge and supporting every group – not just the big names. Every single Open venue seems to have so much fascinating history that it just has such a very special unique feeling when you stand on the first tee. It is a tournament like no other.

GREG NORMAN (AUSTRALIA)
1986, TURNBERRY; 1993, ROYAL ST GEORGE'S

My mother was a very good player – she played off a three handicap at one stage. She won numerous club championships, so she understood what competitive golf was all about. As I was improving at this dramatic rate, I said to her, 'The Open Championship is the tournament I want to win because it is *The* Open Championship.' Little did I know, the Claret Jug would be sitting on that mantelpiece. (From *Chronicles of a Champion Golfer*)

MARK O'MEARA (UNITED STATES)
1998, ROYAL BIRKDALE

I am a firm believer that The Open Championship is truly The Open of the World as it reflects the international game that we have all been able to enjoy. Coupled with the role that The R&A has played in establishing the game as well as protecting the integrity of golf makes it historic in all proportions. The fact that it is played on some of the best links courses in the world, and awards the Champion Golfer with the coolest trophy in the Claret Jug, just sets it even farther apart from all the other golf tournaments in the world.

LOUIS OOSTHUIZEN (SOUTH AFRICA)
2010, ST ANDREWS

It's an unreal experience as The Open Champion, and it's something that I would work to achieve again, to be known as The Open Champion for the year. And it's been a great experience. You know, just having the Claret Jug with you for a year is enough. (*Press conference, 2011 Open*)

GARY PLAYER (SOUTH AFRICA)
1959, MUIRFIELD; 1968, CARNOUSTIE;
1974, ROYAL LYTHAM & ST ANNES

It is simply the most important tournament in the world to me. It was my first Major Championship victory. It changed my life. I love the constantly changing challenge it presents. The weather, the golf courses, the people, the atmosphere. The fond memories are indelibly part of who I am today.

NICK PRICE (ZIMBABWE)
1994, TURNBERRY

The Open was the first championship that most of us were really aware of because back in the sixties we didn't have live television back home. In fact, we saw most sport through promotional films and that was how for the first time I got to see Tony Jacklin and Bob Charles playing. And, obviously, Gary Player, Jack Nicklaus, Arnold [Palmer] and they were just icons. To us, The Open Championship was *The Open* of golf. We were so inspired by watching. It was the ultimate challenge and seven years later [in 1975] I played my first one. (From *Chronicles of a Champion Golfer*)

BILL ROGERS (UNITED STATES)
1981, ROYAL ST GEORGE'S

You can't think about The Open Championship without thinking about the history of the game, a game born out of a beautiful place in the world, the British Isles. It's been about the fans and The R&A, who have supported it and made it into what is really the 'world's championship'. Occasionally I will pick up the Jug and look at the names and I'm just blown away by being included in that cast of characters that have won The Open Championship. It's very meaningful to me, to the extent that hardly a week goes by that I'm not reminded of it in some way that I've been the Champion Golfer of the Year.

JORDAN SPIETH (UNITED STATES)
2017, ROYAL BIRKDALE

The Open Championship is unique and one of my favourite weeks for many reasons, including its storied history, the constantly changing weather, its knowledgeable fans and the incredible links courses which challenge every shot. Every time I play The Open, I feel connected to the roots of the game and all that makes golf so special. It's a deeply important part of our sport, and it is an honour to be an Open Champion.

HENRIK STENSON (SWEDEN)
2016, ROYAL TROON

Watching my childhood heroes compete on the most famous links courses in the world truly inspired me as a junior golfer. I practised hard so that one day I could play in the Championship. Going on to win it is nothing short of a dream.

LEE TREVINO (UNITED STATES)
1971, ROYAL BIRKDALE; 1972, MUIRFIELD

I had no clue there was an Open Championship or anything like that until 1961, 1962 or 1963. My first Open was Lytham (1969). Hated it, didn't like it! I thought there was a lot of luck involved. Hit a drive down the middle of the fairway, I mean, it would start bouncing and jump on the train and go to London … didn't like it. And the more I went there and the more I played it, the more I fell in love with it. I mean, it is absolutely terrific. The Open Championship carries a lot of weight, but I was excited because this was what everybody was talking about … To touch the Claret Jug is a special thing, a very special thing. But it's even more special when you touch it and you know it belongs to you. That's what is really exciting about it. (From *Chronicles of a Champion Golfer*)

TOM WATSON (UNITED STATES)
1975, CARNOUSTIE; 1977, TURNBERRY;
1980, MUIRFIELD; 1982, ROYAL TROON;
1983, ROYAL BIRKDALE

To me it is the 'world' Open. It brings people from all over the world to play a great Championship and it always has been. I remember back in the day Mr Lu coming over and almost winning, and the resurgence of the Americans coming over in the 1960s when Arnie came over and qualified even though he was the defending Champion. The Open is a world championship now, everybody wants to play in it.

TOM WEISKOPF (UNITED STATES)
1973, ROYAL TROON

Believe me, to win my first Major Championship in the country where golf started is something you can't explain. It is the most inspirational place I've ever played golf and I'm very proud to be your Champion. (*From victory speech*)

TIGER WOODS (UNITED STATES)
2000, ST ANDREWS; 2005, ST ANDREWS;
2006, ROYAL LIVERPOOL

It was fascinating to watch, but it was so different that I didn't truly understand links golf until I actually got the chance to play it. Once I got that first chance to play it, I fell in love with it … Peter Dawson says 'Champion Golfer of the Year'. To hear him say that on that green [at St Andrews in 2000], that's something that I will never, ever forget. (From *Chronicles of a Champion Golfer*)

THE REWARDS
AND TROPHIES

The Rewards and Trophies

When Darren Clarke claimed the 2011 Open at Royal St George's he received a winner's cheque worth £900,000. Fortunes from sponsor bonuses and commercial backers inevitably followed; they always do for Open Champions. But the greatest value came from having his name engraved on the historic Claret Jug. 'That is beyond price,' he told reporters the morning after his triumph. 'For all my golfing career, to get my name on here, it means more than anything.'

Clarke was aged 42 at the time and his words surely sum up the emotions of every victor in the 149 Opens to date. Ever since it was first played in 1860, the Championship has been all about the glory of lifting one of sport's most prestigious trophies.

Initially, when Prestwick was the Championship's sole venue, there was only one prize, the Challenge Belt. It was worth £25 and first won by Willie Park. The idea for this reward is believed to have come from the Earl of Eglinton and James Ogilvy Fairlie, the prime instigators of the event. 'The Earl of Eglinton was interested in lots of sports, one of which was prize fighting, and he had already given a belt to be competed for in a prize-fighting competition,' says Angela Howe, The R&A World Golf Museum and Heritage Director.

'Sport was already something that he was very much involved in. He might have said: "Let's also have one for this golf competition that we are starting." It is made of red Morocco leather, decorated with silver embossed golfing scenes. The big buckle in front is quite an elaborate design.'

Prize money was not introduced until the fourth Open, played in 1863, and then the winner only received the Belt, with £10 split between the minor placings. A year later the overall purse rose to £15, with £6 going to the Champion.

There was also a stipulation that anyone who won the Belt three years in a row would be allowed to keep the trophy. 'This was a commonality with other sporting competitions,' Howe reveals. 'I'm not sure to what extent they thought it would happen or how often in other sports it did actually happen. But obviously it occurred in 1870 when Tommy Morris won the Belt outright.'

This left the fledgling Championship without a trophy and as a result it was not played in 1871.

The following year, on 11 September, came the ground-breaking agreement between The R&A, Prestwick and the Honourable Company to restart the event.

They agreed to contribute £10 each for a new trophy, which was to be a claret jug made by Mackay, Cunningham and Company of Edinburgh. It is hallmarked 1873 and is officially called the 'Golf Champion Trophy'. 'In the initial discussions they were talking about resurrecting the competition for a belt, but then decided at some point that they would have a claret jug instead,' Howe says. 'Between our minutes, the Honourable Company and Prestwick, we don't have anything telling us why they chose a claret jug over another belt. Maybe they felt it was time for a fresh start.'

With the new trophy not ready in time for the 1872 Championship, again won by Tommy Morris, a gold medal was presented instead. It is a practice that still continues. Indeed, the victor is always formally announced as 'the winner of the Gold Medal and the Champion Golfer of the Year'. 'I think it is a really nice tradition that has continued,' Howe says. 'The design has changed over the years. Originally it was a big oval gold medal, and it has altered shape and size as time has gone on.'

Although he did not receive the new trophy, Young Tom Morris's name became the first to be inscribed on the new Claret Jug and the 1873 Champion Tom Kidd was the first to be presented with it. Those who triumphed in the era of the Belt are not included, but the identities of the earliest winners of the Jug are engraved on its spout and subsequent names are found on plinths at the bottom.

'In the old days the Champion used to get the Claret Jug engraved himself and bring it back the following year,' recalls former R&A Chief Executive Peter Dawson. 'When Fred Daly won he had it engraved "Fred Daly, Holyake" not Hoylake! Then in 1968, Roberto De Vicenzo came back with the Claret Jug un-engraved and that's when we called in our own engraver. A couple of years later it became a permanent arrangement.'

Scottish jeweller Alex Harvey was the man appointed to the role and he remained in that position when Dawson took over from Sir Michael Bonallack ahead of the 2000 Open at St Andrews. A couple of years later, the new Chief Executive began to wonder if it might be time to appoint a new engraver. 'I went to London and lined someone up,' Dawson admits. 'But when I came back to The R&A, Alex was in the trophy room engraving the club trophies with someone else alongside him helping.

'It was his son Garry and he now does the job. He's also a professional golfer who had won the Boys Championship way back and so he ended up engraving his own trophy, which I think is a great story.' Harvey was the 1972 winner of the Boys title at Moortown, having been beaten by future Ryder Cup star Howard Clark in the final 12 months earlier.

'Dad did it for 35 years before I took over when he retired,' Garry Harvey explains. 'My first one was Todd Hamilton's win in 2004. My hardest one was when Padraig won at Carnoustie. Padraig Harrington is a longish name and The R&A like the full name to go on the trophy and with it being a play-off that was a rush job! Peter Dawson was the main man at the time and he was standing right behind me saying, "We're under pressure, Mr Harvey." It's the last thing you want, to be rushed. I've got to keep myself calm otherwise you'll make a mistake.'

Harvey began engraving by helping his father as a teenager in the evenings after school. He usually arrives at an Open on the day before the final round and the next day goes to the course around midday to check the area where he will be working at the end of the Championship.

'I do the number of strokes and the venue first, so I've only got the name to add at the very end,' Harvey says. 'I have done it before the final putt drops, but only if the guy is three or four shots ahead and he hits his second shot onto the green. I'd normally get the nod then. If there's any chance that he might take a double-bogey, or whatever, then I have to wait to get the go-ahead.'

Harvey uses the draw sheet as his point of reference for the correct spelling of the Champion's name. 'It is a real thrill when you see the Champion look at the trophy and they see their name on it for the first time,'

Harvey admits. 'It's a wee part of history that my work will be on there for as long as The Open is played; it's a great feeling.'

The moment the trophy is handed over is one of sport's most important and emotional occasions. Dawson admits his role announcing the Champion was an intimidating prospect. 'I was part of the closing ceremony at Carnoustie in 1999 when I was on training,' he remembers. 'The size of the amphitheatre was quite daunting, so I suddenly realised the enormity of it.'

Dawson then became involved in a great debate over whether it was more grammatically correct during the presentation ceremony to refer to the Champion Golfer *of* the year or *for* the year. 'A Canadian professor wrote in about it,' says Dawson. This led to a trawl through the archives, where it was discovered that his predecessor, Sir Michael, had used both versions. 'The split was 50/50!' Dawson laughs. 'I tried to say *of* but I might have failed once. I think *of* is the grammatically correct version.

'It's a huge crowd moment. People stay in their seats for the ceremony in huge numbers, whatever the weather, and I think it's important that TV continues to cover it.'

For Peter Dawson's successor, Martin Slumbers, who took over in time for the 2016 Open at Royal Troon, the presentation rituals have proved equally worrisome. 'You stand there and it is dead silence and you know the golfing world is watching,' Slumbers says. 'You know what is about to come out of your mouth is going to be there for history and it is quite emotional.

'The first time, you pinch yourself and say, "I'm one of just a handful of people who have had that opportunity to do this." It is a huge honour and it's a huge responsibility. You practise a lot.'

Slumbers admits to an inner fear of not being able to pronounce the winner's name correctly. 'Two months before my first presentation I woke up in a cold sweat, terrified,' he says. 'I had been dreaming of that 18th green moment and saying, "With a score of whatever and the winner of the golf medal is Kiradech Affffff …" and just lost it! This was when Thailand's Kiradech Aphibarnrat was playing really well and I thought he could win.

'Seriously, though, for the players being called the "Champion Golfer of the Year" really affects them and so for them you want to get it just right. It's quite humbling.'

The presentation involves what has become one of the most recognisable prizes in world sport. Slumbers says the Claret Jug has 'magical' properties.

'You realise how much that one trophy means to so many people,' he reveals. 'There's an R&A video we did at Royal Troon where we asked lots of spectators about the Claret Jug. Then the interviewer asked, "Have you ever held it?" And then completely unannounced it appears. And you see a look of raw emotion. There was a Dutch gentleman who said, "I wonder if they knew when they created this how much it would mean to people."'

This shared emotion between players, fans and administrators has developed through The Open's glorious history and forms a vital by-product. 'I think our professional sport is fantastic but the Majors and particularly The Open has a responsibility, as the oldest, to create that emotional attachment,' Slumbers adds.

The original Claret Jug was retired after Bobby Jones won it in 1927 and, along with the Belt, resides in the The Royal and Ancient Clubhouse in St Andrews. 'If people want to see exact replicas, they are on display in the museum opposite the Clubhouse,' says Angela Howe.

The Jug was replaced by what's known as the 'winner's trophy', which the victor is allowed to keep for the year he is the Champion Golfer. It is not just the Champion who receives silverware to mark their achievements at an Open. Since 1949 the Silver Medal has gone to the best-placed amateur in the field, provided they have completed all four rounds. The Tooting Bec Cup is in fact a medal and it goes to the player who scores the lowest round in the Championship.

If a member of the Professional Golfers' Association wins The Open they also receive the Ryle Memorial Medal, named after former PGA chairman Arthur Ryle. And the highest placed PGA member is the recipient of the Braid Taylor Memorial Medal, which commemorates the extraordinary achievements of the greats James Braid and J.H. Taylor in the early twentieth century.

Since those pioneering days, The Open has grown immeasurably in every respect. Prize funds are now paid in American dollars and exceed $10 million, with around $2 million going to the winner.

Such inflated figures reflect the ever-expanding value of the Championship in particular and golf in general. The trophies have grown in mystique, prestige and historical resonance, while remaining constant emblems of genuine sporting glory.

OPPOSITE Zach Johnson cuddles golf's most historic trophy at the 2015 presentation ceremony.

LEFT Garry Harvey engraving the Champion's name on the Claret Jug in time for the presentation.

Open Reach

Smiles as wide as the fairways that have just been played upon, they beam from ear to ear as youngsters enjoy a first taste of the magic of golf. It is not only the children who are grinning. On occasions such as these, great happiness is also never far from the face of the seasoned Champion who watches over them. And he is someone who knows the game's ultimate delight of lifting the Claret Jug.

Paul Lawrie, the Champion Golfer of 1999, regularly dispenses medals and trophies to enthusiastic juniors and it is always a thrill. 'When I go to my Foundation events and hand out the prizes and you see their wee faces – my wife and I just love it,' says the man who famously won a play-off against Jean van de Velde and Justin Leonard at Carnoustie in The 128th Open.

Within two years of that triumph, the Aberdeen-based Scot set up the Paul Lawrie Foundation. 'We've had funding from The R&A right from the start and they have been huge supporters,' Lawrie reveals.

This is just one example of how The Open's influence stretches far beyond its annual date, which traditionally coincides with the week of the third

Friday of July. Indeed, the Championship is pretty much omnipresent when you consider the lengthy process of assembling the 156-player field that gathers at the height of British summertime on an annual basis.

Week in, week out, the fluctuations of the Official World Golf Rankings ensure the very best golfers will be on show. The Top 50 are automatically entered. There is also The Open Qualifying Series involving professional tour events such as the Australian, South African and Singapore Opens as well as the Arnold Palmer Invitational at Bay Hill in Florida. High finishers in these tournaments are rewarded with a guaranteed spot in the world's oldest and most historic Major.

There are also regional and final qualifying tournaments which provide last-minute avenues into the Championship, often for highly talented players who have yet to make it on the leading tours.

The four days of The Open are a culmination, but the event's influence is felt and lived all year round, and not by only the world's best players. For example, you do not need golfing talent to be a member of The One Club, which is part of the offering of TheOpen.com website. It provides access to special ticketing and

merchandise deals along with exclusive video and audio content that provide permanent reminders of past Open glories.

Being one of the world's biggest sporting events, the Championship generates revenues to support and promote golf worldwide. The R&A has multiple roles in the running of the sport. Along with the United States Golf Association, the St Andrews-based organisation is responsible for the rules of the game, equipment standards as well as multiple amateur teams and championships.

Crucially, it also plays a big part in developing the game, which is why it supplies funds to bolster projects such as Lawrie's foundation. Determined to ensure golf remains popular and prosperous 50 years from now, The R&A knows continual investment is required. Children from diverse backgrounds must be encouraged to discover the joys of the game.

Celebrations to mark The 150th Open come in the middle of a 10-year period when £200 million is being ploughed into the development of golf at all levels. 'It is pretty much The Open that funds all of our activities,' says Kevin Barker, The R&A's director of golf development. 'The purpose always remains the same, ensuring that golf is accessible, inclusive and thriving.'

Despite being tucked away on the east coast of Scotland, The R&A commands a global sphere of influence. 'There are 158 national federations and bodies affiliated to us,' Barker continues. 'That's what puts us at the top table, able to speak on behalf of those organisations and gives us the opportunity to play a leading role in growing the game. Those affiliates can be big like England Golf or their equivalent in Japan or they can be extremely small like in Malta where there is only one golf course, or Andorra or Georgia. So it spans a lot of different golf environments and cultures around the world.'

With funds generated by The Open, The R&A provides money for participation initiatives, providing equipment and helping with high performance training schemes. 'In terms of coaching, increasingly it's been about coaching the coaches to up-skill them with a view to effectively making such work redundant in a few years' time,' Barker says. 'To make them self-sufficient to do their own thing.'

Of course, not everything goes to plan, as the
coronavirus pandemic made abundantly clear to
everyone. The R&A quickly created a £7 million
emergency fund to help golf cope in a time of
unprecedented disruption. Two million pounds
was distributed overseas, while England, Scotland,
Wales and Ireland split £4 million with an extra million
going to support organisations such as greenkeepers'
associations, the Golf Foundation and the PGA.

'We realised how difficult it might be with golf
shutting down in large parts of the world,' Barker says.
'We recognised that this could be a major moment for
national federations affiliated to us and the countries
they operate in, the golf courses that are their members
and the golfers that play in those countries. We don't
have the funds of our football equivalents like FIFA
or UEFA but we did want to help, so we created the
Covid support fund.'

As a charity that attracts and encourages young
golfers from all backgrounds to enjoy and learn from

the game, the Golf Foundation is a key beneficiary from R&A funding. Since 2018 it has focused on growing junior membership in UK golf clubs. Around 45,000 extra young people are welcomed every year, thanks to the Foundation's HSBC Golf Roots programme. The sport is also introduced in more than 3,500 schools, with over 128,000 pupils receiving coaching from a PGA Professional.

As signatories to The R&A's Women in Golf Charter, the Golf Foundation is committed to taking the game to as diverse an audience as possible. A mixed 'GolfSixes League', an inter-club junior competition, is a cornerstone providing teaching, training and weekend competition for thousands of fledgling golfers.

R&A funding has been key to its roll-out and nearly 500 clubs are involved. That means a lot of smiles on a lot of young faces. 'GolfSixes League gave me so much

confidence to trust my shot and to not worry about anything,' says 12-year-old Erin Woolnough, who plays for Felixstowe Ferry Golf Club in Suffolk. 'Six holes, paired with another junior against others who enjoy the game just as much as me; it's wonderful. I have met lots of friends as a result of it.'

Matches are played over a variety of different courses in a Texas Scramble format which puts the emphasis on having fun. 'If your partner hits an amazing shot then you can tell yourself to just go for it – why not!' Erin says. 'With parents walking around, everyone is there for the same reason. It's a brilliant feeling when you hit a good shot or hole a putt, and the families walking with you all clap or cheer; I love it!'

Who knows, such initiatives might spawn a Champion Golfer of the future. And do not assume it would have to be a British winner. Monies generated

by The Open have supported golf in Norway, from where Viktor Hovland has emerged as a world-class talent. Likewise in Chile, where Joaquin Niemann is making rapid progress on the PGA Tour. Kevin Barker cites both players as examples of future heroes who have come from backgrounds not traditionally associated with golf.

And The R&A's Development Director believes there are more in the pipeline. 'We've really tried to support the Polish Golf Union over the last few years,' Barker reveals. 'They're well organised and we've helped with their coaching. Adrian Meronk is now doing well on tour and that would be a great story for them if he starts winning. If he could take it to the next level that could be really big for Poland.'

By contrast Scotland is the most senior of golfing heartlands and Paul Lawrie's efforts in the Grampian region have helped develop players such as David Law, a winner on the European Tour. Such progress is thrilling, but it is not the primary objective of his Foundation. 'The idea has always been to supply golf clubs with members,' Lawrie says. 'To get kids into the game, to get them enjoying it. It's not about producing tour players but if that happens then great.'

Along with his wife Marian, Lawrie organises 'Flag' competitions to introduce youngsters to the competitive game. 'The children get 36 shots and wherever they hit their 36th shot they put their flag in the ground,' Lawrie explains. 'The furthest round in your age category is the winner and we have gold, silver and bronze medals that we hand out. We have quite a few under 12s that play about 11 or 12 holes in 36 shots on holes of about 175 yards. So the standard is absolutely incredible.

'The ones just starting out might get just four or five holes but then the next week I speak to them and they've maybe got another hole further and that's what it's all about. It's a little bit competitive but it's also fun and they get a kick out of getting further round. You see it in their faces.'

The Lawrie family are always delighted by the progress they witness. 'You've got to feel that way or there is no point in doing it,' Paul says. 'Marian goes to every event; hands out their water and their bit of fruit, the balls, the tees, the bibs and explains how the scorecards work.'

This is only one example of how the proceeds of The Open are developing the game. 'I've always been unbelievably grateful for what The R&A do,' says the man who has won 15 times as a professional. 'Not just for the Foundation but they're always pretty keen to back the ideas I take to them.

'I don't start things and leave other people to do them, and I think The R&A like that. They've always been amazing for me and I feel the Foundation is as important to them as it is to me, which is brilliant.'

It is a project that, in relative terms, is only a short wedge up the road from The R&A's St Andrews home. But it typifies what is a booming international drive for golfing reach across the entire planet.

This, after all, is what The Open is all about.

As the event's pioneers first decreed, it 'should be *open* to all of the world'. Since its inaugural running in 1860, no other golf championship can boast such wide-ranging, globe-spanning influence.

It has created great Champions who have trodden glorious links with style, skill and panache. Iconic sporting moments have been watched by millions, either by those on the course, sharing the stage with their heroes, or by people consuming this great Championship at home via multiple media platforms. It inspires smiling children and aged hackers alike to keep having a go at this maddeningly addictive sport.

So The 150th Open at St Andrews, the 'Home of Golf', is an occasion of great significance for many, many reasons. For anyone anywhere who loves the game of golf, it is a landmark well worth celebrating.

Picture credits

All images copyright R&A Championships/Getty Images, with exception of the following pages:

81: Allsport UK/Getty Images; 271: Allsport/Hulton Archive/Getty Images; 121, 208-9, 218, 241, 245, 262, 288, 310: Andrew Redington/Getty Images; 300-1: Brendan Moran/R&A/ Getty Images; 109: Central Press/Getty Images; 47, 74, 166, 267: Central Press/Stringer/ Getty Images; 12-13, 188, 190: Charles McQuillan/R&A/Getty Images; 129: Charlie Crowhurst/R&A/Getty Images; 314: Chris Lee/R&A/Getty Images; 137: Cowper/Stringer/ Getty Images; 118, 164, 253: David Cannon/Allsport/Getty Images; 8-9, 10, 43, 44, 45, 46, 48-9, 50-1, 53, 55, 56-7, 58, 60, 62, 63, 64-5, 69, 70-1, 73, 75, 76, 77, 78, 83, 84-5, 87, 88-9, 92-3, 95, 100-1, 125, 126, 244, 285, 286, 287: David Cannon/Getty Images; 40-1, 96-7, 99, 135, 289, 290-1, 292, 295, 312: David Cannon/R&A/Getty Images; 157: Don Morley/Getty Images; 183, 184-5: Douglas Miller/Stringer/Getty Images; 113, 211: E. Bacon/Stringer/ Getty Images; 279: Evening Standard/Stringer/Getty Images; 280-1: Fox Photos/Stringer/ Getty Images; 179: Harry How/Allsport/Getty Images; 115: Haywood Magee/Stringer/ Getty Images; 32: Hulton Archive/Stringer/Getty Images; 173, 258-9: Ian Wolton/R&A/ Getty Images; 36: James Hardie/Hulton Archive/Getty Images; 142, 229: Jamie Squire/ Getty Images; 2: Jan Kruger/R&A/Getty Images; 313: Johan Rynners/R&A / Getty Images; 284: John Leatherbarrow/Stringer/Getty Images; 86: Keystone/Stringer/Getty Images; 138, 275: Kirby/Stringer/Getty Images; 307: Mark Runnacles/R&A/Getty Images; 132-3: Mark Runnacles/Stringer/Getty Images; 110-1, 130, 226-7: Matthew Lewis/R&A/Getty Images; 144-5, 150, 152, 197, 199, 242-3: Michael Joy/R&A/Getty Images; 219, 221: Mike Ehrmann/Getty Images; 124, 153: R&A Championships; 20-1, 114, 235, 260-1, 263, 316-7: Richard Heathcote/Getty Images; 4, 66, 79, 204-5, 206: Richard Heathcote/ R&A/Getty Images; 270: Richards/Stringer/Getty Images; 200, 201: Ross Kinnaird/ Getty Images; 120, 122-3, 148, 149, 150, 154-5: Ross Kinnaird/R&A/Getty Images; 250, 251: Simon Bruty/Allsport/Getty Images; 248-9: Stephen Munday/Getty Images; 311: Stephen Pond/R&A/Getty Images; 231: Steve Powell/Allsport/Getty Images; 207, 210, 257, 306, 312: Stuart Franklin/Getty Images; 308-9: The R&A; 48: The R&A World Golf Museum; 23, 24, 25, 26, 27, 28, 29, 30, 31, 33, 34, 36, 38, 39, 54, 61, 102, 103, 104, 105, 107, 210, 269, 302, 304: The Royal and Ancient Golf Club of St Andrews; 315: Tom Dulat/Getty Images; 303: Tom Shaw/R&A/Getty Images; 72, 73, 82, 268, 274: Topical Press Agency/ Stringer/Getty Images; 80: Warren Little/R&A/Getty Images.

Thanks to Getty Images for all their support.

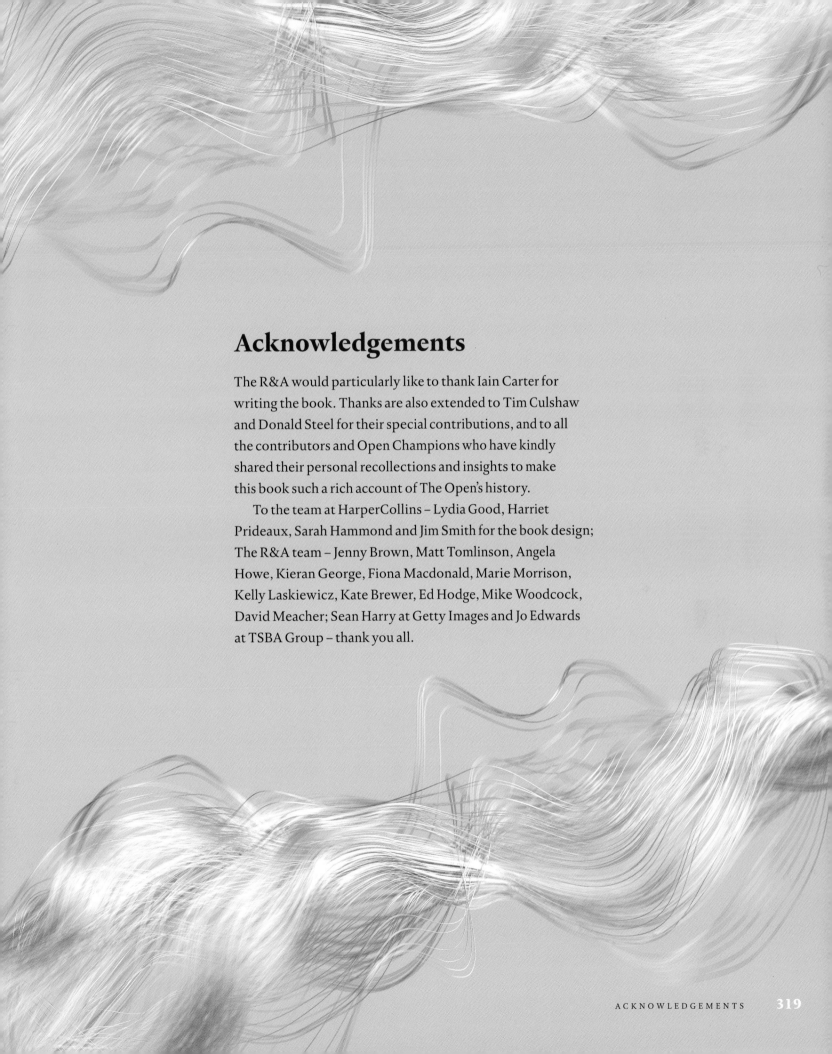

Acknowledgements

The R&A would particularly like to thank Iain Carter for writing the book. Thanks are also extended to Tim Culshaw and Donald Steel for their special contributions, and to all the contributors and Open Champions who have kindly shared their personal recollections and insights to make this book such a rich account of The Open's history.

To the team at HarperCollins – Lydia Good, Harriet Prideaux, Sarah Hammond and Jim Smith for the book design; The R&A team – Jenny Brown, Matt Tomlinson, Angela Howe, Kieran George, Fiona Macdonald, Marie Morrison, Kelly Laskiewicz, Kate Brewer, Ed Hodge, Mike Woodcock, David Meacher; Sean Harry at Getty Images and Jo Edwards at TSBA Group – thank you all.

HarperCollins*Publishers*
1 London Bridge Street
London SE1 9GF

www.harpercollins.co.uk

HarperCollins*Publishers*
1st Floor, Watermarque Building, Ringsend Road
Dublin 4, Ireland

First published by HarperCollins*Publishers* 2022

13 5 7 9 10 8 6 4 2

A catalogue record of this book is available from the British Library

ISBN 978-0-00-839009-9

Design by Jim Smith

Printed and bound by GPS

MIX
Paper from
responsible sources
FSC™ C007454

FSC
www.fsc.org

This book is produced from independently certified FSC™
paper to ensure responsible forest management.

For more information visit: www.harpercollins.co.uk/green